THE
Mushroom
Hunters

THE

Mushroom
Hunters

. . .

*On the Trail of an
Underground America*

Langdon Cook

BALLANTINE BOOKS

NEW YORK

Copyright © 2013 by Langdon Cook

Published in the United States by Ballantine Books,
an imprint of The Random House Publishing Group,
a division of Random House LLC, New York,
a Penguin Random House Company.

BALLANTINE and the HOUSE colophon are registered
trademarks of Random House, Inc.

Grateful acknowledgment is made to Stanford University
Press for permission to reprint as an epigraph an excerpt
from "The Treasure," from *The Collected Poetry of
Robinson Jeffers,* Volume 1, by Robinson Jeffers, edited by
Tim Hunt, copyright © 1938 and copyright renewed 1966
by Garth and Donnan Jeffers. All rights reserved.
Used with the permission of Stanford University Press,
www.sup.org.

LIBRARY OF CONGRESS CATALOGING-IN-
PUBLICATION DATA
Cook, Langdon.
The mushroom hunters : on the trail of an underground
America / Langdon Cook
pages cm
ISBN 978-0-345-53625-9
eBook ISBN 978-0-345-53626-6
1. Mushrooms—Northwest, Pacific. 2. Edible fungi—
Northwest, Pacific. 3. Forage plants—Northwest,
Pacific. I. Title.
QK617.C685 2013
579.6—dc23   2013011039

Printed in the United States of America on acid-free paper

www.ballantinebooks.com

2 4 6 8 9 7 5 3 1

FIRST EDITION

Title page photo by the author
Book design by Barbara M. Bachman

For Martha

Stars burn, grass grows, men breathe: as a man
    finding treasure says "Ah!" but the treasure's
    the essence;
Before the man spoke it was there, and after he has
    spoken he gathers it, inexhaustible treasure.

—ROBINSON JEFFERS

If what a tree or a bush does is lost on you,
You are surely lost. Stand still. The forest knows
Where you are. You must let it find you.

—DAVID WAGONER

Contents

. . .

Outlaws in Lobster Park

...

THE FORAGER STOPS ME abruptly with his hand. *Wait.* I stand motionless behind him and listen. The woods are quiet; not even a bird sings on this clear afternoon at the end of summer, when alders begin to yellow and the nights turn cool. All I can hear is my own labored breathing. Centuries-old Douglas firs loom around us, their wizened trunks craggy enough to house colonies of bats. We have walked a mile of unforgiving old-growth forest to reach this spot, zigzagging through bogs of devil's club and traversing fallen conifers high above the forest floor like construction workers shuffling along suspended I beams. My left hand is pincushioned with tiny thorns. We pause on a forested hillside overlooking a narrow road. In the mind of my guide, this road presents the only real obstacle. He cups a hand to one ear.

"Down!"

He hits the dirt on all fours and flattens himself against a knee-high nurse log. I slump behind a hemlock snag as wide as a front door.

The car is a white sedan, not a ranger's truck. It comes around the corner and pulls into a turnout. An elderly woman steps out with a lap dog. The forager is relieved but still cautious. "I'll wait here for an hour if I have to," he says, still on the ground, leaning back comfortably into the hillside now, with his hands behind his head and one boot crossed over the other, his eyes closed as if he might take a quick nap. This is his element. Even at a distance of only a few feet from me, he blends easily into the landscape, like all the other creatures that use cryptic coloration to avoid detection. He's wearing tan canvas work pants and an ash-gray T-shirt. His plastic five-gallon bucket is painted hunter green, as is his backpack, a simple rucksack with one large compartment that can hold about fifty pounds of product. The product today: wild mushrooms, the sort prized by restaurant chefs across the land for their earthy flavors and meaty texture. These are not the bland white variety found in produce bins at the supermarket. Wild mushrooms grow only in nature, in ragged, untended corners, not in the warehouses or rectilinear, climate-controlled environments used by cultivators. And these particular wild mushrooms—about sixty pounds in all between backpack and bucket—were, until a few minutes ago, growing right here, inside the boundaries of this national park where we're currently trying to hide out of sight. It's illegal to pick them here.

THE STRATOVOLCANO MOUNT RAINIER is in my backyard. To get to my home from downtown Seattle, I drive south on Rainier Avenue, one of the city's main thoroughfares, and on a clear day the white cone fifty miles to the southeast in the Cascade Mountains dominates the view through my windshield. At 14,410 feet and growing, it's the highest peak in Washington State—and it sits smack in the middle of mushroom country, where it forms a golden triangle in the minds of mushroom hunters with two other nearby volcanoes, Mount St. Helens and Mount Adams. Tectonic upthrust here and elsewhere in the Pacific Rim has produced what is known as the "Ring of Fire." We think of the Northwest as a place of water. It is equally a land of fire, with volcanoes through millennia laying down a thick, well-drained pumice that, coupled with ample rainfall, grows enormous trees and a diversity of edible fungi. Like oceans surrounding desert atolls, forests flank the icy volcanic peaks for as far as the eye can see. These are hushed, airy places that can be shot through with warm shafts of light when the sun is out, which is often not the case. Such an otherworldly illumination, sent from the heavens and filtered through a million leafy stained-glass windows, throws spot beams on mosses and lichens, magnifies countless shades of green, and explains why the Pacific Northwest's ancient forests are sometimes referred to as nature's cathedrals.

Mount Rainier and its deep woods are just one stop along what professional foragers call the mushroom trail. Imagine a region that incorporates large tracts of both the western United States and Canada, taking in northern California from about Mendocino and running up through Oregon, Washington, British Columbia, and southeast Alaska, then ranging east to include the Yukon and western portions of Montana and Idaho. Steep mountains, many of them still rising, have blanketed the surrounding area in volcanic soils. They trap weather systems rolling in from the North Pacific that bathe the slopes in precipitation. Rain or snow falls nine months out of the year throughout much of this restless domain, and along the coast it can be hard to distinguish between where the fog and mists leave off and the rain begins. It saturates the great conifer forests, a steady patter that drips from needle to needle, streaming off heavy boughs and down darkened trunks, falling upon vine maples and red alders below, running in rivulets to collect on the parasols of prehistoric-looking devil's club before stair-stepping to salmonberry, thimbleberry, and blackberry, typing a steady beat on the shiny evergreen leaves of salal and Oregon grape, pooling among sword fern and lady fern, coating the club moss with glistening dimples, and pushing little streams through mounds of pine-needle duff. Drip lines form like wet skirts around the trees, and below the ground a mat of thirsty tendrils drinks in the moisture before responding, when the time is right, with a colorful parade of fungi: the fruit of fire and rain.

Wild mushrooms are commercially foraged for the table through-out North America, but it is here, in the damp forests of the Pacific Northwest, where a mostly undocumented commerce has blossomed into big business—with an outlaw edge. The fungi travel from patch to plate along an invisible food chain. It starts with commercial pick-ers who fan out across wooded areas of the region to harvest the mushrooms. Driving beater cars and vans along bumpy Forest Ser-vice roads, pickers follow the great flushes of fungal gold up and down the coast and deep into interior mountain ranges. They spend months at a time in hardscrabble timber communities, pitching base camps in places such as Washington State's Olympic Peninsula, the Central Cascades of Oregon, and California's foggy North Coast. The pickers in turn sell their goods to buyers and brokers; some of these work for large wholesalers, and others maintain a smaller inde-pendent foothold. The buyers also know the whereabouts of the mushrooms and set up their buy stands in rural communities to be closer to the pickers. The top rung of the food chain includes the end users: Many of them are home cooks who purchase wild mushrooms at farmers' markets and gourmet shops; most are restaurant chefs scrapping for a leg up, always on the lookout for a novel product to highlight on their menus, a product that speaks to the renewed en-thusiasm for real, seasonal food.

Today's target species, here in woods officially closed to such har-vest, far below the glaciated peak of Mount Rainier, is one of those foods, and whether obtained illegally or otherwise, it's not hard to spot among the drab hues of the forest. As big as a cantaloupe and flamboyantly dressed in a flame-colored suit, the lobster mushroom is a striking denizen of the woods. It's somehow not of this world, and while it might look like a freak among fungi, in a kingdom rife with weirdness it's really just another organism that has successfully adapted to a habitat and way of life—not to mention the fact that it's actually *two* organisms in one package. The lobster mushroom is a twofer, a parasitic fungus that attacks and lives off another species of fungus, transforming a white, unpalatable, and rather nondescript gilled mushroom into a showstopping orange delicacy. Though such fiery color is often nature's way of saying DO NOT TOUCH, the lobster mushroom, like its boiled crustacean namesake, is a sublime taste of the wild—and, like marine lobsters, the mushroom's flesh is succulent, even silky in texture when properly sautéed, and faintly evocative of the sea.

I have used lobster mushrooms in a risotto with Maine lobster and been fooled by which meat is which. The mushroom's surprising color is an advantage in today's competitive cooking arena. A simple dish of French duxelles—finely diced mushroom and shallot sautéed together in butter and finished with a touch of cream and Cognac—is transformed into an eye-catching treat for the table. Its meatiness and hint of the sea make it an ideal substitute for actual meat. I've had lobster mushrooms in a warm kale salad soaking up a balsamic vinaigrette, bobbing in a homemade tom yum soup, and tossed with squid-ink pasta, sea urchin, and lump crabmeat. One might say the lobster mushroom is emblematic of wild mushrooms in general. Only in the last decade or so has it become a staple in higher-end restaurants. Previously you couldn't pay a chef to use it. The forager says he's been making more money from it year after year. On the mushroom trail the lobster will start fruiting as early as July in certain coastal habitats and then continue on into October. It's not a very cold-tolerant species. As the weather cools and the rains gather force, the mushroom absorbs water like a sponge and develops an unpleasant fishy odor. The best fruitings are found in older forests of Douglas fir and western hemlock, though it occurs with other species of conifer, including pines in the Southwest. In Northwest forests, with their ample ground cover of moss, ferns, and bunchberry, the mushroom stands out brightly against an emerald backdrop. Such Day-Glo color hardly seems possible, much less edible. Almost always there will be more than one mushroom in any location, and often they will form a column, cascading down a crevice of seasonal runoff, where the parasitic spores traveled in a rain-washed slurry to infect a troop of unsuspecting hosts.

———

THE FORAGER IS PATIENT. We wait concealed under forest cover. He makes his living off nature's fickle bounty and understands the virtues of forbearance. He says he's never seen a ranger in these particular woods, and only once has he seen another picker in his patch— just some tourist who stumbled on it while driving through the park. And while the tourist gathered a few pounds for his Sunday table, the forager kept his distance and finished the job. "I got a hundred fifty pounds that day, doing circles around the guy, and he never even knew I was there." I think of mountain lions and other wild animals that watch us in the woods, unseen. Today's wish number is even more ambitious—two hundred pounds—which would mean stashing the mushrooms in the woods until he can return after dark to safely collect them. Two hundred pounds: a number that's hard to believe.

Almost apologetically, my guide explains that he doesn't make trips into the park every year, just in dry years. "Only if it's worth the risk," he adds. In wet years he doesn't need to break the law. In wet years there are plenty of mushrooms for everyone. But this isn't a wet year, and competition is beginning to hurt his bottom line. He needs all the lobster mushrooms he can get. I remind the forager that what he's doing is illegal. He thinks about this for a moment. If he were in charge, he finally concedes, he wouldn't change the rules one bit. He wouldn't open up the park to commercial mushroom picking, and he'd prosecute people like himself who flouted the law. Life is complicated, he says. He needs to make a living, and he doesn't think he's hurting anyone by picking this patch on the sly. Other commercial enterprises work out of the park—the mountain-climbing school, the guides, the concessionaires. "As long as this place allows people to drive through in gas-guzzling RVs," he mutters angrily, "I won't feel bad about picking a few mushrooms." That's it. He doesn't want to talk about it anymore. I can tell the decision to poach a national park weighs on his conscience more than he wants to admit.

After the woman has walked her dog and driven away, we continue down the hillside, parallel to the road. Though the mushrooms try to hide in the duff and moss, their bright-orange complexion gives them away. The forager spots them, and so do I. With each new discovery I am filled with immense pleasure. It's like being a kid again, on a treasure hunt in the woods. Sometimes just a tiny fraction of cap is visible beneath sticks and pine needles. I congratulate myself on sleuthing it out, and into the bucket it goes. The ground here feels soft underfoot—the result of periodic volcanic eruptions and centuries of accumulating forest debris—and it soughs gently with every step. The air is sharp and clean in my lungs. I'm conscious of each snapping twig. All day the forager has been complaining about the hardships of picking mushrooms, the long hours of stoop labor, interminable drives between patches, fluctuating prices, unsavory competitors, adverse conditions in the bush. Now, as he bends down to excavate around a stately one-pounder—a five-dollar mushroom at today's prices—he corrects himself. "I lied," he says. "It sure beats a cubicle."

He sweeps an outstretched arm before him, taking in the trees, the sky, the dirt, even the strange little caterpillar curled up in a dewdrop on the mushroom's cap. Not a bad office place. And I can't disagree. The ancient forests of the Pacific Northwest are some of my favorite places to shake off the tumult of the city. We continue on, and though I'm sweating and thirsty, it doesn't exactly feel like work. "This is the gut," he says to me, as we come over a rise and into a shallow depression where an old grade can be discerned winding among mammoth Douglas firs and red cedars; someone drove pack mules through here long ago, before it was a park. The forager uses words like *honey-hole* and *mother lode* to describe this favored ground. It doesn't take long, though, to see it's not shaping up to be a two-hundred-pound day. The ground is dry and the mushrooms are reluctant. We side-slope for long stretches without a glimpse of cap poking through duff, then come upon a little brood that slows us down and raises spirits. The forager ratchets back his expectations by half. Still, a hundred-pound day, nearly within his grasp, is nothing to scoff at. That's a thousand dollars in mushrooms at market prices, or five hundred in pure profit. The forager fills all his receptacles—his backpack, his bucket, even an extra green canvas bag brought along for the purpose—then hides everything in a thicket of brambles next to the road. We return to the car, which is parked well away from the patch. The plan is to drive back down the road, pick up the load, and get out of the park as quickly as possible. Stealth and speed are critical. The forager isn't even driving his own car today. He's planned every detail, down to the color of his socks. To get caught is to risk arrest, pay a huge fine, and endanger his future earnings as a harvester of wild foods. It's at this point that I realize I've lost my hat. It's a faded, ratty fishing cap, not so much to look at—and, for reasons that I can't begin to explain, I'd like it back. I know just where it is, in a gully near the old grade where I stopped to take pictures. "You pay the fine," the forager says to me, only half joking. We scramble back up the embankment. After I find the hat, he hands me the car keys. "For that, you're driving." He instructs me to coast up to the secreted mushrooms, park, and keep watch while he loads the car. "Whistle if you hear anything," he says, before disappearing into the bushes.

The last thing I want to see is the rectangular grille of a ranger's truck appearing around a corner. I study the road as it vanishes behind a wall of unruly green in either direction. The forager reemerges with his contraband and hides it under tarps in the backseat. I've come here seeking knowledge, immersion in the natural world, perhaps even a form of enlightenment. Now I'm behind the wheel of a getaway car.

THE
Mushroom
Hunters

CHAPTER 1

Among the Recreationals

...

M Y OBSESSION WITH FUNGI arrived like a sickness. It consumed me. In the immoderate manner I approach all new pursuits, I read just about every book, online treatise, and marginalia I could find. It seemed to me I had something of a knack for stumbling on good mushroom habitat. Maybe this was because of all the hiking and bushwhacking I had done over the years, or maybe it was my youthful crush on birds that gave me a facility with field characteristics. Driving along the highway near my Seattle home, I would catalog the woods I saw and try to imagine what species lived there. Mushrooms often fruit in connection with a specific type of tree. I studied and memorized these kinships. Initially my wife, Martha, was supportive of my new hobby. Soon, though, to her dismay, I was sneaking out at all hours to scout likely patches. I started bringing home what some might consider unreasonable quantities of fungi—pounds and pounds of chanterelles, shaggy manes, giant puffballs, the list goes on—first to eat fresh, and then in such numbers that I cobbled together a homemade dehydrator, bought a stand-up freezer, and even did some pickling in the Mediterranean tradition. The homemade dryer gave way to a dedicated store-bought model, and my map collection grew into an unwieldy binder full of tattered and footnoted quads. I took my compass and mushroom knife wherever I went, *just in case*.

ANCIENT EGYPTIANS CALLED MUSHROOMS "the magic food," with powers of immortality fit only for pharaohs; commoners were forbidden to eat them. In Slavic countries, as far back as anyone can remember, families have gathered *beliy grib,* the white mushroom, like a crop, as a hedge against hard winters and starvation. In Africa, edible termite mushrooms grow as big as umbrellas, and a single *Armillaria* fungus spreading across more than two thousand acres of Oregon's Malheur National Forest is considered the world's largest organism. Mushrooms have been implicated in the assassination of a Roman emperor and the surrealistic trip down a famous literary rabbit hole. There's a mushroom that resembles a dead man's foot and one that looks like a frozen waterfall. Mushrooms are colorful, beguiling, hideous, and transformative.

But more than anything, they are thought of as food. Across much of the globe, through the ages, hunting wild mushrooms has been a regular feature of people's lives, a rite of passage even. "All Russians know the mushrooms, not by dint of study as the mycologists do, but as part of our ancient heritage, imbibed with our mother's milk," writes Valentina Pavlovna Wasson in *Mushrooms, Russia, and History*. A popular Russian nursery rhyme even includes points of mushroom identification. It's hard to imagine such children's verse catching on in North America, save for a cautionary tale about deadly blooms in the woods. Yet even here, in the land of fast food and finicky palates, the allure of the wild mushroom is taking root.

Parked in front of a white tablecloth in a trendy Manhattan restaurant, a curious diner might pause to wonder how all this came about. Not long ago, on a snowy evening near Central Park, I browsed the menu at one of New York's finest eateries. The quail came with black trumpets. Shaved truffles sexed up a celery root agnolotti. The garganelli corkscrewed fetchingly in a morel cream sauce. The menu was dotted with calligraphed references to chanterelles and porcini, like little colorful caps poking through the forest duff. The fungi, it turned out, even outnumbered the fish. Such riches would have been unimaginable a generation ago. For a mushroom enthusiast like myself—and an increasing number of home cooks and restaurant patrons around the country who know the fungal difference between a lobster and a hedgehog—this quiet revolution of wild edibles has been a culinary bonanza. More and more, diners are discovering that wild mushrooms can stand on their own and replace traditional parts of a meal, even the meat.

My friends tended to view my mushroom compulsion with detached amusement. Even Martha found it hard to fathom. This surprised me because it was Martha who first showed me an edible wild mushroom, in the early days of our courtship, while on a backpacking trip in Olympic National Park. We harvested several pounds of chicken of the woods, a shelf fungus decked out in bright citrus colors, and made an elaborate Italian feast over a camp stove in the wilderness. After this, the domesticated supermarket variety hardly passed muster. For one thing, it's bland. Selecting mushrooms from a bulk bin—even when they're periodically updated with new and exotic marketing terms like *cremini*—can't begin to match the satisfaction of finding them in the wild. Most people don't even realize that the Continental-sounding portobello is merely an oversize cremini, both of them being the exact same species, the very domesticated *Agaricus bisporus*.

A quick primer. All mushrooms are fungi, but not all fungi are mushrooms. The kingdom also includes yeasts, rusts, and mildews— even slime molds. It is a mark of fungi's otherness that we don't have a proper lexicon with which to discuss them. Though a mushroom is not technically a fruit, we borrow a term from the plant kingdom and refer to its growth as a fruiting. Thus, a mushroom is the fruiting, reproductive body of a fungus, much as a cherry is the reproductive fruit of a cherry tree. The fungus that produces mushrooms usually— though not always—lives underground in the form of thread-like filaments collectively known as the mycelium, a root-like mass of tiny tendrils. When conditions are right, the mycelium produces a mushroom, which contains the fungus's reproductive material in the form of spores.

Mushrooms are the great decomposers and recyclers of the world, and they can be categorized in terms of their survival strategies. Note, again, that they're not plants. They don't photosynthesize. Instead, they get their nutrients in one of three ways. Some are parasites, like the lobster mushroom, feeding off other living things, even animals. Others are saprobes, recycling dead organic material (wood, dung, humus) into soil. The rest are said to be mycorrhizal, which means they partner with plants in a mutually beneficial exchange of nutrients. Skilled mushroom hunters know how to exploit the various mushrooms' survival strategies. They can locate colonies of the parasitic honey mushroom, with its tightly packed clusters of amber-colored caps, by finding the dead trees that are its prey; or they can return to a saprophytic lion's mane mushroom year after year that fruits out of a lightning-struck hardwood. By far the most abstruse relationship is among the mycorrhizal mushrooms. The mushroom hunter seeking chanterelles must understand which plants and trees the chanterelle requires to live. Knowing the trees of the forest is an essential piece of the puzzle.

Only recently has science begun to unravel the mysteries of mushrooms. Turns out, they're evolutionarily closer to human beings and other members of the animal kingdom than to plants. In other words, fungi and animals share a common relative in the distant past, while plants had already split off the family tree. This commonality between fungi and animals can be seen in chitin, the fibrous substance found in the cell walls of mushrooms and the exoskeletons of arthropods. Fungi have had a profound impact on people and civilizations throughout human history, despite our lack of knowledge. Consider for a moment how baking, brewing, or winemaking would have begun without yeast. Or where we would be without penicillin. In the future we may rely on mushrooms to help clean up oil spills, and the Chernobyl meltdown proved that fungi can mitigate nuclear contamination by literally feeding on radiation. The most obvious use through the centuries, however, can be seen on our dinner tables. Meaty, flavorful, and highly textured, wild mushrooms are a pleasure to cook with and exhibit that sought-after "fifth flavor" popularized in Japan and known as umami, a comforting savoriness that spreads across the palate and coats the tongue, making the diner feel good all over. Many parts of the world have enjoyed long liaisons with fungi, notably Eastern Europe and the Mediterranean, much of Asia, and Mesoamerica. North America is largely a mycophobic region, as passed down from an Anglo-Saxon fear of what lurks in the dark woods. But this is changing.

OUR DRIVER PULLED THE LEVER, the door clanked shut, and we lurched out onto Lake Street, a police escort's flashing blue lights leading the way through the rain-soaked streets of Boyne City, Michigan. The yellow school bus passed a row of tent canopies set up along neat sidewalks, their unlikely wares on display: lawn gnomes for sale, ornately designed walking sticks, and phalanx after phalanx of carved wooden toadstools as tall as toddlers, with little white price tags fluttering in the wind. It was the start of the annual Boyne City National Morel Hunting Contest, and everyone on board this bus hoped to find glory in the nearby woods.

I was in the lead bus of five, seated next to a woman named Mary Ellen. Passengers shifted in their seats, making squeaking noises in their rain slickers and plastic pants. A few wore wide-brimmed rain hats and billowing ponchos, even garbage bags. "I'm sizing up the opposition," Mary Ellen whispered to me as she studied each passenger. "That guy might be worth keeping an eye on." She pointed a discreet elbow at the seat in front of us, where a stocky man in a camouflage trucker cap was checking a GPS application on his smartphone. After living on both coasts, with years spent in New York, Los Angeles, and San Francisco, where she once worked as a network news radio anchor, Mary Ellen had recently returned to live a more bucolic life in her hometown, and today's excursion was one of the reasons why. The bus picked up speed. No one on board, save the driver, knew our destination. Secrecy, after all, was paramount.

I had come to Boyne City because I have always been drawn to nature's secrets more than to, say, Hollywood's secrets or the secrets of Wall Street hedge-fund managers. Nature is real. It exists beyond our ability to create it or even mediate it. When I was young, the mystery of birds kept me up at night. Later, it was anadromous fish, such as salmon and steelhead, swimming upstream on their unknowable migrations. Wildflowers, with their constellations of families and their pouting, O'Keeffean lips, seduced me for a spell. But once the mushrooms grabbed hold, I couldn't let go. The others got tossed aside and mushrooms became my fondlings, and before long I found myself going to greater and greater lengths—such as today's morel hunt in a distant state—to satisfy my fungal yearning. This is not to say I wasn't interested in the human element. In fact, by this point the human intersection with the natural world had become something of a specialty of mine. I was most interested in foraging, that age-old knowledge passed down since antiquity that had briefly lost its luster in the glare of whiz-bang modernity and was now being rediscovered all over again. Foraging existed at the crossroads of a few of my favorite pastimes—nature, the outdoors, and food—and foraging for edible mushrooms satisfied my desires like few pursuits could. At the end of the day, birds were just a note in a life list; I could watch them and study them and be enamored of them, yet they remained *apart*. Mushrooms, however, came home with me. They went into a pan and became *a part of me*.

Morels might be the most widely recognized edible mushrooms in the world. In the Midwest they're the favorite, bar none. Across much of Europe, morels form a culinary triumvirate with two other celebrated types of wild mushrooms, chanterelles and porcini. Each season, hunters take to the woods to visit old family patches handed down like precious heirlooms. In Asia, morels are foraged in bewildering numbers in the Himalayas, Caucasus, Hindu Kush, and else-where, with many of those morels funneling into Istanbul before export, just as art and religion did hundreds of years ago. In North America, quite possibly their point of evolutionary origin, morels sig-nify the beginning of a new year of mushroom hunting. The people who gather them come from long lines of mushroom hunters, includ-ing those at the Boyne City contest, many of whom had been picking morels since childhood. "I had some in butter and garlic last night," bragged a man behind me in a flattop haircut. Everyone on the bus within hearing distance perked up. "They're popping now in Illinois—big time," confirmed a woman with a harsh smoker's voice, grasping an oxygen tank. "My eyes aren't what they used to be," la-mented another, and everyone nodded solemnly. "You know what?" said a tiny, ancient woman across the aisle as she banged her wooden walking stick on the floor for support, gripping its morel-shaped han-dle with thin, bloodless fingers. "I don't even eat the darn things and I can't get enough of them." "Sweetie, I'll take 'em off your hands," said her seatmate, and they both cackled loudly as the bus rounded a corner and left the last vestiges of town behind.

Each spring, morel enthusiasts, driven by a lust that's hard to ex-plain and impossible to corral, head for the wooded areas of the coun-try in search of their favorite fungus, hundreds of thousands of them, maybe more. They carry bags and buckets, maps and knives. East of the Mississippi, the morel hunters scour the hardwoods just as the trees begin to leaf out, committing to memory the bark patterns of dozens of deciduous species that might host a fruiting of morels be-neath their boughs: elms and ashes, tulip trees and sycamores, even old weather-beaten apple trees falling to pieces. In the West, hunters learn to distinguish between conifers and keep track of the mountain forest fires that produce morel flushes the following spring. Morel hunters search every state in the union, even Florida and Hawaii. Some are content finding just a few for a single dinner; others hope to lard in pounds for the coming year. Still others, numbering perhaps a few thousand, don't plan to eat any of their catch. For them, the morel might as well be official currency. These people work in the woods for a living, hauling out improbable quantities of fungi as a matter of course, and they don't have the time or inclination to visit a fair or ride a school bus devoted to their pursuit. More than any other mushroom, it is the morel that separates the commercial foragers from what one hunter I know calls the *recreationals*.

The guy in the seat in front of me was from South Bend, Indiana. He'd been coming up here to northern Michigan to hunt morels for thirty years and already had a cooler packed with them in his car, a fact that I took note of should my own efforts come to naught. There were hunters from Ann Arbor, Cincinnati, North Carolina, even the island of Cyprus. "A Cypriot!" Mary Ellen exclaimed. Boyne City was feeling a little more cosmopolitan. After passing a few hobby farms, the bus entered a pastoral landscape of fields and woods, and moments later we pulled into a large meadow by the roadside. Mary Ellen told me she had competed the year before and didn't find a single morel. I found this hard to believe. How could anyone not find morels in a covert location where picking had been prohibited until the contest? "You're optimistic!" she said. But how could I not be? The very essence of mushroom hunting is optimism. We were about to embark on a search for a type of food that humans could claim absolutely no credit for. We didn't plant it, didn't water it, didn't husband it—didn't tend it in any way. Nature was the sole benefactor. All we could do was hope to find it, and therein lay the rub. Finding morels was maybe one of the most difficult avocations that any sane person could adopt. Some devout morel hunters go an entire season without sating their desires with a single, perfunctory find. The professionals, on the other hand, traffic in amounts that would baffle the most successful of the recreationals. The serious commercial hunters didn't even live in this part of the country, despite its long love affair with morels. I told Mary Ellen about the hauls coming out of Oregon, Montana, and British Columbia, how the commercial hunting in the Yukon made everywhere else seem like small potatoes, or so I'd heard.

"A hundred pounds a day?" she asked me as we filed off the bus and gathered in the field.

"That's what they say, anyway. The good ones might do more."

The idea was inconceivable, and I didn't begrudge her skepticism. She had been a reporter most of her life, a dealer in facts. Boyne City was the self-proclaimed morel capital of the country, of the world perhaps—and yet a good day of morel hunting here was counted in numbers, not pounds. A hundred morels was a grand day. A hundred pounds was a fantasy.

And then the master of ceremonies made a horrible noise with the bullhorn, a tsunami warning blasting through the hills. Mary Ellen kicked up her legs like a nervous thoroughbred and crashed headlong through a briar patch at the edge of the woods. She was gone. I entered the newly leafed-out forest on my own. White trilliums bloomed everywhere. There were trout lilies, jack-in-the-pulpits, and Dutchman's-breeches, and in places the ground was hidden ankle-deep in the lush green foliage of a type of wild leek called a ramp. I walked farther into the woods, leaving the timid behind. I'd forgotten my compass and didn't have a map—no one did. In a broad vale I found my first keeper. Then, just like that, the siren sounded again and I started to make my way back to the buses. Ninety minutes had gone by in a flash of squinting at the ground. A tent was set up in the meadow where the buses waited. Morel hunters came out of the woods and waited in line to have their findings officially tallied by judges at the tent. The man who expected to take first prize had a group of hunters gathered around him in the meadow. He'd been picking all week. "There's too many good spots," he said with a winner's twinkle in his eye.

A bested hunter shook his head. "If I could have had that valley all to myself . . ."

"You've got to get down where that leaf material is," the champ was advising someone.

My new friend Mary Ellen appeared. She had averaged exactly zero mushrooms per ninety minutes. A goose egg. She was mortified.

"What happened?" I asked her. "You took off like a rocket."

She looked at her feet, now soaking wet. "I know, I know. I crashed and burned."

"We need to get you at least one." But she had already reported in at the tent. Never mind that, I insisted, this is for pride. We wandered off during the final tallying and, sure enough, right among a patch of ramps at the edge of the forest, Mary Ellen spotted one. Her eyes lit up as she caressed this impudent little mushroom in her hand.

Fifteen minutes later everyone re-boarded the buses and headed back to town. I found the hunter from Indiana and followed him to his minivan in the parking lot to do a deal. We passed vendors on the sidewalk hawking their big yellow morels for sixty dollars a pound. "How about thirty?" the man said, handing me a Ziploc that might have weighed a bit under a pound. I handed over the money quickly, as if this were a drug deal, not realizing that most of the morels at the bottom of the bag had already turned bad. Plastic is a terrible way to store mushrooms. It seals in the heat and moisture, rotting the fungi in no time, yet in my embarrassment I was too shy to inspect the goods.

IN TRUTH, BY NOW I was not after only morels. I was after the morel hunters, and not just any hunters. I wanted to meet the best. I wanted to know who they were, where they came from, what they did, and how they had learned to find morels—and maybe why. My inquiries kept leading back to a single morel hunter, a furniture builder in town named Anthony Williams.

Tony, as he's known, is the patron saint—or agitator, depending on your point of view—of the Boyne City festival. He's a third-generation resident of Michigan's northern woods, a sturdy, bearded, soft-spoken man with a slight lisp. I found him in a little tourist shop that sold jewelry, folk art, and Tony's distinctive wooden furniture, some of it massive, like the four-poster bed in the middle of the place that was going for thousands of dollars. The bed was the first thing I noticed when I walked in. It was impossible to miss. Tony had fashioned it from four solid trunks of pine, roots and all, which must have required painstaking effort to make level. A latticework of twisted branches formed a canopy overhead, and the effect was one of natural beauty. Sleeping in such a bed would be like laying down your head in a shady grove, comforted by dreams of fairies and wood nymphs. "We're not farmers," Tony likes to say about mushroom hunters. "We go way back. We're gatherers. This is what the planet is handing us."

I asked Tony what made him so successful. "I go to the woods and I move fast. Morel picking is moving. It's not lollygagging around. Right now I'm looking for mature ash trees and poplars. I pick morels from a distance. See that hillside over there?" He pointed out the window to a blurry hump of green in the distance. It looked like any other hump of far-off green. "I can pick out poplar and ash trees from here. Once I'm in the woods, I look for the big mature trees. Early in the year I look on the south sides. Keep moving. I pick where people won't go. I love picking the ridges. There's a million little tips like that. When my mother was pregnant she still picked. We'd pick in the morning, stop for lunch, and pick in the afternoon. We did some hellacious morel picking within a mile of where we're sitting."

Though he lived in a fairly conservative part of the country, Tony wasn't one to conform. He played in a rock band as a young man, did a year in jail for smuggling pot out of Mexico, owned a barbecue joint for a while, and now made his living as a craftsman. "When I was a kid, the festival was kind of a joke. It was this hillbilly northern Michigan thing." The contest, he explained, was born in a tavern. "Guys were arguing over who was the best morel hunter—a bar fight!" A group of about twenty men met the next morning to settle it. One of them, a Lions Club member, suggested they organize the contest for the city. Since no one else was doing it, they decided to call it a *national* festival. By the mid-seventies the festival started to catch on. Tony first joined the competition in 1980. "Between you and me, I was stoned. I'd had a gig the night before, up all night partying. They said, 'Jeez, it starts in, like, fifteen minutes,' and I'm like, *Awwwlright*. I drive down there and I just kick everybody's ass. I hadn't been to sleep in twenty-four hours. I won it five years straight." After that, he retired from competition so that others wouldn't be scared off. He said this not with bravado but with slight embarrassment. "I have this label of being the world's greatest morel hunter. It's weird. In my own family I was second." Tony's mother was hands down the best. "She was a waitress, a hard worker, and she'd get in the woods and just boogie." Tony's dad owned eleven laundromats. One of Tony's most memorable morel hunts was the day they dumped out the baskets of dimes from the laundromats and filled them all with morels.

Sports Illustrated, Audubon, and *USA Today* have all written stories about Tony Williams, champion morel hunter. "I've gotten a lot of ink," he admitted. "You know, I'm a great morel picker, I really am. The world's best? That's pretty heavy." After retiring from competition following his fifth crowning, Tony joined the festival board and took charge of trying to bring it up to date, with a greater emphasis on the commerce and cuisine of morels. One year another board member asked him if he knew who Emeril was.

"You mean the chef on TV?"

"Yeah, him. He called."

"Emeril called?"

"He wanted to come to the festival and cook."

"What did you tell him?"

"We told him no."

Tony has been trying to get hold of Emeril ever since.

Eventually he'd had enough of the small-time approach. "We have every pickup truck in northern Michigan trying to be the best morel picker. If we're going to capitalize on this, we need to make this a morel town. We have to make this a festival where every restaurant is serving morels and you can buy morels off the street." The new approach worked. The festival now attracts thousands of people each year, at a time when the summer tourist trade has not yet kicked in in other northern Michigan towns.

"I'm into it," he went on. "I love the fact that so many people do this. You get 'em all: rich, poor, the guy outfitted in five thousand dollars' worth of L.L. Bean, CPAs surrounded by drywall and metal desks. It's one of the reasons why my furniture is so popular. I've brought nature into your house. To me, one of the problems is the young people aren't doing it. During my seminars, I say, 'Where are your kids? Why aren't they here?' They're home on the damn computer. Get kids into the woods to understand that food doesn't need to come from the grocery store or McDonald's. By picking morels we're helping to save the planet, we're educating people. I want to get the word out about stewardship and young kids, all these things."

LATER, AT CAFE SANTÉ, on Water Street in downtown Boyne City, the special was a plate of fettuccine with veal meatballs and morel ragu. After dinner, with a full stomach, I strolled a couple of blocks along Lake Charlevoix to Veterans Park, where a country band played Lynyrd Skynyrd covers under the festival tent and you could buy a thirty-two-ounce souvenir cup of beer for five dollars. I ran into Mary Ellen. She had been hunting right around her house that morning. "I got, like, a dozen," she said, her eyes popping. "It was amazing. I feel . . . I don't know . . . *redeemed*."

After the morel fest, I started to attend other mushroom fairs. I became a connoisseur of lawn gnomes and walking sticks. In the high Rocky Mountains of Colorado, I joined dreadlocked mushroomers at the Telluride Mushroom Festival, and in California I met oenophiles who paired their wild fungi with local wine varietals. Back home in Seattle, at my local mycological society, I met Japanese Americans in love with matsutake, Italian Americans motivated by the earthy aromas of porcini, Eastern European Americans who vacuumed the forest floor clean, and a host of other fungi lovers who hailed from all over the world. There were mushroom hunters known for their zipperlip patches and hunters known for their inability to find anything at all, teenage mushroom hunters knee-walking through farmers' fields for blue ringers, and elderly mushroom hunters who couldn't stomach a supermarket button. I met stage actors and academics, newspaper reporters and housewives. All these people were united by their infatuation with a little-known kingdom and their drive to uncover its secrets.

But these were all recreationals. When it came to wild mushrooms for the table, most of them knew almost nothing in comparison to those who hunted for profit. Like a decent beer-league softball player, I knew there were actual professional foragers out there who made my amateurism seem like an altogether different game. The professionals did this for money. They made a living from the wild mushroom trade, and it was their business to know where the most productive fruitings of mushrooms happened, out of sight from the prying eyes of the public and me—an undercover economy that one researcher in the early 1990s valued in excess of $40 million. Since then, the trade had continued to expand, though it remained mostly hidden, as did the harvesters. With a knowledge of the woods that would put your average survivalist to shame, they quietly bushwhacked miles into untrailed forests and resurfaced hours, days, or even weeks later with overflowing baskets of gourmet delicacies. And in exchange for what? An itinerant life on the road, continually moving with the seasons? A low hourly wage and no chance for health insurance? A garden variety of potential wilderness pitfalls, including injury, exposure, even wild animals? Or, perhaps most alarmingly, the hazards of competing with other territorial pickers, some of whom supposedly carried firearms?

Disappearing into a forest at dawn and exiting just before dark with a hundred pounds of delicious, enchanting chanterelles—this idea gnawed at me. How did they do it? I liked to think of myself as an accomplished naturalist and outdoorsman. I understood the fine nuances of habitat, the need to think strategically, the fact that there was no substitute for boots on the ground. Still, the expertise of the pros remained unfathomable. So I vowed to find these mushroom hunters and learn their secrets. Infiltrating the hidden world of the commercial pickers, in particular, would require caution. Martha objected outright. I explained my plan to an acquaintance in Oregon who was in the process of starting a truffle farm. "These guys are very territorial," she wrote back, "and most pack guns. They can be dangerous. I'd think long and hard about hanging out with them." Despite such dire warnings, I was already too far gone. To learn the ways of the mushroom hunters, I would need to stand on their turf, to pick alongside them, and maybe even sell some of my labor at a local buy stand.

THE FIRST HUNTER TO let me inside the circle was in his midthirties and had been foraging for money for nearly half his life. I met him through a friend of a friend. He took me along on the condition that I never reveal his patch or even his name. I tried to wheedle a location out of him ahead of time. "I can't tell you," he said without apology. "Where are you going?" Martha asked me as I filled a backpack with supplies. I said I didn't know, and she gave me that look that said all her worst suspicions had been confirmed. Secrecy is synonymous with mushroom hunting. Stories of prevarication, falsified maps, cloak-and-dagger tactics, and deathbed revelations are passed around like family lore. I'd heard about one desperate competitor who lay in wait—"like a gator in the weeds," the story went—for his rival to come driving by, so he could tail him to a secret patch. As with most mythologizing, there's a high quotient of exaggeration and also a kernel of truth. Mushroom hunters do indeed know one another's car makes and license plate numbers. They keep tabs. Questions of secrecy aside, the anonymous forager's precautions weren't so much about protecting his patch from others as they were about avoiding arrest and prosecution. His patch, it turned out, was inside the boundaries of Mount Rainier National Park.

Like most national parks, Mount Rainier is closed to commercial-scale foraging. I shadowed the forager as he slipped through the forest like a commando behind enemy lines, quietly picking his lobster patch. As far as I could tell, he didn't have a gun, just a pocketknife made in China. In little more than a few hours, we gathered a hundred pounds of mushrooms, then the patch gave out. It was a strangely exhilarating feeling to walk among such hidden bounty. When it was time to go, the forager surprised me by suggesting I drive. "This makes me an accomplice," I said. "Yes," he answered. I carefully drove the speed limit and watched my rearview mirror. A mile outside the boundary of the park, he told me to pull over. In the back, covered in tarps, was a thousand dollars' worth of mushrooms. We both got out of the car. The forager said he wasn't sure if it was smart to have brought me. He preferred to work alone during risky picks, and having a tagalong jeopardized his bottom line. "You understand, right?" he said without animosity. I said I did. But now I'd had a taste. Where could I find someone who would be willing to continue my education? He thought about this for a moment, digging his bootheel into the ground, then looked up. "I know someone you need to meet."

CHAPTER 2

The Circuit Picker

. . .

DOUG GLEN CARNELL REGARDED me sternly. "I've got nothing to hide. Use my whole name—first, last, and middle," although he wasn't sure about the spelling of the middle name. That was just about the first thing Doug said to me, and the policy never wavered as he showed me everything he knew.

To say Doug is a woodsman is to make an easy understatement. Doug has worked as a logger, sure, but he's also served in the military, pounded nails, cut steel, and captained a crab boat. When you drive around the Pacific Northwest's moldering timber communities with Doug in his five-hundred-dollar midnight-blue Buick Century sedan, you spend a lot of time waving to the people you pass, all friends or former colleagues: shake rats, long-liners, Cat drivers, metal scrappers, and those three old coots jawing outside the general store. He might spin a yarn about the ghost of a little girl who haunts Willapa Bay's oyster flats or point out the eroded tops of cedar posts used long ago as an Indian salmon weir. He's skied with Olympic medalists and sold peaches for profit. He's been thrice married and thrice divorced. But, above all, Doug is a mushroom picker.

The first time Doug took me picking, we agreed to meet in Hoquiam, on the scruffy southwestern rim of the Olympic Peninsula, a place known for its ragged edges and old salts. I was looking for a tall rangy guy, middle-aged, with ramrod posture and nervous hands—a stalk of wild asparagus gone to seed and waving in the wind. Unfortunately, our chosen rendezvous, a 7-Eleven across the street from Sasquatch Pizza and the Hum-Dinger Drive Thru, was buzzing with police activity—a hit-and-run—and I worried that my new guide might spook and head in the opposite direction. For all his virtues, and there were many, Doug Carnell was a man with at least one major vice in the eyes of the law.

But at ten A.M. on the nose he rattled up in his muddy Buick. Though Doug says he's six-one, he looked taller, with long arms and legs and the energy of an itchy adolescent. He had a shock of graying shoulder-length hair, a bushy mustache that partially covered his upper lip, and the deep, soulful brown eyes of a born lady-killer. Forest debris littered his shoulders; this was Doug's lunch break, not that he would be eating anything more than a Twinkie. We shook. His hands were rough, shaped and coarsened by a life of labor, with dirt caked under the nails and knobs at the joints. He was definitely not the picture of a modern recreationist. Self-consciously, I looked at myself: hiking boots, convertible pants, pink hands poking out from a shiny blue layer of swaddling Gore-Tex. Doug sat back on his heels, thumbs in his belt loops, wearing the traditional uniform of the rural outdoorsman, which is to say the man who works in the outdoors for a living: soiled blue jeans, black lace-up boots, faded green hoodie. The sweatshirt said SCREAMING EAGLES, not that he could remember exactly where these loud raptors resided, maybe near Pendleton, Oregon, he thought, where he sometimes picks morels in the spring. Doug has harvested mushrooms up and down the West Coast for three decades, and each little town consignment store has its own rack of cast-off high school garb for sale when you're in a pinch.

Doug is what's known as a circuit picker. He follows the wild mushroom trail year-round, picking his home patches near Westport, Washington, in the fall, traveling south through Oregon into northern California for the winter, and then marching right back up the east slope of the Sierras and Cascade Mountains in spring, sometimes deep into British Columbia if the pick is good. Along the way he'll sell his mushrooms to a favored buyer or visit the buy stands that appear ephemerally like insect hatches in rural communities near the patches. The stands are often no more than a tarp or wall tent strung up in a gas station parking lot with a foldout table, scales, and maybe a wood-stove. Regular pickers know they can expect to find buy stations in places like Willits, California; Brookings, Oregon; and Trout Lake, Washington. This is a cash-only economy. Doug doesn't write or deposit checks. He doesn't use a credit card. He doesn't even have a bank account.

PEOPLE HAVE BEEN PICKING mushrooms since humans first came down from the trees. As a way to make a living, though, the U.S. wild mushroom harvest is a relatively recent development. It didn't get going in any sort of meaningful way until the 1970s, when select restaurants started using wild mushrooms and other foraged foods on a more regular basis to show their commitment to regional flavors, seasonal eating, and quality ingredients. As a product of nature that doesn't require the clearing of land or profligate irrigation, much less pesticides and herbicides—that doesn't require any attention from human beings at all—the wild mushroom is perhaps the signature ingredient in the pantheon of natural foods. Restaurants such as Chez Panisse in Berkeley, California, prided themselves on their local and seasonal produce, and as this new way of eating caught on in the 1980s, foraged foods became increasingly desirable all over the country. On the West Coast, the new market for wild mushrooms happened to coincide with a downturn in the timber industry, so many of the first professional mushroom pickers were ex-loggers. They knew the woods and needed the money. Today the pickers are more likely to be recent immigrants, often Southeast Asian refugees who fled their native countries in the post-Vietnam era, or, more recently, Latinos on the migrant trail, mostly out of Mexico but from other Central American countries as well. Doug was one of the few white pickers still in the game. He was, as I was later told, a picker's picker.

It was late September, end of the dry season, the brief Cascadia summer officially put on notice. The mushroom harvest had shifted from mountains to coast, where fog and damp maritime air rolled in thick and heavy like spilled paint, coating the woods with necessary moisture. Come morning, the dense underbrush shone with condensation. Conifer needles dripped slowly in the silence. Mushroom pickers call this the drip line and know to go to these places first. I told Doug I wanted to shadow him, see how it was done, maybe even try my own hand at picking commercially. If this interest in his work came as a surprise, he didn't let on. "We'll get you into some mushrooms," he said in that laconic way of his, the sort of understatement you might hear from firefighters or jet pilots. "But understand it's not a simple walk in the woods." In the convenience store, Doug got an oversize refill of coffee—his main nourishment in the field—before making a plan. We stood together outside the 7-Eleven, drinking coffee and looking up. To the west, heavily laden clouds bunched up like ships at a lock, and a few rays of sun shoehorned their way into the sky. The day took a deep breath, poised between the unknowable and the suspect. "It won't rain today," Doug finally decided. "Not for a while yet anyway." We got in his Buick and drove north on Highway 101.

MURRAY MORGAN, WHO WROTE a popular history of Seattle in the 1950s called *Skid Road,* considered Washington's Olympic Peninsula to be the last wilderness in the Lower 48 and enumerated all manner of iconoclasts who lived there, including "latter-day Thoreaus, Marxists in tin-pants, kelp-eaters, single-taxers, theoretical and practicing free lovers, and cooperators of assorted kidney." The peninsula is bordered—or barricaded, you could say—by water: Puget Sound to the east, the Pacific Ocean to the west, and the Strait of Juan de Fuca to the north. Much of its interior rises to the saw-toothed, glacier-studded peaks of the Olympic Mountains. Just shy of eight thousand feet, Mount Olympus is the tallest peak in the range, though so remote as to be rarely visible from almost any vantage save the tops of other surrounding peaks. Several of the peninsula's storied salmon rivers begin at the foot of its glaciers, notably the Elwha, Hoh, Queets, and Quinault. I had backpacked through these heavily forested valleys, fished the rivers for steelhead, and ventured as deep as the rocky moraine of Mount Olympus on foot, a good twenty-five miles from the Hoh River trailhead. It's an area of immense contrasts. The alpine slopes of the Olympic High Divide are arid enough to support a small population of golden eagles that hunt sunbathing marmots, while the rain forest below is among the dampest places in the temperate world, with parts of it receiving nearly two hundred inches of rain a year—sixteen feet of precipitation, twice the depth of the average swimming pool's deep end. The creeping mildew never lets up. This rain forest—tall, dark, imposing—discouraged homesteading, and a citadel of steep mountains blocked overland travel. Not surprisingly, the Olympic Peninsula was one of the last regions of continental America to be settled by Europeans. Even as the twentieth century approached, much of its territory still had not been explored, and in 1889, a year before the closing of the American frontier, a motley crew of cowhands and would-be adventurers led by Scotsman James Halbold Christie set out to be the first to traverse its peaks and valleys, in the middle of winter, no less. Perhaps all one needs to know about this foolhardy band of mostly novice explorers and liversots is that they quaffed their full allotment of whiskey before making it five miles up the Elwha Valley. After that they built a boat and endeavored to travel by river. When the boat sank, they rented two mules, Dollie and Jennie, to pull the reconditioned barge upriver. Dollie fell four hundred feet to her demise; Jennie quit after weeks of punishing labor and was allowed to fend for herself. Months later the Press Party, named for newspaper sponsor the *Seattle Press*, arrived on the other side of the mountains near Lake Quinault and wired its patrons for a hot meal.

Today the same route can be followed by trail during summer months in a long weekend.

Olympic National Park occupies much of the peninsula's interior, with nearly a million square acres of forests, mountains, and rivers. In President Theodore Roosevelt's original conception of the reserve, it was meant to safeguard the largest subspecies of elk on the continent, now known as Roosevelt elk. By the time the park was finally written into law by the Bull Moose's cousin, Franklin Delano Roosevelt, the acreage had been cut in half, with the lumber interests successful in largely excising the most lucrative timber reserves. Small remnants of the great temperate rain forests—the Bogachiel, Hoh, Queets, and Quinault—are all that's left of the ancient tracts. Outside the park's borders, the big trees fell in swift order across thousands of square miles. To a faller or timber baron, even as late as the 1920s, the forests of the Olympic Peninsula must have seemed like a limitless resource. The first settlers and loggers used hand axes and saws. A single Douglas fir with a ten-foot diameter at the base and more than two hundred feet in height—as high as the Golden Gate Bridge's car deck—might take weeks to drop. Then came mule teams, followed by steam donkeys (large steam-powered winches that initiated industrial logging in the late 1800s). The railroad logging of the early 1900s picked up the pace, while the advent of gas-powered chain saws in the Depression era wrote the forests' epitaph. Driving 101 through the peninsula today is an exercise in marveling at America's amazing can-do spirit—and an unhappy reminder of how that spirit can lead to unchecked desire, greed, and overconsumption.

Environmentalists tried in vain to slow the cutting. It wasn't until the 1980s, during the "timber wars" of antilogging protests, that they were able to leverage the Endangered Species Act, thanks to a retiring, little known, and quickly disappearing bird, the northern spotted owl. Spotted owls depend on old growth for hunting and nesting. Researchers tracked their decline in tandem with the disappearing ancient forest.

There used to be a house on the approach to Aberdeen (city motto:

"Come as You Are") with a front yard given over to a vast collection of rusted logging equipment. A large replica spotted owl, made from plywood and carefully painted, hung from a tree, with a halo over its head. The message seemed ambiguous, though probably not to local residents. The once-thriving cities of Hoquiam and Aberdeen, on either side of the log-choked Hoquiam River, are probably best known now as the formative grounds of Nirvana front man Kurt Cobain. A half century ago, these aspiring communities and high school rivals enjoyed a bustling local economy of shops, restaurants, and even stage theaters, most of it supported by timber. The shuttered downtown buildings and denuded hillsides tell how that story played out. Hoquiam, home of the much-ballyhooed Loggers Playday and its competitive feats of strength (log-rolling, ax-throwing, choker-setting, tree-topping, and the "hot saw" contest), now draws more tourists to the Bowerman Basin Shorebird Festival. And so it goes for scuffling timber towns throughout the Pacific Northwest. The answer to redevelopment, in many cases, can be found in the woods themselves, not as milled lumber but in the form of outdoor recreation, restored salmon streams, and a host of products the logging industry refers to plaintively as "non-wood timber products": wild edibles, medicinals, and floral displays.

DOUG HAS DONE HIS fair share of logging. He remembers cutting coastal old-growth cedar in the 1980s. He's not proud of this work, in hindsight, though at the same time he wants me to understand the ritual of it, how in a place like this the logger was king, how the men on a logging crew shared an identity not unlike men who go to war together: Mere civilians could never understand their work or their bond. To be an old-growth logger was to have membership in an exclusive club. The work was dangerous and the pay good. Paradoxically, the same loggers who felled jumbo Douglas firs and Sitka spruce also spent their off-shift hours in the forest, hunting, fishing, trapping, camping. Many of them lost jobs during the spotted-owl controversy. These were high-paying jobs, and no one, save the tree huggers, wanted the logging to end. Everyone on the peninsula either worked in the timber industry or knew someone who did. Handmade signs in store windows famously said: THIS BUSINESS SUPPORTED BY TIMBER $$$. Everyone was in on it.

"Still, we shouldn't have cut it all," he says finally. "Have you ever seen a brown creek? I'm not talking about spring melt—I'm talking about a creek that runs brown after every rain. All that sediment and crap in the water, washing down from the hills, it smothers the salmon eggs. They don't have a chance." As a mushroom picker, he's learned to see the forest in a different light. The trees and the salmon and the mushrooms are all part of the same picture. "It's like a spiderweb," Doug told me. Shake one corner of the web and sure as hell the spider will feel it on the other side. To be a mushroom picker is not all that different from felling trees or netting salmon. It's outdoor work that requires an intimate knowledge of the natural world and a willingness to labor in abject conditions that would test anyone's resolve. "But," said Doug, "picking mushrooms don't hurt anybody. Not when it's done right."

Doug exudes confidence in the rural arts: hunting, fishing, woodworking. He'll tell you stories. He'll show you a river where the silvers are running thick or offer you a haunch from the elk that he'll no doubt get later that fall. He'll tell you about the old-growth cedar roots he found that he intends to fashion into bedposts (because his most recent ex-wife made off with all the furniture). Sit down with him for a drink—more likely a tall Styrofoam cup of 7-Eleven coffee than a beer—and you'd be forgiven for assuming he was a born-and-bred country boy. He isn't. Doug was raised in Rainier Beach, a tough neighborhood in South Seattle. A latchkey kid, he spent a good part of his childhood playing on the streets to keep his distance from a difficult father, and it nearly cost him his life at the age of twelve or thirteen when, during a rare Seattle snowstorm, he impaled himself clear through the neck on a tree branch after a wild episode of unchaperoned sledding. The branch nicked his jugular. With blood spurting, he managed to pull himself up, wrap the wound with a scarf, and make it the two blocks to an ER before collapsing.

This near-death experience didn't change his trajectory. At the age of fifteen or sixteen, after one too many petty crimes, he was shipped off to a ranch in Texas, a reform school of sorts, in lieu of juvenile detention. On his first day, he and another kid stole a ranch vehicle and went joyriding. It turned out to be the principal's truck. The bad behavior continued until he was faced with a choice. Rather than do time, Doug enlisted in the Army and was sent to Alaska for basic training. "Those were good years," he says about his three-year stint in the military. He came home to Washington State and started getting into trouble again. In the agricultural community of Yakima, east of the Cascades, he found assorted farmwork and partied at night. This was the eighties. In addition to being a famous apple hub, Yakima was notorious as one of the smallest U.S. cities with its own DEA office, a by-product of the migrant-worker trail out of Mexico and the steady stream of narcotics that followed. Doug got into cocaine and discovered he didn't have the "shutoff valve" that recreational drug users have; neither did his friends. Of the people he remembers from those years, most are dead: overdoses, AIDS, car accidents. Winters, he worked at the White Pass ski area an hour away in the mountains, where the Mahre brothers were training for their Olympic runs. Doug explains his termination there as the day he got drunk and "tried to punch out the entire U.S. ski team." He went back to Yakima and got deeper into the other local snow, freebasing for the added high and finally resorting to shooting up. He remembers being in his early twenties and trying to go cold turkey at his grandmother's funeral, the sweat pouring off him, his eyes wild. He called Narcotics Anonymous and somehow found himself at a rehab center, where he jumped the line to get in. "They knew I needed help, and quick." That was the end of Doug's hard-drug career. After leaving detox, he pointed his car west to flee the scene, arriving a day later at the appropriately named town of Westport, on the edge of the Pacific, where he still lives today.

In Westport, Doug worked as a commercial fisherman for a while, even ran his own boat. When he went down to Crescent City, California, one year to fish Dungeness crab, he made the mistake of sending the checks back home, where a nonstop party was going on in his absence. Powerful, speed-like drugs that could be easily manufactured with cheap household products—drugs such as methamphetamine—had cut a path of destruction through rural communities across the country. The day after Doug got home, the bank repossessed his boat. "You feel like a loser," he told me, the implacable face of the Pacific just beyond the car windows. "It's one thing to lose your house. To lose your boat . . . In the eyes of the community, you don't know how to do your job." That's when Doug gave up fishing—and his second wife—to become a full-time, semi-itinerant mushroom picker.

NEAR THE COASTAL TOWN of Moclips, we ducked inland and followed a gravel road into private timberlands. Doug calls this "shake rat" territory. The shake rats are, in many ways, the final phase of industrial logging, gleaners of the scraps left behind. Everyone calls them shake rats, even the shake rats themselves. In the old days before the spotted owl, the shake rats enjoyed a bonanza. They felled enormous coastal red cedars and cut the logs into bolts to fashion the world's greatest shingles, or shakes, with the help of mechanical splitters. With its imperviousness to water, cedar is an ideal wood for siding, decks, and any other exterior building use. Now, with the functional end of old-growth logging, the shake rats were combing through the leftovers of a bygone era—they were the dumpster divers behind restaurants, sifting through piles of garbage for anything palatable. Doug prefers a different metaphor. Like paleontologist fossil hunters, he says, they uncover traces of an epoch that's passed into history's dustbin. They spread across the land and search for old cedar stumps, even excavating them from underground. They pull weather-beaten logs and snags from the reproduction stands that were left behind for whatever reason. Logs that were deemed too twisted or too small—logs that might have been forgotten merely because of a shift change thirty years ago—are now treated like found treasure and turned into shakes. Such cedar deposits, Doug explained, also attract mushrooms.

We drove past a clearing with a collection of shotgun shacks clustered around a small, run-down mill as if huddled around a smoldering fire. The community resembled a nineteenth-century gold-rush town hastily carved from the wilderness. I'd seen pictures of company towns from the early logging booms, and this didn't look much different. Simple one- or two-room shanties, some of them with trailers annexed to one side, squatted in the dirt. Smoke curled from a dozen stovepipes. Those with more aesthetic aspirations displayed collections of detritus found in the woods: corroded saw blades, old wooden signs, a doll's head nailed to a stump. Your average passing motorist with a flat tire would hesitate to knock on any of these doors. We idled past the mill, announcing ourselves with Doug's muffler— meth-head tweakers had stolen the catalytic converter for quick cash—and Doug waved to the shake rats visible inside the open, barn-like interior. The guy working the saw nodded. "Got to be tough to do that job," Doug said with admiration. "When the saw breaks, you lose a finger. I knew a guy who cut off his finger in the morning, had the hole sewed up, and was back to finish his shift in the afternoon. That's tough. Most guys would be drinking by then."

Past the community of shake rats, we turned onto another spur, this one barely passable. We barreled through a forest of alder that was closing in on the jeep track, the branches singing on the sides of the car. At a puddle as deep as a hot tub, Doug told me to hold my breath before he gunned the engine. Water splashed up on the hood. We bottomed out and then parked before the road deteriorated into a goat path, got out, and examined steam coming off the radiator. Doug ran his finger across the accumulated moisture and licked it. No worries, just water. He patted his Buick. "The Blue Pig has been good to me."

We had arrived at our first pick of the day. "There are two kinds of patches," Doug explained to me. "Friendlies and hostiles." I wondered which one we were visiting now. He surveyed his sparse gear: old five-gallon paint bucket with lid; unsheathed steak knife from the Dollar Tree ("two for one"); and, in the trunk, several plastic rectangular baskets that resembled a supermarket basket without the handle. The baskets, I knew, were becoming a scarce commodity. Everyone needed them—pickers, buyers, restaurants. They got traded back and forth on a regular basis. Mushroom pickers everywhere were constantly on the lookout for cheap baskets. Each one held on average between ten and fifteen pounds of mushrooms. Like produce boxes, they could be stacked: on the backseat of a car, in a walk-in cooler, or even up a packboard, a modified backpack frame designed to carry several baskets through the bush. Someone was manufacturing them abroad, in Asia or somewhere, just not quickly enough.

With a touch of alarm, I also took note of what Doug *didn't* have. He didn't carry a map or compass or GPS unit. In fact, I doubted he had any of the hiker's so-called Ten Essentials on his person. He didn't even have water. I asked him if he'd ever gotten lost or spent a night in the woods. *Never.* How did he get around? He just *knew* these woods, as if the entire Olympic Peninsula were his sandbox. Surely, I said, there must have been a time when he got turned around. Doug thought about it and decided, *No,* he'd never had an issue. And animals didn't worry him either. "I've only had two scary animal encounters," he said, one involving a pack of aggressive coyotes that closed in on him because he was in the woods at night without a flashlight. He "bellered" at the coyotes, which only seemed to set the pack off, and they started to dart in at him as he swung a big stick to keep them at bay. Luckily, his friends had heard his roar and, knowing he was in trouble, ran through the woods with lanterns and scared the pack away. I told Doug that a few years ago I might not have put much stock in this tale—coyotes were viewed as harmless, after all— but recently a woman in Canada had been killed by a pack. It appeared that the animals were getting more belligerent as they grew in numbers.

"There you go," Doug said. "I swear God's truth it happened. Put my hand on a Bible." Doug had gotten religion recently, though he said it was more of a modified spiritualism (and later, at quitting time, he would tell me the best thing about going to Catholic reform school as a teenager was all that sweet virginal poon). The second memorable animal encounter Doug neglected to get into, said he'd save it for later when we were around the campfire, telling ghost stories. Instead, bucket and knife in one hand and the other hand free to fend off the brush, he dove into the forest. Salal gave way to evergreen huckleberry and then to a dense mix of young cedar and western hemlock. It was a jumbled mess, a forest reinvented after the calamity of industrial logging. Through the trees you could catch glimpses of old stumps that dwarfed the new growth around them. Relics from the first cut, when the forest was a howling wilderness, the stumps held on in various states of decay, some of them as wide as a garage door, with slot-like gouges visible where preindustrial loggers had placed their foot planks for better purchase before working a two-man crosscut saw back and forth across the thousand-year-old trunk. Smaller stumps from successive harvests gathered round the giants in tight clusters, like children at the feet of a storyteller.

I followed Doug deeper into the woods, already knowing he was the one I'd been looking for, someone willing to share the mysteries of a nearly unknown trade with a total outsider. We parted the bushes as we went, the underbrush shedding its water like a wet dog. Despite such slick conditions, Doug loped ahead on his long legs, leaping over logs and straddling deadfall. This dark grove, already logged two or three times in the past hundred years, was dense and unsightly, with a bedraggled look that is typical of industrial forest. Once it was giant red cedar, now spindly hemlock and Douglas fir. Everywhere there was tangled undergrowth and leftover logging slash. Doug moved through the brush like water through a stream, with fluidity and purpose, immune to its thorns, burrs, and sharp, jagged ends. I struggled to keep up. Soon I fell behind and couldn't find him anywhere. It was suffocating in there, and sound didn't travel far. Scanning left and right, I failed to pick him out among the snarl of regrowth. A paranoid thought crossed my mind. Maybe it was tradition, like with cops or soldiers, to haze the new initiate, to spin him around blindly in the forest and see how he did trying to find a way out. The realization of being lost in the woods: Few moments are scarier. Almost immediately I could feel my heart knocking wildly against my ribs. Then I heard Doug's voice up ahead. He was waiting for me to catch up, and I chastised myself for doubting.

Near the top of a rise, we stood together on an elevated nurse log, a dozen saplings sprouting around our feet from its mossy hide, and looked down into a shallow ravine. All around was rot and decay cloaked by a carpet of bright green, and from this moist ground protruded the creamy white caps of mushrooms, hundreds of them. Standing there, looking out upon such bounty, was like deciphering the answer to a perplexing riddle. "It's just a small patch," said Doug.

Doug has patches up and down the West Coast, has in fact forgotten more patches than most pickers will ever know. When you follow Doug through the salal and huckleberry and old cedar slash, you're following a man who has created little trails through the forest, just as the elk and deer and bears do. These trails lead directly to mushrooms, which end up in his bucket by the pound and are later emptied into baskets to be weighed by the buyer so that Doug can get paid and have gas money to make the next trip into the woods. Each patch is different. This was a cedar bog, the place to find the first hedgehog mushrooms of the season.

THE BEGINNING OF ANY SEASON is a time cherished by mushroom pickers. They get to pick a new species, for one thing, which helps to break up the monotony that can set in after picking one type of mushroom for too long, and, perhaps more important, the prices are high. The vanguard of a mushroom flush always sees the best prices paid to a picker. Chefs clamor to be the first to offer such seasonal delicacies and pay top dollar. Doug hoped to get six or seven dollars per pound for these hedgehogs, which would be a few dollars more than the current going rate of four dollars for chanterelles.

The other advantage of picking a new species was the change in scenery. For someone like Doug, a good percentage of the enjoyment is in spending time in the woods. It is most certainly not about the money. Most pickers live hand to mouth and routinely scrounge around to make a little extra to pay bills. As with any manual labor, no one is getting rich picking mushrooms. But there was something to be said for this line of work, it seemed to me at that moment, as I whacked another huckleberry branch out of the way and kneeled down among the delicate fronds of maidenhead fern to pick a trio of hedgehogs in the moss. There was something to be said about working in the outdoors far from the madding crowds, being your own boss.

"Madding crowds, huh. Is that like crowds gone mad? Sounds like the city." Doug wiped the sweat out of his eyes. "I should have gone to college. This is okay. Each day I wake up and decide where I'll pick. I've got no regrets. How many college-educated get to play in the woods for a living?" Granted, on some days the alarm clock goes off at three A.M.—as it will tomorrow. Tomorrow, Doug tells me, he plans to visit one of his best patches up north. It's a long drive and he needs to be there by dawn, before the other pickers—the lazier pickers—descend on it. He was there last week and picked a few mushrooms. Tomorrow, he's sure, the flush will be *on*.

But today was a hedgehog day, at least for starters. The hedgehog is the underdog of the edible-mushroom crowd. Though it doesn't get invited to the same fancy parties as chanterelles, porcini, and morels, the hedgehog perseveres when those other varieties have had too much to drink and call it a night. It's a member of the toothed-fungi group, with two species regularly picked by commercial foragers in North America. *Hydnum repandum,* the larger of the two, is known as a "spreader" on the circuit, for its habit of growing a wide, hand-sized cap over a short stem. The smaller *Hydnum umbilicatum* is called a "belly button." Though diminutive, belly buttons can grow in vast colonies across the forest floor. Chefs like them because they're cute and look good on a plate. Each species is sometimes referred to as a "sweet tooth" mushroom, though the taste is more spicy than sweet. Like good wine or chocolate, hedgehogs have a complex flavor profile that can be different things to different people. Hints of clove, cinnamon, and black pepper intermingle with the deeper, earthier fungal underpinning that is characteristic of most wild mushrooms, giving hedgehogs a versatility in the kitchen that lends itself equally to rich, heavy preparations such as risottos, casseroles, and cream sauces as well as to lighter fare such as vegetable stir-fries.

"Here now," Doug said, crouching beside me. "You want to give 'em a clean cut, like this." He brandished his large knife and swiped at a clump of hedgehogs with a single, deft movement. The mushrooms parted from the base of their stalks and fell into his open palm, their cut ends smooth and the toothy undersides of the caps plainly visible. Hedgehogs are one of the easiest of the edible mushrooms for the neophyte to identify. Instead of gills, they have rows of small teeth resembling the spines of a hedgehog. Their coloration is creamy to pinkish orange, sometimes causing them to be confused with chanterelles—until picked, that is, when the brittle spines underneath the cap give them away. Their flesh is dense and white inside and holds up quite well in the pan, and though they bruise easily, requiring extra care from the picker, they're also tough, enduring cold snaps, hard frosts, and light snowstorms well into the season. This cold tolerance also means they have a long life both in the field and on the refrigerator shelf, making them a supremely useful wild ingredient for the restaurateur, at a time when most wild ingredients have gone to bed for the winter.

"Cut your hogs clean," Doug said again. "You don't want any of the dirt coming home with you." If any dirt gets into a bucket of hedgehogs, it finds its way into the spines and is nearly impossible to remove. Stems that are left jagged or tattered develop unappetizing bruises. This same bruising effect can stain the caps if they aren't handled gingerly.

Though I had been picking hedgehogs for several years, I thought of them mainly as an occasional treat. They weren't as widespread as chanterelles, and my patches were in such random locales that I had trouble making any clear distinctions about their habitat. They tended to be a surprise that I enjoyed each fall, late in the season. My best patch had been in a block of old-growth hemlock near Snoqualmie Pass in the North Cascades, in an area that was otherwise cut to ribbons by timber harvest. There was an informal shooting range nearby, where gun nuts would bring their semiautomatics and squeeze off round after round all day long. Despite the noise, the local wildlife seemed to sense they were in no danger, and on each occasion that I picked this patch I saw some form of megafauna, including bears, elk, deer, ravens, and secretive woodland hawks known as accipiters. On steep slopes running up to a ridgeline just above four thousand feet, I found the hedgehogs in clusters at the base of conifers and among the bear grass. Once I picked them in an inch of fresh snow; their tan caps stuck out of the powder at angles and they looked to all be having a lively conversation despite the weather. Another year the patch didn't fruit at all. I asked around but no one knew why. Mushrooms are largely a mystery.

More recently I had found hedgehogs while backpacking up the Elwha drainage of Olympic National Park, where the Press Party had made their clumsy crossing. Ten miles in from the trailhead, I started seeing them in the moss where the forest was darkest and wettest. While this should have told me something, I needed Doug to articulate it. The hedgehogs here in this cedar bog fruited in similar conditions: dark, wet forest governed by cool, coastal fogs, with a significant presence of older trees, in this case the decaying stumps of cedar. Doug told me to look for the seams. Bright green moss grew luxuriantly in the moister pockets unclaimed by the salal and huckleberry and on top of rotting logs that looked like long humps of upheaved earth or burial mounds. The hedgehogs fruited in the crevices of these logs, in the holes left by rotted-out stumps, and along the upwelled margins of underground seeps. We found them in groups and all alone. An important realization struck me: Recreational mushroom pickers often distinguish between the age classes of trees when discussing habitat—not, usually, whether those trees are alive or dead. I had always thought of the hedgehog as an old-growth-loving species; now I understood that the old growth need not necessarily be standing. Doug scouted for such cedar bogs, where the earth feels as if it's moving under your feet, with dark-brown, nearly red splinters of cedar piercing the blackened dirt like shipwrecks towed to the surface. Even dead cedars take multiple human lifetimes to decompose. In these swamps the ground was virtually made up of dead and dying cedars, some of them left over from past logging, some of them part of the natural cycle of death and rebirth that has gone on for millennia, since the oceans first receded from this spot and the cedar forests evolved out of the muck.

One of the single best bites of food I've ever had involved hedgehog mushrooms. I was at a beef tasting, holding a pencil and a sheet of paper with an intricate grading system. We were eating different brands of artisanal beef—grass-fed, organic, and Wagyu, all of them grilled to the same doneness by the chef for apple-to-apple comparison. I happen to love steak, and this was some of the best available. Yet the bite I remember from that night was not beef at all. It was served on a white porcelain spoon, an intermezzo to clean our palates before the next round of beef tasting. The spoon contained a mixture of sautéed wild mushrooms, including hedgehogs and chanterelles, finished with creamy mascarpone and some fresh herbs and spices. I remember cleaning the spoon in one lip-smacking bite and then nearly falling off my chair. The mushrooms were as robust as the steak, with an equally profound flavor. "What was that?" I asked the person sitting next to me. We were on to the next cut of beef, though, and no one could be bothered with questions about mushrooms.

"How do you like to cook hedgehogs?" I asked Doug. He thought about the question for a moment and then said he hadn't eaten a hedgehog in seven, maybe eight years. "I can't even remember what they taste like!" This was one of the small ironies of the business that I would run into again and again. The mushrooms are the equivalent of cash. They get picked, piled into baskets, and then sold for money. Every last bankable mushroom goes to the buyer, except perhaps for a few handfuls that are occasionally used as barter or given to friends.

We worked our way into the bog, catwalking on deadfall and jumping down to soft mossy landings. Hedgehogs sprang from impossible nooks and crannies on the forest floor, many of them wedged under logs, where they fruited out of the decaying wood fiber. Doug sliced them off with his one-dollar knife, careful to ensure that the stem of each mushroom was neatly cut so dirt wouldn't get into his bucket. He was very conscious of his reputation in the picker world, priding himself on delivering clean mushrooms that didn't require a lot of primping before being sent off to restaurants, where a dirty batch might be summarily sent back for refund. Buyers appreciated clean pickers and often rewarded them with a couple of extra quarters per pound. A clean basket saved everyone up the line time and money.

The picking, however, was slow. After an hour Doug had just five or six pounds—maybe forty dollars' worth—and the patch was petering out. Clearly the flush wasn't on yet. Just the same, this was useful information. "Half of my trips are scouting," he told me. He might wait another week or more before coming back to this spot. What about permits? I asked him. Did he need permission to pick this area? "Now, see, this is what I'm talking about. This is a friendly patch. No one will hassle us here. So much has changed since I first got in the game. Twenty years ago you didn't need papers for anything, and now you practically need a permit to fart in the wind."

We bushwhacked back up to the car, eating handfuls of evergreen huckleberries as we went. "You like those berries?" Doug asked me. Sure, I said. "Me too. They energize me. They must have good stuff in them, because every fall I eat these berries and wake up each morning ready to run around all day in the woods." Huckleberries, like other *Vaccinium*s such as blueberries, are loaded with antioxidants and other nutrients. These woods, which we once viewed solely in terms of board feet and dollars, were shelter to countless wild foods and medicinals, many of which science had only recently begun to understand.

Doug lined one of his baskets with newspaper and carefully emptied his bucket of hedgehogs into it. We drove back out the way we came. On an impulse, Doug decided we'd pull over at one of the shake-rat shacks to see if his old friend and onetime logging partner was home. Never in a million years would I have approached one of these shanties on the edge of the woods by myself. I studied Doug's expression for clues. Was this a test of some sort? A put-on? We found Johnny sitting in a La-Z-Boy recliner, reading a book on cannabis cultivation. His chair was in the middle of the shack, and virtually everything Johnny needed—food, beer, reading material—was stacked against three of four walls, all within arm's reach. It might have been the tiniest home I had ever seen, not unlike those tourist-attraction cabins built from the hollowed-out stump of a redwood. Johnny's bed was an unmade mattress in a loft above. He stood up slowly, wearing ticking coveralls and a denim shirt. From the looks of them, his clothes hadn't seen a washbasin in more than a week. A shiny patina of grime caught the light slanting through his doorway. He squinted. Across his forehead stretched an ugly wound, a brownish slit a few inches long and sewn haphazardly together, perhaps by Johnny himself. He followed us back outside where there was room to talk, blinking in the light. A fifty-gallon drum beside a fire pit overflowed with empty cans of Busch. Riotous tangles of multicolored nasturtiums had taken over the small vegetable garden. Doug pulled off a red flower and ate it. "You know you can get a nickel a flower in Seattle for these."

Johnny considered this for a moment. "You're shittin' me," he finally said.

"God's truth."

"I always learn something from you, Doug. It's a weed here. *Bam,* just took over. You still picking mushrooms?"

"Hogs. Slow day."

Johnny tilted his head and looked around. A pickup pulled up, with two shifty-looking guys in the front. Doug waved hello, the way he did with everyone. They wouldn't look at us, just waited in their cab, windows rolled up and eyes averted.

"See you later, Johnny. Watch out for the Who-Hit-John," Doug advised. I followed him back to the car. "Those fellers in the pickup have whatever it is they all plan to drink, smoke, or snort for the rest of the day. I can't hang out in a scene like that no more. Let's go."

We drove out of Shake Ratville. "Now, that was a friendly patch," Doug explained to me carefully, so I would understand. "Next we visit the hostile."

CHAPTER 3

Kings for a Day

...

COMMUNICATION WITH DOUG WAS a haphazard affair. He had no phone or email address. Sometimes he used the phone of his roommate in Westport, a guy who claimed to have once been a stockbroker and a documentary filmmaker and was now living on disability after a Navy diving accident. Other times Doug borrowed a phone from a friend or relative. Calls came through at odd hours on lines listed as BLOCKED or RESTRICTED. As frustrating as this could be, it was hard to be annoyed when the voice at the other end impersonated a game-show host or IRS flunky. "Allo, allo? Ees dees Monsieur Cook? Congrat-u-lations! You are zee winner . . ." Whatever I was doing, I always dropped everything to join Doug for a day of picking mushrooms. Even when it meant a hostile patch.

Doug looked out at the sea stacks and sighed. For once the Pacific was living up to its name. He pointed to some rock piles offshore. "On a calm day like today, you'd get into some serious rockfish jigging right out there. Or surf perch off the beach. It's a day to fish." Though Doug took pride in his past as a commercial fisherman, he wasn't too happy that both his sons were now fishing up in Alaska. "It's a macho thing," he said to me. I wondered if he really thought so. Doug loved to fish and dig clams. His crab boat had been his prized possession before the bank took it away. It was hard to believe that he disapproved of his sons' decisions to fish, even if such jobs were among the most dangerous imaginable. We drove across the hardpan beach, Doug stopping every now and then to scope a tasty-looking rip or rock pile, until we came to a spot where the woods met the dunes. It was the intersection of past and present, a spot where Doug's working life could be viewed nearly in its entirety. To the west, ocean; to the east, woods. Signs everywhere declared the place private property. He turned to me, his brown eyes wide, trying to make me understand what was ultimately indefensible. "I've been picking this patch for twenty-five years. A few lousy signs don't make no difference to me."

Trees standing at the edge of the continent look shell-shocked. Storms blow in off the Pacific and batter the shoreline. The coastal fringe of forest gets tossed and pounded, sprayed by salt and lashed with sand. This happens storm after storm, year after year, and after a while the bravest among them begin to falter. They spill down the slope in contorted fits, like drunks stumbling down bleacher steps at halftime, and get swept away. It's a landscape of perpetual disintegration.

Here and there, weathered shore pines twisted up beneath a line of stunted spruce, determined to make a stand. Briars filled in the pockets. Signs nailed to the trees, in contrast to the vegetation, looked fresh, like a new coat of paint on an otherwise dilapidated house. The property had recently changed hands, and the new owners of this oceanfront acreage were keen to announce that its management would be new too. We got out of the car and walked up the beach, then turned to face the land. No one was around. "Don't worry, I won't get you in trouble. Just stay behind me." We walked up and over the dunes. I followed Doug on a guerrilla trail, one he'd obviously made himself, through a thicket of beach scrub, then into a desultory woods of shore pine and spruce, until we could go no farther.

A six-foot-tall high-tensile woven wire fence marked the property line adjacent to the public beach. A taut strand of barbed wire ran along the top as if it were a prison camp.

Doug paused before the fence. "This is where I get in," he said plainly, as if judgment never existed. He pointed to a section that had been bent back to allow a gymnastic sort of entrance. Golden chanterelles, bright blips of brilliant yellow, bloomed in darkness along the length of the fence. We could see troops of them marching up the hillside. These were a type of chanterelle variously called fluorescents, rainbows, peaches, and spruce chanterelles. Unlike the most common species of chanterelle in the Pacific Northwest, which grew in Douglas fir forests, these mushrooms were mycorrhizal with spruce—Sitka spruce on the coast and Engelmann spruce in the mountains—and they flashed an intense neon color in the light. Some mushroom fanciers considered this the most beautiful and best tasting of all the North American chanterelles. *Cantharellus cibarius var. roseocanus* was the scientific name. Nearby a stout king bolete stood all alone, beckoning us. The king is the BMOC of mushrooms, the quarterback, the one voted most likely to succeed. Modesty doesn't become the king. It juts from the earth on a solid, trunk-like stem. Its head swells with the rain: broad, dome-shaped, a trophy atop a solid foundation. Pedigree demands that it attend only the best habitats: high mountain passes and exclusive coastal real estate.

I narrowed my eyes to get a better view. It was dark inside these stunted woods, nearly dark as nighttime. I could hear the surf rolling in, could smell the salt water. Doug looked this way and that, shifting his gaze like a bank robber in the middle of a heist. The week before he had been picking another favorite old patch that had recently changed hands. The new owners were scions of some sort—Doug couldn't remember what business or which family—and had hired an entire army of guards to police their new estate. It occurred to me this might have been added incentive for a man like Doug to poach the patch. He took a friend with him, and they snuck in through a quiet corner far from the main compound. Buckets filled fast. Doug thought he was in the clear. That's when they heard the voices. *Hey, you, hold it right there!* They took off through the woods. His friend lost his bucket right away. Doug clutched his close and tried to bull his way through the underbrush without spilling anything. It was right out of *The Most Dangerous Game,* one of his favorite movies. Doug could hear a call for backup on the radio, so he and his friend split up. Surprisingly, the guards kept pace. These guys were good. Like a hare at the betting track, Doug led his pursuers in frenzied circles and was starting to put distance between them when, just as he was about to launch himself free from the scrub and make a hasty exit, he tumbled. The mushrooms went flying. No time to gather his prize, he abandoned bucket and mushrooms where they lay and vaulted a roadside thicket of blackberries to make his escape. In the end, even though he didn't get caught, he called it a "Pyrrhic victory." That patch was off the list.

For a moment I thought Doug was going to pull his lanky frame over the barbed wire. Instead, he spun around and paced along the fence line.

"We won't get you in trouble today," he said again.

We both admired the bolete on the far side of the fence. In the darkness its silhouette looked like a hamburger bun atop a pedestal. It was impossibly large and beefy. "I guarantee you that whole hillside is loaded with kings. Them people don't even know. Don't even know what *royalty* lives in their backyard." This made Doug chuckle slightly, his mustache twitching on either end. I could tell it took restraint not to leap the fence and go grab that big mushroom. It looked so fat and vulnerable there. I wanted to pick it myself, and the more I looked at this one lone king bolete, with its promise of nearby kin, the more I was prepared to break the law.

"What do they call information in the CIA?" Doug asked finally, interrupting the sort of long silence that is a prelude to misbehavior.

"Intelligence?"

"Right. *Intel.* What we have here is intel. Kings are on. We'll pick a different patch tomorrow." He ducked back through the brush to the beach, where he stood upright in the light and gazed out across a leaden expanse that stretched to the horizon. Sea and sky looked like a dish rack of pewter mugs in need of polish. "Yes, a new patch tomorrow, laddy. We'll be kings for a day." The ocean view seemed to take Doug elsewhere momentarily, and then he snapped to and strode away down the beach.

Back at the car, he was looking for and not finding a soda can with which to fashion a smoking pipe. In the eyes of law enforcement, this was Doug's one big vice, aside from the occasional trespass. A couple of years ago he received a diagnosis of Parkinson's disease, and now he was a habitual marijuana smoker. The drug helped calm his nerves. When he smoked pot, he didn't get the shakes and his hands remained steady. I asked him why he didn't simply get a note from his doctor and a medical-marijuana prescription card. Doug grimaced. He told me a complicated story that involved the VA, lawyers, doctors, and his own frustration with bureaucracy. In the end, it appeared, he was more comfortable being an outlaw, even if it meant smoking out of old cans that wouldn't be noticed by a police officer and keeping a stogie in the car to mask the sweet, skunky smell of quality herb. After all, he was a mushroom picker; the cops knew that all the pickers smoked weed.

After an intensive search through back and front, Doug accepted the fact that he must have thrown out his last can and went back up to the hostile patch, where he picked a single chanterelle through the fence and returned to the car. "I bet you've never seen anyone do this before." He pushed a thin twig through the chanterelle's stem and bored it out, then scooped out a little bowl in the cap, into which he packed a small green marijuana bud. I watched Doug smoke his pot through a mushroom. He was right. I had never seen anyone do such a thing. Afterward, we drove back down the hardpan beach in the gray, splintered shards of the Pacific and onto Highway 101.

. . .

THE NEXT DAY, a fall morning that reflected a mercurial mix of light and dark like a spun nickel, I met Doug at the Walmart in Aberdeen. This time he was accompanied by his friend Jeff. Bearded and heavy-lidded, with a graying ponytail, Jeff was about the same age as Doug. He, too, had worked as a commercial fisherman—until a rogue line whiplashed across the deck and took with it twenty feet of his small intestine. Jeff told me the story. He had been fishing for mackerel in 2004 off the coast of Cape Cod. With a hundred tons in the net during a paratrawl operation, the block broke and Jeff was called upon to fix it. He was about to thread the last screw into the block. "I heard someone yell 'Line broke!' It almost cut me in half. Lost a third of my insides." He lay in a murky pool of blood and salt water on the deck, clinically dead. That's when he went into the tunnel, he told me, a shiny tunnel "like a veil of water." It was glimmering. There was a junction, with dark apparitions floating about. He understood he could either stay where he was with the shadow people or continue on. Just as he was about to make his decision, there was a whir of wings and two angels put him on a bed of feathers and whisked him away to a strange hospital. "There was a guy at the top of the hospital, and he was the watchman. I started coughing and choking and he said, 'If you don't stop coughing, you will surely die.' I said there was a scratch in my throat." The next thing Jeff knew, he awoke in an actual hospital and he was alive. His fishing career, however, was over. A year later, his old friend Doug lured him out to the West Coast for the morel harvest. He'd been picking ever since.

We drove north toward Olympic National Park. Doug pointed out a V of sandhill cranes flying high overhead. "They get in that jet stream and just haul ass," he said, with an admiration that bordered on longing. A moment later the forest closed around us for the first time since getting on 101 an hour earlier. Doug knew this stretch due south of the Quinault Indian Reservation. He knew it well. The state had planned to cut it, he claimed, using—incredibly—the lame excuse that it was unsafe for vehicular traffic. A letter-writing campaign did nothing, so the day before the cut was scheduled to start, Doug and a friend skulked around after dark in camouflage clothing, tearing down every survey marker they could find. The loggers arrived to a scene of total confusion and gave up in frustration. Authorities decided it wasn't worth antagonizing the locals and called off the cut. "My only civil disobedience," said Doug now. I thought this over and then told him I might do a little fact-finding research on the cut, not because I didn't believe it, I reassured him, just because it was an interesting story. He told me to go ahead. "You won't find nothing," he said. "The state's always covering up one thing or another."

The dance between loggers and those who make a living from non-wood timber products is a difficult one. Many of the people harvesting mushrooms, berries, floral greenery, and a wide variety of plants and fungi for medicinal use are former loggers themselves, just like Doug. They know the woods inside and out. Plus, there is the adrenaline of it all, a feeling an ex-logger never fully gets over. "You have to understand, old-growth logging, it was a thrill," Doug told me once. "Dropping a thousand-year-old tree, that fucker cracking and popping . . ." Jeff was less conflicted. "I hate loggers," he said without malice. "They fucked up the fishing."

Hanging out with this pair reminded me of the sort of male camaraderie that develops in close quarters. You'll find it in school dormitories, on fishing boats, in the military. Old pals, they knew each other's foibles and weaknesses all too well and exploited them in an ongoing raillery of inside jokes, ragging, and general good-natured BS. They talked about women, football, and more women. Neither one was a paragon of the married life, and they goaded each other endlessly about their exes and sins of the flesh.

"We don't need no stinkin' wives," Doug cried, grabbing the steering wheel with both hands and accelerating as if he'd momentarily lost his sanity. We sailed along on the Buick's pillow-like suspension at a clip that had me thinking about rescue strategies in the event of a rollover, until Doug remembered the illegal substances in the car. He stomped on the brake and Jeff dutifully lit up the cigar. Doug pointed to a ramshackle tavern sagging on the side of the road; the place looked as though it had survived more than one grease fire. "Get you some for free in there."

"Don't ever come for free, man," said Jeff from the backseat.

The tavern slipped behind us. "I tell you the story about the lady I met in that place once?"

"The one with the beard? Yeah, a hundred times."

"She kinda tickled."

"Like I said, never free."

"Don't go in that place," Doug said to me. "Seriously, not good people. Full of rednecks. Hell, I'm a redneck, but you know what I mean."

"Takes one to know one."

"What I said. Rednecked rednecks. The worst kind." Doug turned to me, deadpan. "You know I'm just kidding about the redneck thing." I said I understood. "Because I wouldn't want you to get the wrong idea." Doug had a habit of doing this, letting me know when he wasn't serious, as if I might not catch the subtle cues, a clueless college boy such as myself. He liked to use the phrase *off the record* too, invariably circling back around after a long, off-the-record digression about his dope-smoking or womanizing to say, "Ah, hell, it's all on the record, I don't care. Print whatever you want. I'm an open book." He laughed at this, though he was careful not to show a mouth full of bad teeth, the one thing he was really insecure about.

We drove a ways north on the peninsula to check out a chanterelle patch, only to find out another picker or crew had beaten us to it. While settling for the dregs—only about eight or nine pounds' worth—we stumbled on a few king boletes that had just come up. They grow fast, much faster than chanterelles, and it's likely they hadn't even broken through the duff when the competition cleaned out the chanties a couple of days earlier. Like the lone mushroom back at the hostile patch, this was a key piece of information. The kings were definitely on.

———

THE KING BOLETE IS a member—indeed the favorite son—of the *Boletaceae* family, which is distinguished by its spore-bearing tissue under the cap. Unlike typical gilled mushrooms, boletes have pore-like tubes that form a sort of sponge. These tubes emit the reproductive spores. *Boletus edulis,* the king bolete, is the most coveted of wild mushrooms in Italy as well as in Russia, Poland, and other Eastern European countries. Russians call it *beliy grib,* the white mushroom, for its pure white flesh; the Germans call it *steinpilz;* the French *cèpe;* the Brits *penny bun.* Italians call the king and a few other closely related species *porcini,* and this is largely the accepted term of commerce. Restaurateurs happily pay big bucks for the privilege of printing this evocative word meaning "piglet" on their menus. In Italy, virtually everyone in their right mind hangs on the starting gun of porcini season like swimmers on the block, and people go positively mad in produce markets, pawing over the many varieties and grades available. In North America, the king is widespread yet mostly unknown except for those small, overpriced packages of dried porcini imported from Italy. My favorite kings come from the Cascade Mountains in late summer, a firm, flavorful variety that can fruit in astonishing numbers if conditions are right, which is rare. Their timing is something of a mystery that even professional foragers can't always predict. By far the most anticipated harvest, and the most predictable, is the annual beach pick.

Each fall, usually starting around the beginning of October on the Washington coast—though sometimes as early as mid-September, depending on when the rain starts—king boletes will appear quite literally at the edge of the ocean beaches, even right out of the sand dunes. Of course, the sand has nothing to do with it. The boletes are mycorrhizal with Sitka spruce and shore pine, both of which grow near the beach and sprout root systems that spread underground beneath the dunes. The flush marches steadily southward as the season progresses, into Oregon late in the month and northern California before Thanksgiving, all the way south to the Monterey Peninsula. Probably these fruitings once extended up and down the Northwest coast. Now much of the habitat is gone, mowed down into golf course fairways and leveled for ocean-side condominiums. Where the habitat hasn't been plowed, it's now posted. The beach pick is almost entirely relegated to coastal state parks, many of which prohibit mushroom picking. The habitat is so limited in California that punitive laws have been enacted to keep the pickers out.

Unlike chanterelles and several other varieties of wild mushrooms, kings have a very short shelf life. Their flesh softens, and any bugs that might have been missed during the grading process will run rampant unless the mushroom is continually refrigerated—an impossibility for markets trying to show off their goods. This is a consequential problem for the kings of the Rockies; though they can be found in abundance scattered across high-elevation meadows and mountain passes, especially in Colorado and New Mexico, getting them out of the mountains and into the marketplace poses a range of difficulties. Rocky Mountain kings fruit earlier than their West Coast counterparts, usually during the monsoons of July and August, when Denver International Airport is often ninety degrees in the shade. The logistics of trying to outmaneuver such mushroom-spoiling heat is just one of the many obstacles facing a commercial forager in the Rockies who wants to export his stuff. And so the cooler West Coast supplies most of the market.

In recent years, Southeast Asian immigrants have figured out the beach pick, a development that galls old-timers used to having the patch to themselves. "I don't mess with it anymore," says Doug. He admits he lacks the patience to wait for the beach mushrooms to pop. "The Asians find their spots and sit there, pacing back and forth until the mushroom is big enough to pick." This is an exaggeration, though not by much. Once the flush starts, the boletes grow fast and furious. Unlike chanterelles, they mature rapidly, so rapidly that you could conceivably shoot a stop-time video of their growth from imperceptible blob of cells to large iconic mushroom in a few days. This fast growth presents a problem—or an opportunity. Even though a patch might be picked clean one day, it can have a whole new crop twenty-four hours later. Mushroom picking is already a competitive enterprise; with king boletes it becomes downright cutthroat, as the pickers rush to and fro, claiming productive spots and making their presence in the patch known. So Doug leaves the beaches to others and picks his kings farther inland, where the flushes are smaller yet less contested.

It's an open question as to just how the many varieties in the *Boletus edulis* complex will one day get sorted out by mycologists. Currently there are a number of closely related mushrooms classified under the same species name in both the Old World and the New, a taxonomic combobulation that's likely to change with advanced DNA sequencing. In North America alone there are several varieties of *Boletus edulis* that beg for deeper study, including a Rocky Mountain form with a dark-red cap and a Northwest form with a lighter-tan cap. Already, a pale whitish variety known primarily from the pine forests of the Southwest has been awarded its own species status, *Boletus barrowsii,* while another variety, perhaps the largest in the world and found mostly on the California coast, is now called *Boletus edulis var. grandedulis*. Porcini snobs who have been to Italy are generally quick to point out that none of these North American varieties, which seem to be mostly mycorrhizal with conifers, tastes as good as the hardwood-loving kings of the Boot, especially those found in common with chestnut trees. Of course, what they might not realize is that much of Italy's prized porcini is now imported from Poland and China.

Whatever future mycologists have to say on the matter of classification, a porcino by any other name is still pretty damn sweet. Chopped and roasted in olive oil with a little seasoning is a classic way to enjoy fresh porcini. The mushroom has a distinctively nutty taste, and it's great on a cheeseburger or crostini. Add more butter and some cream and you're getting into the decadent corners where I like to operate. And of course there's the famous dried porcini. This is how you'll see it most of the year in the gourmet markets, though remember that porcini are generally dried because they couldn't be sold fresh, whether because of age, worms, or whatever. No matter: Dried porcini have an earthiness that is quite frankly mind-blowing to the newcomer. Put your nose in a bag of dried porcini and inhale— and be prepared to suck in the woods and the duff and the very dirt where the mushroom lived. It's a big aroma: toasty, terrestrial, rugged. I like to pulverize my dried porcini into dust—"magic mushroom dust," I call it, not to be confused with the *Psilocybe* genus—and then reconstitute it with warm water to use as stock. Porcini stock is the secret ingredient in my cream of chanterelle soup. It's also the bass note in my red sauce and essential in any self-respecting oxtail ragu. I go through bags of the stuff every year and give it away as presents at birthdays, weddings, and baby showers. As a consequence, I need to find lots of porcini on an annual basis.

Serious recreational porcini hunters know where to look. Beginners are usually, and understandably, flummoxed. King boletes require dedication. Knowing which tree species the mushrooms are mycorrhizal with in your region is essential. In the Pacific Northwest it's largely spruce and shore pine; along the California coast it's often Bishop or Monterey pine; in the Rockies it's spruce; and in the Northeast it's various conifers as well as hardwoods, in some cases. There could be many more hosts in any of these regions, though. You'll know when you're zeroing in on a porcini flush. You'll see a few outliers and then they'll be all over the place. A good porcini patch can put out more than you can possibly use. Frequently they'll be hobnobbing around with the toxic fly agaric—*Amanita muscaria*—that iconic red-capped mushroom festooned with white warts. The largest fruiting of either species I've ever seen happened in the same place, a lonely corner of Wyoming where the mushrooms fruited along a wooded trout stream in such profusion that I felt as if I were hiking through a magical fairyland.

Nowhere is porcini fever more intense than in Italy. Unfortunately, I have not experienced this Old World mushroom lust *in situ*. A friend of mine recently traveled through Tuscany and had the opportunity to hunt porcini in the heart of it all. He plays the stand-up bass in an old-timey band named the Tall Boys, and he was hardly surprised when I found him at a gig recently and went right up to the stage during a bouncy rendition of "Pig in a Pen" to inquire about his porcini-hunting success in Italy. He just grinned and gave his bass a few extra plucks.

DOUG CALLED THIS ONE of his absolute favorite porcini patches. He figured it would yield for about two weeks, during which time he would visit it every other day to pick the newly emerged mushrooms that would start popping like bonus balls in a pinball machine. The patch was near the Hoh Indian Reservation. In fact, it might have been *on* the Hoh Indian Reservation. Neither Doug nor Jeff seemed to know for sure, nor did they care. Land ownership on the Olympic Peninsula is a farrago of state, federal, Indian, and private property lines, with sketchy boundaries and often little signage. Even within those general categories there are numerous designations, each with its own rules, rules that—when it comes to mushroom harvesting— are often fuzzy to begin with. Federal land includes Olympic National Park, Olympic National Forest, and several wilderness areas, each governed by its own specific statutes, while state land includes parks and Department of Natural Resources (DNR) areas. Private timberlands make their own rules, though as tax-exempt lands they are supposed to be open to the public. And no one seems to know exactly what's up on the rez.

Commercial pickers, I was quickly learning, don't think highly of the patchwork quilt of rules that's been stitched together to regulate their work. The vast majority of mushrooms are harvested on public lands, places overseen by a hodgepodge of local, state, federal, and tribal bureaucrats, most of whom know nothing or very little about the ecology, life histories, or populations of fungi within their own jurisdictions. The regulations—where picking is allowed, how much, and what documentation is required—strike the hunters as totally arbitrary. More difficult to grasp than the rules themselves (which are rarely posted or even readily available online) are the processes and policy goals that led to these regulations. Some of those policies are the result of long-standing battles between the timber interests and environmentalists that culminated in the Clinton-era Northwest Forest Plan, which would ultimately preside over a major shift in emphasis from industrial-based forestry to ecosystem-based forestry. The word *sustainability* comes up a lot. For their part, the pickers have tried to argue that harvesting mushrooms is no different from plucking fruit from a tree. Provided you don't harm the underground mycelium, the fungus should continue to produce more mushrooms the next year. The fact remains, however, that many concerned citizens, including environmentalists, look at mushrooms as a finite resource, like fish stocks, that can be mismanaged and overharvested, even though there is no hard data to support this belief, and they view commercial harvesters as a ragtag army of resource extractors. Because the harvesters move with the seasons—and because many don't speak English—they almost never have a voice in decisions made about their livelihoods. Not surprisingly, they see the heavy hand of Big Brother at work. The rules seem designed to regulate *them* rather than the resource. Already occupying a marginalized corner of society, the pickers in many cases simply ignore the regulations. Rangers and other officers on the ground often don't know what the rules are themselves. They have bigger problems to deal with, like big-game poachers, outdoor meth labs, timber rustlers, and writing tickets and collecting campground fees for cash-strapped state coffers.

We pulled off the highway onto a winding road. This was Doug's first visit to this particular patch since the previous fall. He sped up and then slowed down, scanning for familiar landmarks. Just looking at the croplike rows of even-aged trees, he figured the forest here was a private timber parcel, which meant an entirely separate regulatory apparatus from that of public lands. "All the king's deer!" he brayed. That was his response to many of these timberlands, an allusion to medieval laws that outlawed hunting for anyone other than royalty, and he enjoyed yelling it out the window as we passed the timber-company holdings. In theory, private, tax-exempt timberlands were supposed to be open to public use wherever logging wasn't in progress; in practice, more and more of the access points were being closed except to those who paid for a permit or recreation pass. On the Olympic Peninsula, the owners used a color-coded system. A green dot on a spur gate meant the road was open, while a red dot meant it was closed. Doug said more roads were being red-dotted, and in many cases, he believed, the closures were meant to benefit elk hunters, who paid for the privilege. *All the king's deer.*

We continued down the road at a herky-jerky pace, trying to find our destination. This was a secret patch, one ferreted out by Doug years ago when he was working on some theories related to bolete mushrooms. He scouted the area scientifically and discovered his theories to be correct. It was, he said, a killer patch that cranked out porcini like nobody's business, and he wasn't about to be deterred by some dumb regulation that didn't know the first thing about mushrooms. When we turned the corner, though, Doug was dismayed to see another car in the pullout. "Well, Christ almighty!" he bawled, letting out a string of coarser invective. We all jumped out, anyway, with our buckets.

"You two go that way," Doug said, pointing to a far corner of the patch. "I'll see who's invited themselves to the party."

"Crashed the party is more like it," Jeff replied, scowling.

"Let me deal with it."

"Might not be mushroom pickers at all," I suggested, fearing a confrontation.

"And I might be the prince of Monaco. Let me do the talking. I'll holler if I need backup." With that, Doug made a beeline for the heart of the patch. This was a spruce reproduction plantation, all of it planted after the first cut of old-growth spruce, which might have happened nearly a century ago. Doug and Jeff called it "reprod." The trees were all about the same size and growing in a grid pattern. It was dark inside. Unlike the average chanterelle patch on the fall line of a fir-choked ravine, this was easy going, despite the overwhelming sense of gloom. We found a far corner and started to walk the rows. A plush carpet of moss covered the ground. Right away we saw the handsome tan caps of porcini buttons peeking from the duff.

A king bolete patch in full flush is a lovely sight to behold. Chanterelles may be beautiful nuggets of gold in the dark woods, but kings are something special. Even after years of picking king boletes, I still get a thrill with each find—and this thrill would come a hundred times over on these few acres of second-growth timber as we settled down and started picking. For reasons beyond my understanding, certain individual trees hosted three, four, even a dozen mushrooms. They rose from the duff and moss with their classical mushroom form: bell-shaped cap and thick stem. Thinly sliced lengthwise, these boletes were the silhouette of a perfect mushroom. Small yet dense, they made a satisfying *plop* sound as they landed in our buckets. We pulled each one out of the ground, trimmed off the dirty tip of stem, and moved on to the next. Later, the mushroom buyer would grade them. Young buttons such as these were known as "number ones" and commanded the highest price. The number twos were generally larger and softer than the ones. The number threes, also called "dryers," were past their prime and got sliced up and dried for later use. My pulse quickened as my bucket filled. I raced through the forest with eyes glued to the ground, intent on the next score—too busy to even recognize the inexorable pull of a new addiction. I had porcini fever.

An hour later, Doug reappeared. "No threat," he reported. "Just a Mexican guy and his wife." He said he had a friendly conversation with the couple and even gave them some pointers about cleaning their mushrooms. A glance in their bucket suggested they were picking only the number twos, a grade that generally earned the forager about half of what a number one was worth, and sometimes they were wormy at this stage and worth nothing at all. The number ones were our prey, buttons that had just fruited, some of them only a few inches tall. Often their caps were barely visible in the duff. You had to train your eyes to see them. Once you found a bolete, you needed to look closely for others nearby. Frequently they ringed a particular tree that, for whatever reason, was putting out boletes that year.

"This is what's known as a day-saver," Doug said. A near skunking in a chanterelle patch had nevertheless led to a beautiful pick elsewhere—a pick that was just getting going and would go strong for a couple of weeks at least. "But you wait," Doug cautioned. "Jeremy will find something to complain about." This was the buyer. "He'll bitch and moan about something. It's never good enough for Jeremy." Doug told me not to get the wrong idea. "See, we're friends and all, and we'll pick together, but when he wears his buyer hat he has other concerns."

"Car payments," Jeff said. "House payments."

"Yeah, *concerns*," said Doug, "Maybe a vacation in the Bahamas." The pickers laughed together and then Doug told me he was just kidding around. "We like Jeremy, he's a straight-up guy, just like to flip him some shit, you know?"

What I knew, based on the little I had gleaned so far, was that the relationship between pickers and buyers was complicated.

After a few hours, the patch played out. It was time to meet up with the buyer, who was driving the two-plus hours from Seattle in an empty van so he could fill it up with wild mushrooms to take back to restaurants all over the city. Doug was feeling good. He tuned in a pirate radio station broadcasting from somewhere in the hinterlands.

We drove south, listening to obscure soul singles, and passed the derelict-looking tavern again. "Those kings really did come through for us today," Doug said. "It'd almost be worth stopping by the watering hole for a drink, like the old days after cutting cedar." But the gray afternoon light was giving in to a gathering darkness, and just as soon as the thought occurred to him, he vetoed it and kept driving. "We'll kick back somewhere else after we make our money," he decided, changing the radio station to a news program with the usual ominous reports from around the globe. "Not too many pickers that can find NPR on the dial," he said. Jeff snorted at this and called him a hippie. "I'm okay with that," Doug said. "Most of these guys around here are all *rah-rah, nuke the towelheads*. The white guys, at least. Hardly none of them pay taxes." As for the mushrooms, within twenty-four hours they would be for sale at a farmers' market, perhaps even on display, perched on a throne of tasteful ferns, with a piece of parchment tented nearby: *$30/lb.* in gracefully looping ink. Or they'd be packed in baskets in the walk-ins of a dozen different one-syllable restaurants in the trendiest part of town, where glass and brick fronted busy sidewalks and people dressed in long coats perused window menus as they passed.

. . .

IT WAS DUSK WHEN we pulled into the small coastal community of Raymond, Washington, to the south of Aberdeen and Hoquiam. A logging and fishing town of fewer than three thousand souls, Raymond was twice that size in 1900, before beginning its long decline into a tourist town that attracts very few tourists. We parked behind a tidy house on a residential block. A Japanese sports car and a large American SUV occupied the gravel driveway. Inside, a Vietnamese man sat cross-legged on the kitchen floor, a stack of large king boletes arranged by size on newspapers spread at his feet, fastidiously cleaning his mushrooms. Doug and Jeff stood outside by the back door. Everyone was waiting for the buyer.

After looking at the immaculate kings inside, I wondered what the buyer would have to say about Doug and Jeff's work. Doug had told me he took great pride in delivering the best product, though it would be hard to top what I had just seen in this kitchen. I was feeling protective of my new companions. Meanwhile, the picker inside, a man named Sang, who appeared to be in his forties, worked patiently with a penknife, scraping away every last speck of dirt from the stem and whittling away each little imperfection. He wielded a piece of foam packing material like a stiff-bristled brush, using it to clean and shine the caps of his boletes. In front of him on the newspaper was a small midden of forest debris and dirty mushroom shavings. The mushrooms themselves looked so clean and perfect that you almost wanted to bite into one like an apple.

I went out back to check on Doug and Jeff again. The buyer had arrived and they were in the process of unloading their baskets. As I had feared, the transaction didn't seem to be going well. The buyer looked over a basket of dirt-flecked kings, then another, and shook his head. "Now, Jeremy—" Doug started in, and the buyer stopped him short, pulling out a soiled bolete and holding it up. Exhibit A. Doug turned away. He and Jeff stood tight-lipped in the driveway, hands in their pockets, shoulders hunched, shaking off the chill of the evening. The buyer looked over more baskets.

"This is hours to clean this up," he said finally. "It's game day to-morrow. Watch the game, clean some kings." He weighed the baskets and loaded them into his van anyway, not even bothering to grade the mushrooms for quality. "Come on, guys," he said, thumbing hundreds and fifties out of his money clip for the pickers. "I know you can do better." That was it. End of transaction. The buyer, clearly in a hurry, collected his scale and a stack of empty baskets and went into the house. The pickers stuffed the bills into their jeans pockets without counting them, without even looking at the money. The day was over for them, though it didn't exactly feel like happy hour. More pickers started arriving, pulling into the driveway and idling on the street. I decided to stay and watch the grading process, figuring I could catch a ride back to my car in town. I bid Doug and Jeff goodbye. We shook hands hastily and they drove off to Westport, the vandalized muffler audible long after the car rounded a corner and disappeared out of sight.

CHAPTER 4

The Buyer

...

D ON'T CALL JEREMY FABER a control freak. He'll tell you, in
his typically blunt way, that that's the stupidest thing he's heard
all day—and he's heard a lot of stupid things. Yet control is exactly
what he needs to maintain over the next few hours as he plies his trade
in the unorthodox way he's learned it, in what might seem at first
glance a strange place among strangers.

But these were not strangers. They just happened to speak a very
different language. Faber, owner and chief operator of Foraged and
Found Edibles, set his portable electronic scale on Sang Tran's kitchen
counter, zeroed it out with an empty basket, and got to work. He
moved about the kitchen with a barely contained intensity, like someone who's had too much coffee and maybe a few candy bars, though
he's skinny as a rake. When he wasn't talking to Sang, he mumbled
aloud a litany of things he'd forgotten to do that day or would need to
do later when he got home—well after midnight—sounding like
nothing so much as a human Post-it. Within minutes, word circulated around the neighborhood, and a line of mostly Asian men appeared at the back door, holding overflowing baskets: golden
chanterelles, porcini with caps the size of softballs, scarlet lobsters,

and the odd cauliflower mushroom, looking like something that might wash up at high tide. The pickers arrived one after another: Cambodians, Lao, Hmong, Mien. This was the main reason Faber had come to Raymond: to buy several hundred pounds, maybe more than a thousand tonight—worth in excess of fifteen thousand dollars by the time they sold tomorrow to restaurants around Seattle and beyond—from a community of mostly first-generation Southeast Asians who foraged in their adopted Pacific Northwest nearly year-round. Virtually all of them had been touched by war. Many had military backgrounds or grew up in military families. You could tell them by their magic tattoos—elaborate *yantras* of animals, deities, and spells blessed by monks and designed to ward off bullets and grant invisibility. They had been anti-communists, rebels, guerrilla fighters, U.S. allies, and finally refugees. They took to the forests and mountains of their new home with an ease that spoke of their rural roots. As combatants and refugees, they had hunted jungle fruits, frogs, rats, anything to keep the pangs of hunger at bay. Some were children at the time; others were parents trying to keep families intact. As wild harvesters in their new country, they worked in the woods as family units. Everyone agreed—even the competition— that the Southeast Asians made first-rate mushroom pickers.

Faber cultivated relationships with the Asians. His business depended on it. Get to know one and a whole family network stretching up and down the West Coast would soon reveal itself—a sister in Sacramento, an uncle in Weed, stepbrothers in Springfield. They all knew their mushrooms. They picked huckleberries in late summer, bear grass and salal for floral displays, medicinal plants that got exported to China. The Southeast Asians perfected the idea of seasonal mushroom camps in the woods. They convened by the thousands in little tent cities in central Oregon during the matsutake pick. They camped in Cave Junction, Brookings, and Weitchpec, their encampments as much about keeping native culture alive as they were old-style settlements on the frontier.

For the next few hours Faber would banter with these immigrants, sometimes seeming as if he was just talking to himself, all the while sorting, grading, and weighing mushrooms—and then he'd peel off newly minted hundreds, fifties, and twenties from his money clip to pay the pickers. The job demanded a high level of control: control over rigid numbers and control over a much more slippery cultural transaction. Sang's wife, Srey, prepared a pot of rice, while his mother-in-law, Chay, walked around the kitchen, greeting everyone and making small talk. Sang was Vietnamese and his wife Cambodian, an unusual union for highly tribal people. They had first met in the United States. Sang spoke to Srey in her native Khmer (Cambodian) and in broken English. Srey and her mother both spoke good English. They were refugees of Pol Pot and the killing fields. This much I knew. Later I would hear the full story, and it would make me think about randomness and fate and how we reconcile the two. Sang was thirty-six; his wife, thirty-five. Though physically fit, Sang looked ten years older, his face not so much lined as hardened. Srey was petite and sassy. Together they had three children, and Srey had a teenage son and daughter by a previous marriage. Chay, the mother-in-law, clearly relishing her position as the matriarch, hugged Faber and the grading began.

As it was his house, Sang stood first in line. To his disbelief, his basket of beautiful-looking boletes was overrun by insects. Any number of microscopic pests can spoil a basket. One was called a "hopper" by the pickers, for its habit of hopping around on the mushroom. Another they called "stem worm," the larva of a type of fly known as a bolete gnat. The stem worms start at the bottom of the stem and tunnel their way up. Another was a "cap worm," which specializes in tunneling through the cap and into the spongelike tubes underneath. There was even a barely visible maggot whose presence could be discerned, in its earliest stages, only by a tiny yellow blotch when the mushroom was sliced in half. Sang forced a weak smile as his basket got sorted. He wore a Dodge truck ball cap and a plaid green-and-blue work shirt. Faber took his cleaver to a handsome king, and before the two halves had come to rest on the cutting board, he was already pushing them aside to his pile of "wormed-out" boletes. It looked white and clean inside to me, and I could see Sang do a double take. Although I was supposed to be an impartial observer, I found myself wrapped up in the travails of the mushroom pickers. I wanted them compensated for their hard work. Like watching a boxer struggle in the ring, I caught myself reacting viscerally to the grading of each mushroom—sighing with relief when it ended up in the basket on the scale and flinching in frustration when it didn't. There was nothing to do except watch. None of the pickers put up an argument.

This wasn't always the case. On another day I would watch Faber get into it with three Mexican pickers. "You want this as a number one?" he asked the first Mexican. "Yeah, that's a one, man." Faber told him if he came back tomorrow he'd grade it a one. The picker protested on the very next mushroom. "Look at the white stuff," he said, meaning the pores. Faber agreed to grade it a one. His leniency was becoming a problem, though. The picker complained about the next mushroom, a large, soft bolete that was probably wormy inside and that Faber generously called a number two to keep the peace, without even slicing it in half. "It's a one," the picker badgered. Fed up, Faber took a cleaver to the mushroom and, sure enough, it was wormy inside and now got tossed aside with the number threes. The picker's two friends took their baskets and left.

"What?" Faber said.

"They don't want to sell to you."

"I'll be nice."

"How much you pay?"

"Twenty-one. That's a good price, right? Bring them back tomorrow and I'll grade you nice." It was too late. The delicate balance between cultivating new clients and grading tightly had been lost.

Sang's house was different. Faber could grade tight and no one complained. Otherwise they could always make the half-hour drive to Aberdeen. I watched another pristine-looking bolete get shoved to the side. Against my better instincts, I started to protest, just like the Mexican pickers, but before I could get the words out, Faber was pointing to a barely perceptible yellowing in a corner of the cap. "Believe me," he said impatiently. "By tomorrow this will be a worm-infested mess. Do you want to eat a worm-infested mess at a restaurant?" His pickers nodded; they trusted him. One mushroom after another got sliced open and shunted to a pile that would be dried and sold for a fraction of the worth of a fresh, worm-free specimen. "They wormy," Sang said, watching his profits shrink as the discard pile grew larger. I was mentally exhausted by the end of this first transaction and had to take a breather. A dozen other pickers waited quietly in line for their turn, with more arriving. Most of the pickers were men. They formed a line while their wives waited in a cluster on the other side of the kitchen island. The men watched stoically as Faber sliced porcini mushrooms in half and looked for bug infestations. The wives tried to remain calm, whispering and gossiping among themselves, their expressions—along with their profits—rising and falling with the grading process, like sails filling and luffing in a blustery wind.

Faber looked tired. Srey came over and put a hand on his shoulder. "Jeremy, you need wife," she said. A few of the other women giggled. They all liked Faber. They considered him tall, handsome, and successful. More important, he was connected. This was a quality they valued. Faber knew important people in Seattle—restaurateurs, chefs, caterers—who kept his business humming. And yet no wife! Faber ignored the little smiles and exchanged glances. He sliced and graded, writing down final tallies on a receipt for payment. Today he was paying thirteen dollars for number ones—young, firm, and wormless king boletes—and six dollars for number twos, the less desirable mature mushrooms. The dryers would fetch a dollar fifty. One picker walked out with $234 in new bills. Another made ninety-five. Despite his wormy boletes, Sang still managed to clear more than a hundred, although this was a disappointment. For the use of his kitchen as a buy station, he would receive a commission as well.

"Too expensive, gas," Sang groused.

Faber couldn't let this statement go without comment. "You

wanted the Durango, Sang." Big trucks were a sign of prestige for many of the new immigrants around town. There was a time you could tell a mushroom picker by his car—the conversion vans, old pickups, and dented hatchbacks. No more. Nowadays a picker, especially a Southeast Asian picker, was just as likely to drive a shiny Toyota Tacoma, even if it meant buying everything else at the Dollar Tree.

Sang said he needed a new transmission and told Faber about a deal he was considering for a used one out of Seattle. "Eight hundred dollar. Ninety thousand mile."

The buyer was a sounding board for such decisions. Faber looked at Sang skeptically. "Guess how much my van cost, Sang?" Outside in the driveway, Faber's 1992 Astro van cut a pale figure next to most of the other vehicles parked there.

"Nice car, Durango," the picker protested with a hint of desperation, as if saying the words would make it so. His other vehicle was a Nissan 3000 sports car. Fast cars and big trucks—the American Dream, on wheels, at least.

"Nicer when it's running," Faber said curtly.

Sang couldn't contest this point. "Soon," he said with a rueful laugh.

Faber wasn't done. "And how do you get to the patch? Chay's car?"

Sang nodded shamefully. He was reduced to driving his mother-in-law's vehicle.

Faber, just under six feet, towered over the Southeast Asians. Thin and long-limbed, he moved the way he talked: in quick, sometimes confusing bursts. Even after a string of all-nighters to buy mushrooms, he still exhibited the quick reflexes of an athlete. He was in his midthirties, with a mop of wavy brown hair, close-set eyes, and a prominent beak. Doug, who liked to get a rise out of the buyer, sometimes called him "old hooknose" or even "that hook-nosed Jew bastard," and Faber didn't discourage easy shorthand bigotry. Counting his money while driving seventy on the highway, he'd say, "I like the feel of cash. I'm Jewish. It's in our blood." He worked this angle frequently, because to be a New York Jew in Seattle was something of a novelty, and to be one in the woods of Washington was even more exceptional. Faber enjoyed his notoriety, and bantering with his pickers like a typical smart-ass New Yorker was just one of many traits that separated him from other buyers, along with his ethnicity, education, and social position.

Though Faber's involvement in the rough-hewn mushroom trade might have been an anomaly, no one denied his willingness to work harder than the next guy. This work ethic meant scouring high and low to find the best products to bring to market. It could be a lonely business. He crisscrossed the Northwest and beyond, usually by himself. He often picked alone. When he bought mushrooms from his pickers, he liked to catch up with their affairs and joke around in a way that would be familiar to anyone from the tristate area. The Southeast Asians made good sidekicks. They could gossip with the best of them. Their families were large, often shifting with new lovers, divorces, and intrigue. They liked to party. With the non-native speakers, Faber took a particularly avuncular tone, helping them with their English and also matters of finance and local custom. He encouraged Sang's family to send the children to college and made constant fun of their vehicular decisions, hoping his message of thrift would sink in. He had a sentimental streak despite the outward appearance of tough-love pragmatism, and he was a believer in the basic tenets of hard work paying off. Faber honestly wanted his pickers to succeed. Sometimes his generosity cost him. He told me one time about a woman to whom he'd extended credit, how she got ahold of his cell phone and called home. "An eighty-dollar call to Laos? Really? That is not cool." He didn't expect to see her again.

Next came the chanterelles, gathered mostly by Sang's in-laws. Sang's eighteen-year-old stepson, wearing a basketball jersey, emerged from a bedroom as if just waking up from a deep sleep. "Where's the girl?" Faber kidded him.

"We could ask you the same question," Srey said to the buyer.

Faber brushed off the comment. "Every time I see him, there's a new girl!" The boy, much taller than his parents and sturdy, rubbed his eyes and frowned with embarrassment. He spoke without an accent and clearly had no interest in the mushroom trade; more important for him, he wasn't quite good enough to play for the community-college team and now he needed to figure out what to do.

"What's his problem?" Faber asked Srey after the boy left the room. He couldn't believe this second-generation immigrant was already comfortable enough to consider bailing on his education.

Srey shook her head. "He doesn't like school. If he can't play basketball, what's the point? That's his opinion, not mine." Her English was easily the best among the adults in the extended family. In a loud voice, she made a joke in Cambodian that got the other women tittering again, something about a TV show for eligible bachelors.

Faber shook his head. "Like a hole in the head," he said.

"He say that," Srey went on, "and nobody believe him." She guided me by the elbow to another room, where framed photographs lined the wall, portraits of her family and herself as a young girl. Srey had emigrated to the United States in 1980. "I was six year old," she said, as a picture of Buddha looked placidly down at us. "We walk until we get to Thailand. My father came first, because they were looking to kill him. Then they went after us and tried to kill us. We got out of that place. They caught my brother. They tie him up. They go, 'Where's your dad? Where's your mother and your sister?' He didn't answer and they kill him." From Thailand, they fled to the Philippines, where a church sponsor helped get them to Canada and then the States. They moved from North Carolina to California and finally to Washington State, where Srey met Sang, the Vietnamese son of a U.S. GI he had never met. Next to the Buddha was a photo of Sang's father in his neatly pressed uniform.

"Sometimes when I talk about it, I get scared," Srey said. "I saw everything. Step on people who died. Step on the wrong place— boom! Bad, bad people." Srey showed me a picture of Angkor Wat before the Khmer Rouge occupied it. We walked back into the kitchen, where she pointed to a photograph of herself as a young woman. Her voice rose an octave. "You know what's famous about me when I come to the United States? I'm Cambodian dancer." In the photo she's standing with five other young women, dressed in a shiny red dress and black high heels, with thick bracelets around each ankle and both wrists, a golden tiara perched on her head. Her three-year-old daughter sat against the wall below the photo, eating dry cereal out of a plastic bowl. Faber stood nearby, still grading mushrooms and talking to the pickers. Chay was last in line, and, after closing her hand around the bills, she stepped up on her tippy-toes and gave Faber a theatrical kiss on the cheek.

. . .

BACK IN SEATTLE I stopped by the Foraged and Found booth at the farmers' market one day to see Faber. Piled high in a wicker basket were the gleaming caps of porcini, selling for about twenty dollars a pound. A chalkboard listed wild greens, including watercress and medicinal plants, all kept in a cooler. I had gathered many of these items myself, though it was hard to imagine trafficking in the sort of volumes that paid a living wage. Faber clowned with shoppers as they passed by, convincing a few of them to shell out for an ingredient they'd never imagined buying. Usually, he told me, he had a couple of cute girls who ran his booth, but they were off today. Later I arranged to meet him at his home. A gold plaque above the front door announced the wood-frame bungalow as IDLEWILDE. Faber, barefoot, greeted me with barely a nod as he pushed open the door with his elbow, a fat T-bone steak in one hand—last night's leftovers, now breakfast—and a thick wad of cash in the other. I mentioned the few press reports I'd managed to dig up, which described him as "shy," "retiring," "elusive," and he wasn't interested in dispelling this image. He told me he didn't much care for people (a fabrication, I would learn). Money, on the other hand, he admitted to liking. The money in his hand, crisp, copious, and freshly counted, wouldn't have seemed out of place in the hands of a back-alley blackjack dealer—or, as it turned out, in the dirt-stained grip of a man who brings wild mushrooms, greens, and berries to market. Such wild edibles, coveted by the best restaurants across the land, pay the mortgage on Idlewilde, a spiffy house in a neighborhood where similar residences fetch nearly a million dollars. The question on Faber's mind: Would his business eventually earn him a return on investment that could buy a well-appointed retirement cabin in the woods, the sort of place where no one would bother him and a man could "sit on his own porch drinking whiskey and firing guns"? The question on my mind: How did mushrooms pay a mortgage on anything?

You've got to be willing to get dirty, Faber likes to say. Most of the time he's busy driving around the Northwest, buying from a carefully cultivated network of pickers so he can sell directly to restaurants or at farmers' markets. When the pick is good, though, he'll be out in the field himself, alongside his pickers, trying to boost his margins. He'll tell you that's the only way to make money in this business. He runs his company out of the basement of his home, where he stores his products in a restaurant-style walk-in cooler and, from the looks of it, wherever else he can find room. When you first set foot in the basement, the overpowering aroma of fungi hits you like lawn-mower clippings on a humid day. Bags of morels, porcini, lobsters, and other dried mushrooms litter the floor. Fresh products wait in the cooler for shipment. Strewn about are towers of shipping cartons and mailers.

Faber deals mostly in what is known as "fresh market." Though he'll dry and freeze a portion of his products, the bulk of his capital comes from selling fresh directly to restaurants. In this respect, his business model differs from that of other wild-food purveyors, especially the wholesalers who work with middlemen. Big companies operate sizable warehouses and ship their products all over the world. They run multiple field buyers and dry a significant portion of what they buy. Yet, in keeping with the largely clandestine nature of the business, you aren't likely to find much of a public presence with these companies. If they have a website at all, it's buried in the search results. The business works largely by word of mouth. Smaller companies throughout the Pacific Northwest do business with the wholesalers. And then there are the players like Faber—independently minded outfits that prefer to cultivate their own networks and sell directly. The margins can be much higher, the volumes smaller. Business relationships are largely personal too. If a restaurant isn't happy about an order, Faber will hear from someone he probably knows on a personal basis, and he will take pains to correct the situation. Like every business with a long-term vision these days, Foraged and Found Edibles is obsessed with customer service and satisfaction. In Faber's case, the final arbiter is the restaurant patron or home cook who takes a bite of his product. At a time when so-called USDA-approved organic greens, grown in factory-farm conditions, can become contaminated with *E. coli* by a pack of feral hogs, many consumers are looking for a purer sort of "all natural" food to grace their tables and impress dinner guests. Found well beyond the fence lines of Big Ag, wild foods are by definition organic, and they offer an authentic taste that can't be duplicated in domesticity. Faber figures every big city has at least one dealer like himself: a backwoods-savvy merchant in the delicacies of the wild.

Becoming such a woodsman was Faber's first trick. He was raised on Long Island, where, by his own admission, he got into New York City's rave scene at a young age and first developed an interest in, shall we say, natural products and all-cash business. When he was seventeen, his parents sent him to rehab, even though by then his inclination wasn't so much to indulge in his own product as it was to make money from it. He majored in forestry at the University of Vermont and then transferred to the Culinary Institute of America in Hyde Park, New York. For most of his life he had worked in restaurants—greasy spoons and fast-food joints as a kid, and later at more-upscale places like Perry's Fish House in Burlington. After graduating from the CIA, he moved west and took a series of restaurant jobs in Seattle, working at such stalwarts as Ray's Boathouse, Serafina, and the now-defunct Brasa before landing a job at the re-

nowned Herbfarm in the suburbs east of Seattle. There he appren-
ticed under James Beard Award–winning chef Jerry Traunfeld, who
taught Faber how to use wild ingredients in imaginative preparations. The Herbfarm was one of the first restaurants to champion foraged foods in a big way, and it routinely lands on Top 10 lists for the
Pacific Northwest's best eateries. There Faber met one of his closest
friends, Matt Dillon, before Dillon would go on to make a name for
himself with his own restaurants. He also worked with Christina
Choi, another wild-food enthusiast, who had bright, expressive eyes
and an infectious smile, and who would become his girlfriend.

Faber and Choi explored the wilds of Washington together, camping all over the state and experimenting with the little-known foods
they found during long hikes through mountains and woods. Meanwhile, Faber worked up to sous chef. All the while he was also running a little grow operation on the side, housed in an attic crawl space
above his rental room. Though not much of a dope smoker anymore,
growing pot satisfied his yearning to work with actual currency. He
grew and sold several crops over the course of a few years, until an
ex-roommate threatened to rat him out if he didn't pay hush money.
Rather than split profits with the blackmailer, Faber ripped out all his
plants and went legit.

At the Herbfarm, he was spending more and more time outdoors.
He brought his finds back to the restaurant and incorporated them
into dinner specials. Soon he was known as the house forager. In 2001,
he and Christina Choi started Foraged and Found Edibles together.
In a smallholder echo of the Microsoft and Amazon legends, they
used Choi's garage as the launching pad for their effort to supply the
Herbfarm and numerous other Seattle-area restaurants with wild
foods. A year later Faber left the Herbfarm altogether to concentrate
on his business, while Choi, in time, decided to travel and pursue her
own interest in wild foods down a different path. Though Choi's
departure—and the end of their romance with it—gave Faber full
control over the fledgling company, Doug and others liked to call her
"the one that got away," and Faber himself would continue to refer to

Christina Choi as both his best friend and the heart and soul of the business. Choi's interest was purely culinary and spiritual. She championed wild foods for their unique qualities and also because they were products of nature rather than agriculture. Her cooking, a fusion of her Chinese–Swiss heritage, was forever changing with the seasons and whatever foraged foods were available nearby, and though her financial interest seemed nonexistent, unlike Faber's, this passion would lead eventually to the opening of Nettletown, a Seattle lunch spot that could boast quite possibly the highest ratio of wild to conventional food of any restaurant in the country.

A commercial forager's life is hard on relationships. This was something Faber would learn in the coming years. The money, on the other hand, was steady. Despite the Internet bubble, these were boom years in Seattle. Flush with high-tech capital, the city built a baseball park with a retractable roof, a football stadium, and a new opera house. Swanky restaurants opened in droves in trendy neighborhoods like Belltown and Queen Anne, catering to Seattle's new breed of young, moneyed professionals who wanted to eat well and to eat local.

. . .

ON A WARM MORNING in June that suggested peaches and cherries more than fungi, I joined Faber for a day in the field. "When should I expect you home?" Martha asked me before I left. I couldn't answer. Faber was known to disappear into the woods for days on end, though I figured that today, among the longest of the year, we'd be home before nightfall. He was taking a rare day off—we would drive my car. Dressed like a Gen Y snowboarder (sweatshirt, baggy army pants, faded T-shirt, not a shred of fleece), he had me pull over in the mountains an hour east of Seattle so he could pee—and, more important, so he could take over the driving. Faber is used to spending hours and hours each week behind the wheel. He gets visibly uncomfortable in the passenger seat, legs drawn up, dirt-encrusted fingers drumming on his knees. We drove past craggy, near-vertical peaks of the North

Cascades on Route 2, over Stevens Pass (near the site of a horrific avalanche in 1910 that swept a Great Northern passenger train off the
tracks and killed ninety-six people), before descending into the gen-
tler east slope valleys of the Columbia Plateau. Turning north, we
followed one of the tumbling rivers that rise from Glacier Peak, an
inactive volcano at the center of a designated wilderness area that
some consider the crown jewel of the U.S. public-lands portfolio. But
we would not be venturing into wilderness today. Instead, Faber
pulled over on the side of a gravel forest road. This was an area known
for "multiple use," a Forest Service term for public lands that, though
far from pristine, are usually not obliterated by industrial-scale logging. Multiple-use forestland is not just the domain of the hiker; it's
used by the equestrian and the off-road-vehicle enthusiast, by the
small-scale logger and the miner. It's neither unbroken old growth
nor a tree farm. Often such woods are good mushroom habitat. They
have tree stands of varying species and ages and the sort of low-level
disturbance (trails, selective logging) that, for reasons beyond our
ken, encourages certain mushrooms to fruit. Some theorists have suggested that the pantheon of choice edible mushrooms is in part determined by those species that, through the ages, have volunteered
themselves as food, the ones that thrive in areas used by people, and
that finding them near trails and other "edge" habitats is hardly surprising.

My guide was out of the car and into the woods before I could
shoulder my daypack. I hurried after him. Faber can seem awkward
and angular when cooped up in a typical home or office; in the woods
he becomes graceful and expansive, using his long limbs to bound ef-
fortlessly over deadfalls and to swing like an ape-man on vines down
forested slopes. Even at a rather unsafe trot I continually fell behind,
finally catching up (and catching my breath) in front of a massive
cedar. "You probably didn't know that spring porcini like cedars," he
said to me, and he was correct. Faber delights in pointing out the ignorance that surrounds his business. Unlike the more wide-ranging
fall porcini that I had picked with Doug and Jeff, spring porcini (*Bo-*

letus rex-veris) inhabit only the interior mountains of the West Coast, fruiting east of the Cascade Crest, in the Blue Mountains, and along the eastern flanks of the Sierra Nevada—arid places not known for their moisture-loving cedar trees. These mushrooms are usually associated with ponderosa pines and true firs (grand fir in Washington and white fir in California). Yet here we were standing before a hulking cedar with exposed roots that spread out from the trunk like elongated toes on a foot. I looked down and around the roots and didn't see anything resembling a mushroom. Faber, a slight smirk now creeping onto his face, bent down and casually brushed away a layer of sticks and debris. The pale-red caps of three plump porcini mushrooms, each one a bit shy of half a pound, stood out against a brown background. He pulled them from the dirt and trimmed off the ends with a slice of his pocketknife. This single cache of wild food was worth nearly thirty dollars to Faber.

We visited more individual trees, with the same result. Faber had mapped an entire neighborhood of porcini in his head, all of them linked to individual trees that might as well have had names. He knew the zip codes of each cluster. In time I would learn just how important it was to have steel-trap recall for mushroom patches. Recreational pickers rely largely on map notations and handheld GPS units with their megabytes of electronic memory, while the best commercial pickers have a Rolodex of patches in their heads. One time, while Faber was buying morels and spring porcini in Sisters, Oregon, his station was visited by some familiar faces from Raymond. They were new to the spring pick and had only a few porcini to sell, nothing to get excited about. Faber suggested they focus on picking huckleberries instead, breaking the news with characteristic bluntness: "You won't make any money on boletes. You need three or four years before you see money. People say, *They're in the woods,* but you don't know exactly what tree they grow under. Might be one tree in there with five pounds under it." Smoking cigarettes while crouching on the roadside, the pickers mulled this over as their Grand Cherokee Laredo idled loudly nearby, a spare tire lashed to the luggage rack.

Faber counted out a few bills for their efforts. He encouraged them to set up a huckleberry camp in the next month and even offered to pay the five-hundred-dollar permit if they would agree to sell to him exclusively. "I'll need a lot of huckleberries this year. I didn't get enough last year. Buy the permit. I'll pay for it. I'll bring beer and cigarettes up. I'll camp with you guys. It's nice up there." After they drove off, Faber turned to me. "Was I convincing? They'll make a lot more money picking huckleberries."

In many ways, spring porcini mushrooms are an apt metaphor for North America's wild mushroom culture. Italian American immigrants in northern California, especially those who settled near the huge volcanic cone that is Mount Shasta, in communities such as McCloud and Dunsmuir, have picked this mushroom—commonly called a spring king—for a hundred years or more, as it reminds them of their beloved porcini of Italy. Yet spring kings didn't receive species status until 2008, with the binomial *Boletus rex-veris* (translated, naturally, as *spring king bolete*). One would be hard-pressed to find a commonly eaten food in either the plant or animal kingdom that lacks a taxonomic name and official species description. The fact is, science is only just beginning to catch up with what generations of mushroom eaters—*mycophagists* being the term of art—have known all along.

Spring kings differ from their fall cousins in several respects. They fruit in different habitats and in association with different trees; they have a tendency to cluster, sometimes even sprouting from the same stem; and they're largely hypogeous, which means they do most of their growing below ground. The taste and texture are similar, however, making them a favorite mushroom of European immigrants in the western United States, enthralled as they are by the rich, woodsy aromas of porcini. A classic way to enjoy spring porcini is to slice and marinate them in olive oil and garlic, then grill over a charcoal fire. The finished slices are plated on a bed of fresh spring greens. Done correctly, they're crisp and golden on the outside with a chewy white interior; their meatiness explains why Italians call porcini "poor man's steak." These days, with the prices spring porcini are fetching, a person of lesser means might be more apt to have marinated New York strip on the grill.

On that first hunt with Faber, I followed him over hill and dale, continually amazed by his unwavering haste in the woods and his familiarity with specific trees. We drove to half a dozen locations on the east slope of the Cascades, and at each patch of woods Faber had a specific matrix of known trees to visit. We bounced from arbor to arbor, exhuming chunky porcini buttons as we went. There was nothing haphazard about it. Unlike a recreational hunter, who might choose a picking area based on habitat, or a general feeling, or maybe nothing at all, Faber made the rounds with efficiency and speed. I peppered him with questions as we went. He had patches all over the place, and each one was meaningful in its own way. One of his favorites he referred to as his "late spring bolete patch." It was above 4,500 feet on Blewett Pass and overlooked the snowcapped Stuart Range to the west, most years not coming on until July. He found it while camping with Christina Choi. The way he talked about the patch, I could tell that it evoked for Faber a younger version of himself, when he was both carefree in his twenties and also down in the trenches, working ridiculous restaurant hours with a confederacy of other kitchen mules. The patch was a place for him and his friends to go and wind down—drink a few beers, build a fire, bushwhack around the woods, sleep on the ground. He could look at Mount Stuart for hours on end, that huge heap of granite and ice, imagining its couloirs and ice caves. In fall, the campsite blazed a brilliant yellow as larch trees turned before dropping their needles; in spring the ground was carpeted with wildflowers: queen's cup, Solomon's plume, cinquefoil. Goshawks ghosted through the timber, on the lookout for a careless Douglas squirrel or a love-drunk grouse drumming on a log. The fact that he and Choi had gone there one time in the midst of a phenomenal porcini pop made it that much more special. They picked buckets of spring boletes right out of camp. This reminded him of another patch to the south, on the edge of canyon country, the domain of rattlesnakes and redtails. It was another camping spot, near a good swimming hole on a forested hillside covered in elk sign, a place where no one would ever think to look. On dry, south-facing slopes nearby, Faber and Choi had picked wild onions, the mushrooms and aromatics making a fine spring mountain stew together. As he remembered this, I could see a darkness suddenly descend on him. "Anyway," he said, cutting himself off. I asked him about other patches that had memories connected to them, but he was done talking about it. On the way home, slightly annoyed now, Faber asked me if I had any other interests besides mushrooms, so we talked baseball.

. . .

THE GRADING OF WILD MUSHROOMS has an operatic quality to it, even though haggling is taboo. Often, pickers will stick around the buy stations at the end of the day to watch the process unfold and shoot the breeze, sharing news of good flushes, new patches, prices being paid here and there. (It helps when the buyer keeps a cooler of free beer and soda just for that purpose too.) The U.S. Forest Service has produced technical reports that suggest the buy station sometimes functions as an educational center, where pickers can learn important words and phrases in English, find out news pertaining to closures and other regulations, and generally immerse themselves in the process of learning the local cultural habits. On the flip side, the buy station can also be a tribal center, where people of similar backgrounds meet to share in their native culture. I saw this sort of activity again and again just by hanging around with Faber when he was buying mushrooms. One Lao woman looked as though she had gotten dressed up before arriving with her basket. She wore a pink velour sweat suit, bright lipstick, mascara, and large dangly hoop earrings. She might have been drinking, I couldn't quite tell. She mugged for some Lao men in line and made a few lewd gestures. Another woman, a Cambodian, showed up in a long, woolly, red hooded sweater with a large, inexplicable number seven sewn onto the breast and a green skirt with a yellow floral print. Faber told her she looked nice. "All number ones!" she shouted with glee. Everyone whooped, and as Faber took up his cleaver she spoke in an indecipherable clucking tongue. A man standing at the table asked Faber if he'd like to know what she said, to which he answered, "Sure."

"She said she's afraid you might ruin your hand."

Faber admitted he was tired and said he'd go slow and careful with the grading. "I've been working a lot, you know? Driving back and forth. What's she saying now?"

"She says she's half Chinese and can't see."

"Am I fair?"

"You're a fair person," said the man.

MUSHROOM BUYERS ARE CAGEY by nature, and trying to talk to them—especially if you're just some curious passerby and not a picker—can be a one-sided conversation. I was grateful to Faber for allowing me a glimpse of his world. This was something of a coup for me, and other recreational hunters who knew of my introduction to Faber sometimes assailed me with questions. Mushroom hunting will always have a patina of the occult. This is part of its allure. Yet Faber was surprisingly generous with his knowledge. He shared patches freely and revealed secrets of the trade—unusual tree species that produce mushrooms, habitats not generally recognized in the literature, preservation and cooking techniques. In contrast, another large, well-known buyer in the Northwest couldn't be persuaded to open up under any circumstances. His business wasn't listed online; a picker gave me his mobile line, so I gave the buyer a call to see if we might meet. Immediately he wanted to know how I had gotten the number. I explained that I wanted to visit one of his buy stations and just observe the process, not get in anyone's way. "It's like with the cops," he said to me. "We're not interested." What a strange thing to say, I thought.

It's true that we live in a world with increasingly few secrets. Secrecy, however, was only part of it. When friends of mine said they planned to swipe my maps so they could learn all these new patches I was going to, I had to laugh. I'll take you to one of these patches, I told them. It wouldn't be the same experience, though, as going with Doug or Jeff or even Faber. The world revealed had borders well beyond the patch itself. Faber brought me around to meet his pickers, showed me his basement warehouse, and even allowed me to see the more banal details, such as the packaging of products and delivery runs around town. In a bid to build his business, he was expanding into the New York City market and had recently dispatched a new hire from Seattle to the East Coast to establish a toehold. He had also hired two new employees to be dedicated to some of the business's less glorious tasks at home. You'd have to be insane to leave your job as sous chef at one of the country's premier restaurants to pursue the evanescent pull of foraged foods, yet that's exactly what Jonathan did—just as his new boss at Foraged and Found Edibles had done nearly a decade earlier, and at the same place. Faber had taken on Jonathan at the beginning of the year, and the new hire was still learning the ropes. We stood in the spotless kitchen of the Herbfarm, his old employer, while Jonathan, another CIA graduate, talked with his former colleague who was now the head chef. To a competitive cook in today's *Top Chef* climate of food-as-competition, Jonathan's move might seem lily-livered, a sign of weakness. And to do what? Deliver a box of fungus to his former competitor in line for the plum job of chef de cuisine? It didn't make sense. Why bother attending the most famous cooking school in the United States if you were going to bail out?

To hear Jonathan explain it, the reasoning was as plain as a freshly laundered white tablecloth. He was married with a five-year-old boy, a son he wanted to spend time with. As chef at the restaurant, he'd be pulling eighty-hour weeks and getting home well after everyone else in the family was asleep. For Faber he worked a regular daytime shift and didn't take a pay cut. In fact, Faber gave him a raise over his restaurant salary. Wild foods excited Jonathan. He saw his new job as cutting edge. Sure, a lot of his daily work involved the more mundane aspects of the business: cleaning and packing the products, tracking orders, making deliveries. On the other hand, he got to visit with scores of Seattle's finest restaurants, and, perhaps more important, he was periodically given a chance to join Faber in the field, where he could learn hands-on the tricks of the wild-food trade. These were not ordinary ingredients, after all. Laying hands on truffles and porcini and Saskatoon berries and fiddleheads was like browsing through the bins of a gourmet produce shop. It was one thing to grow a nice tomato or pepper at home, quite another to uncover nature's hidden garden deep within the folds of the misty mountain forests of the Pacific Northwest.

The delivery for the Herbfarm weighed in as the biggest and most diverse of the day. The restaurant was in the middle of its Mycologist's Dream menu, an annual event that celebrated the region's fungi. Today Jonathan was dropping off a ten-pound box of golden chanterelles, a ten-pound box of porcini split between number-one buttons and number twos, and some additional oddballs such as cauliflower, saffron milk caps, and man-on-horseback mushrooms. Owner Ron Zimmerman came out in a smart black tunic to check on his order.

"We had a two-point buck in here last night," he told me with a combination of pride and wonderment at the extraordinary foods he was lucky enough to serve. Apparently a regular patron had shot the deer in the sagebrush country of eastern Washington over the weekend and rented out the whole restaurant to feed his friends and family. "We broke it down right here." A cook whisked by, carrying several racks of seasoned ribs on a tray—"not the buck," noted Zimmerman— while another picked up a box of apples. We ate fat green grapes from a bowl on the counter. Zimmerman ran his hands through the chanterelles and chortled like a pirate sifting his pile of golden booty. "The riches of the woods . . ."

Back in the van, I told Jonathan about an order I'd placed with my local butcher for a pound of veal sweetbreads. I planned to pair them with a half pound of chanterelle buttons. Jonathan loved sweetbreads and recommended I try poaching them in chicken broth and herbs. My plan had been to pan-fry them, which is fairly standard practice, and while there's something irresistible about little nuggets of meat that are crispy on the outside and fork-tender on the inside, the pan-fry method also masks some of the flavor nuances that remind you you're eating offal. He suggested roasting a medley of root vegetables in the oven along with the chanterelles in a separate pan, then combining the vegetables and mushrooms with the sweetbreads just as the stock has reduced to a thick glaze. The dish wasn't for everyone, he explained, certainly not for the average squeamish American eater. For those who truly loved sweetbreads, though, the almost slippery, melt-in-the-mouth texture would be heavenly. I wondered if Jonathan engaged in such conversations every day. Even though the restaurant and high-end food business had become fashionable in recent years for the rock-and-roll tattoo that bad boy celebrity chefs had etched onto it, at its heart the business was still populated by dreamy food lovers like Jonathan, the sorts who planned a family vacation around Italy so they could go truffling in Piedmont.

At our next stop, Café Juanita, we delivered a ten-pound box of wild watercress and a box of chanterelles. On the north shore of Lake Washington in the Seattle suburb of Kirkland, Café Juanita has enjoyed its reputation as an outstanding neighborhood bistro for more than a decade, and chef-owner Holly Smith was rewarded in 2008 with a James Beard Award. I watched her face brighten at the sight of the watercress. She ripped open the bag with impatient fingers and teased out a sprig, munching her way down the stem. She closed her eyes for a moment and feigned a swoon. "I just love this stuff."

Our final delivery of the day was in direct contrast to these first two stops. After searching for and failing to find a back door in the parking garage for this newish account, we carried our boxes through the street door and made a beeline for the kitchen, nodding to the hostess and hoping we weren't making a scene. One of the cooks was attending to a vat of meatballs and pouring braising liquid over a pot of sirloin and onions. He ignored us for a while, until Jonathan offered a game "Hey, how's it going?"

"Busy!" the cook snapped. He was tall, pear-shaped, baby-faced. He took a dishrag off his shoulder and slapped it down on the counter behind him, then snatched Jonathan's receipt book from his hand and plastered it against the wall with a loud *thwack* before scratching out his initials. He kicked the box of watercress aside and had a minion take away the mushrooms. Our business was done. We retreated to the van. Working in a kitchen could be stressful, there was no doubt about it. "That guy's always like that," Jonathan said. "A couple weeks ago we showed up at one-thirty and he told us next time to come before one. Last week we delivered at noon and he said that wasn't a good time either."

. . .

JUST BEFORE THE HOLIDAYS, I wangled a dinner invitation for my family to Idlewilde, Faber's home. My kids sat themselves before the woodstove while Martha and I joined Faber in the kitchen. The day before, he had taken twenty pounds out of his black trumpet spot, a rare mushroom in Washington State, and he figured this would be the high-water mark before he set sail for northern California, post-holidays. Right now he had pretty much abandoned Washington State, driving down to Eugene, Oregon, every few days instead to purchase chanterelles. He didn't really get this obsession with the chanterelle. To underline this fact, Faber passed me a tray of crostini just out of the oven. "You said you weren't a big fan of yellowfeet," he said, as I plucked one of the appetizers and dispatched it in two bites. True, I *had* said that. Sometimes called a winter chanterelle, the yellowfoot (*Craterellus tubaeformis*) is a wispy, hollow-stemmed relative of the golden chanterelle. It had always struck me as insubstantial. Now I recognized my misjudgment. Despite the yellowfoot's flimsy stature, its flavor was pronounced, if delicate, with both a savory element and a slight fruitiness. Like so many wild mushrooms, its taste was hard to pin down, as if the proper adjectives hadn't yet been invented. Faber gave the sauté pan a stir. "I dry-sautéed these with soy sauce and liver." The mushrooms, cooked whole, were nearly unrecognizable. A deep brown, they resembled the tentacles of squid or some other slinky cephalopod on the toasted bread. Martha, not one to shop for liver, was impressed. "You need to make this at home," she whispered to me.

Faber opened a bottle of white Bordeaux and carefully dressed a platter of Olympia oysters, a gift from one of his clients. Recently he'd received a batch of cranberries from Doug, who was without a vehicle at the moment and staying close to home. Doug had arranged to buy more than a thousand pounds of cast-off cranberries from a local bog out at the coast. Rather than collect his berries at harvest time, which was three weeks earlier, Doug had negotiated a much cheaper price to gather whatever berries remained along the edges post-harvest. These would be much riper and sweeter than the berries that get picked, packed, and shipped around the country well in advance of Thanksgiving. Faber sliced several cranberries in half, garnishing each oyster with half a berry, cider vinegar, and shredded scallion.

An old girlfriend of Faber's came by. Allison was a pretty blond-haired woman of about thirty who worked as a nanny. They'd broken up earlier in the spring, when the stress of Faber's job was taking him away from home for weeks at a time to pick morels, one of his big cash crops of the year. At the time he thought he was doing her a favor, though now he regretted the breakup and was patiently trying to win her back.

"Do you always eat like this over here?" I asked Allison.

She smiled, unembarrassed. "Not lately."

Faber had confessed to me that even though his ex wasn't ready yet to welcome him back, he was willing to put in the work, just as he was willing to put in the hours it took to bring wild mushrooms to market. For a kinetic, brusque sort of guy, he was oddly patient. Lately, a strange feeling that he'd never expected had come over him: the desire to settle down and raise a family. "Allison would make a great wife," he'd said to me matter-of-factly before she arrived. "And a good mother." I could still remember what it was like to be in my mid-thirties and starting my own family. That was around the age when I had to accept that driving all night through darkness on lonely highways wasn't in the cards anymore, or that backcountry skiing might not be the best hobby with a one-year-old at home.

"How much longer can you make these marathon drives to Eugene and back?" I asked him. He admitted that soon he would have to allow one of his employees to make the trip. Paradoxically, the growth of his business also required a certain letting-go.

For the soup course, Faber braised sliced leeks in the liquor of manila clams and bay mussels plus a healthy shot of sake. To this he added thinly sliced matsutake mushrooms, cooked them together briefly, and ladled the broth into bowls over the shellfish meat. "It's a classic flavor combination, matsutake, clams, and leeks," he said, handing me a bowl. Somehow I had missed the memo on this classic flavor combination. As soon as I tucked into the soup, though, I could see what he meant. Matsutake has a spicy cinnamon-like flavor that is revered in Japan. Cooking the mushroom in traditional Japanese ways with ingredients such as sake, soy, and rice vinegar makes use of this unusual flavor, much more so than Western techniques and various forms of dairy. Next to me, Martha was inhaling her soup. "You need to make this at home," she said.

The final course was pan-seared game hen, plated with a butternut-squash soufflé and finished with a black truffle gravy. The truffle, as big as a golf ball, sat on his kitchen chopping block. I took a whiff. Its pungent aroma reminded me of overripe pineapples mixed with other loamy forest smells. In general Faber was not a huge fan of our native American truffles, most of which come from the second-growth woods of Oregon and Washington, though he conceded that a good one was comparable to an average European truffle. White Italian truffles were his favorite. Martha tore into the game hen with uncharacteristic knifework and made sure to catch a slice of truffle on her fork before taking her first bite. She closed her eyes and turned to me.

"I know," I said. "I need to make this at home."

CHAPTER 5

New Frontier

...

W HEN PEOPLE ASKED ME what it was like out on the mushroom trail, I struggled for appropriate analogies. Commercial fishing? No, not quite. Fishing was a highly organized industry with strict regulations. Hard-rock mining? Definitely not. Serious mining was backed by serious funding. And the mushroom trade was a far cry from illicit narcotics, a comparison I sometimes heard (for one thing, it was legal, or mostly legal). Yet it shared certain similarities with drug smuggling. The players preferred anonymity. They worked largely in secret. It was an all-cash business. Really, though, there were no easy comparisons. The mushroom trade struck me more as a legit—though freewheeling—type of frontier-style capitalism that was mostly gone nowadays. Maybe it was one of the last vestiges of a nearly vanished Wild West.

It certainly seemed this way when I met up with Jeremy Faber in Montana. Spring in the Rocky Mountains had arrived a little late and he had business to do. Together we drove around Missoula, looking for the biggest bank around, and while this might have been a college town—the cultural hub of the northern Rockies even—it was overrun with rinky-dink banking institutions with names like Mountain

West, Montana First, and Farmers State. He dismissed the place as pathetic and sounded embarrassed that he'd even considered attending the university years ago. "There's the Snowbowl," he said, pointing to a decent-sized mountain visible in the distance between a cleft of sagebrush-covered foothills. "Twenty-six hundred vert. Not bad." Even back then, skiing was the main draw for him—and it was what he did now when he wasn't working. We pulled into the nearly empty lot of a U.S. Bank. Faber hated U.S. Bank, hated it the way you hate child abductors or mass murderers, but he had no choice. This was the only bank in town with a Seattle branch besides Wells Fargo, and he'd already vowed to never bank at Wells Fargo again.

Faber prided himself on efficiency. "Ten minutes," he said to me. "Check your watch."

We walked into the bank. Faber made a quick scan—two tellers up front twiddled their thumbs, and, unbelievably, there were no fewer than six senior clerks scattered throughout the right side of the room, each unoccupied at a capacious desk with a sea of blue carpet between them, like desert-island castaways, all of them pretending to do something important. Faber pursed his lips, trying not to laugh. If they were busy at all, it was probably in trying to defraud homeowners yet again with some ingenious mortgage scheme. No one looked up. Maybe they smelled him. Faber could have been homeless or deranged. Week-old stubble, disheveled hair, same shirt and pants for the past four days. Undeterred, he strode forward, his heavy boots muffled by the carpet. He performed a little vaudeville move, one foot forward and arms spread wide. *Ta-da!* "Who'll have me?" he cried, a big smile now on his face.

The clerk with the closest desk finally cracked, losing the game of chicken, and glanced up, putting on a happy face. "That would be me."

Faber didn't waste any time. "I want to open the fastest, simplest account you've got." He sat himself down in a heap and stretched his arms. His steel-blue Marmot jacket was ripped at both sleeves, his hands black with dirt.

"Personal or business?"

"Business. No, personal. Wait—what's the difference?"

"If it's for doing business, it has to be a business account." The clerk pulled out a brochure and started unfolding it—five, six, seven pages, and counting—until he had a big paper accordion in hand. He started to enumerate the differences. Faber sighed.

"Personal," he interrupted. *"Personal!"*

"All righty, then," said the clerk, folding up his accordion.

When it was finished, Faber looked at his BlackBerry. "Thirteen minutes," he said triumphantly. "What's three extra minutes?" Faber now had an account where he could withdraw five or six thousand dollars every day, provided his employees back in Seattle got the day's receipts deposited. For the next month he would be a daily customer at the U.S. Bank branch forty-five miles down the road in Hamilton, Montana.

. . .

THE BITTERROOT VALLEY WAS once a place of breathtaking natural beauty, and its craggy mountains still impressed, yet an endless procession of sprawling one- and two-horse towns, gravel pits, fast-food franchises, trophy homes, storage lockers, and neon-lit casinos now marred the hour-plus drive from Missoula to Darby, the old hitching-post-turned-small-time-tourist-destination where Faber intended to buy as many morel mushrooms as his new bank account would afford.

In the early years, Faber could get away with picking morels by himself or with a partner such as Doug. All he needed was several hundred pounds a week to keep Seattle restaurants in morels. Now, with the New York operation up and running and constant calls from wholesalers looking for product, Faber was faced with the dilemma of small businesses everywhere. He had to grow. Had to grow just to hold on to his current market share. Everyone wanted more. The business was right at the million-dollar mark for gross revenue. He wanted to avoid 20 percent growth year over year—that was a recipe for disaster, he was sure—yet 10 percent seemed necessary to keep clients happy. This meant filling orders for up to three thousand pounds weekly, an impossibility even for a very talented small crew of pickers. There was only one way to do this kind of volume: Faber had to join the fray and set up a buy station in town to attract the hundreds of mostly Mexican and Southeast Asian pickers who had come to the Big Sky State in search of morels.

While Faber prepared his tent canopy and slick new sandwich board (two slabs of varnished wood duct-taped together, with MUSH-ROOM BUYER in black letters and a few drawings of morels and chanterelles), I walked around downtown Darby. At the state liquor store down the road from Sober Automotive, the clerk apologized for not selling beer, only the hard stuff. She said the mushroom pickers were in town just about every spring, starting around Memorial Day. At the main intersection, a couple drank shots of tequila outside the Sawmill Saloon, while more ATVs than cars rumbled by. A mule deer buck looked both ways and walked across the street. Both the Right to Bare Arms gym and Big Bear Taxidermy looked closed. At the People's Market, I found a Cambodian picker in the beer aisle, wearing a wool watch cap and a navy-blue mechanic's jacket with a Miller Lite patch on the breast. He shook his head. He was just admiring the labels, not buying, since it was definitely not Miller Time. He'd picked three pounds today, his wife two. "Five pound very bad," he said wearily.

I bought a six-pack and drove back to the buy station, which was set up in the gravel lot of a cabinetmaker, Bluebuck Woodworking, beside Tin Cup Creek. Times were tough in Darby, Montana. The landowner was dropping the rent for the cabinetmaker rather than evicting him. Faber's $125 in weekly rent was a welcome infusion. For his part, Faber's costs were mounting and he needed large quantities of morels, and soon. On his way to Montana he'd stopped at a secret patch to pick morels in an inch of snow. His Astro van threw a rod on the rough road to the patch. After picking upward of a hundred pounds, he got the van turned around, killed the engine, and coasted back down the mountain. Once on flat ground, with the engine clanking and spewing oil, he was able to drive the van far enough to reach a boneyard, where he left it for good in exchange for three hundred dollars. Now he was in another of his fleet of Astro vans, and this one was having problems too. The night before, on the way to camp in the Bitterroot National Forest, it had overheated. In the morning Faber poured in a gallon of water, which promptly pooled at his feet. Cracked radiator. Once again, he coasted down the mountain in neutral. When he hit the pavement and put the van into gear, the needle pinned instantly in the red, and he sputtered to a stop. Now the vehicle was waiting for a radiator at Honey Enterprises, where the brother-owners (the one missing a thumb and forefinger did the books, the other worked the wrench) talked too slowly for Faber's comfort and tacked up news stories about crooked politicians and miscreant wildlife ("WOLVES KILL 120 SHEEP"). The wolf story was a bad omen. Faber loved wolves and would have them recolonize every inch of their former stomping ground if he could.

Costs continued to pile up. This was not how he had envisioned his trip to Montana. That first night he attracted zero pickers to his stall. This was somewhat expected. He was new in town. Much of his competition was already here, including Foods In Season, Sierra Madre, Ponderosa, and others. He had counted at least seven buy stands, and there were probably more. The buyers, he knew, were trying to keep prices low. This was technically illegal. It's called collusion. Prices had dropped to as low as eight dollars per pound, and yet the pickers were bringing in minuscule quantities, five or ten pounds, maybe a full bucket for a decent picker. The economics made no sense. Prices should have been higher with such limited supply, and now they were finally inching up. The buyers wanted to top out at ten, but the night before someone had offered eleven dollars, and there was a rumor of twelve. Pickers routinely complain about price tampering and accuse the buyers of colluding. Buyers dismiss these claims as paranoid and suggest the pickers read up on the laws of supply and demand. As with most disputes, the truth is probably some-where in the middle. With globalization, prices today are more apt to be set by an international trade. As good as the Pacific Northwest is for mushroom harvesting, most estimates put it at no more than 10 percent of the world market, a market led by countries with far lower living standards. No doubt buyers have engaged in illegal col-lusion on occasion, agreeing to set price ceilings and other controls. This would be hard to prove without police investigations and wire-taps. More likely it is a passive sort of collusion, an unspoken limit above which no one will go. When a buyer like Faber upsets the bal-ance, the other buyers will sometimes express their displeasure in subtle ways. They'll stop by to say hello, to let the transgressor know they're paying attention, that word travels fast.

Another way that the buyers maintain low prices is by enforcing loyalty. They can do this by paying pickers' costs up front so that the pickers owe them. A buyer might put together a crew and send them out to a place like Darby, Montana, with enough money to pay for gas and groceries to get them started. The pickers are then expected to sell exclusively to that buyer to work off the debt. Frontier capitalism.

The next day, with Faber's van still in the shop and nothing else to do before opening the buy stand, we decided to scout the area in my car and let other pickers know there was a new buyer in town. We drove out past Painted Rocks. On our way to the patch, we stopped in at the West Fork ranger station to get permits. A pert blond woman with a nose ring and a neat pageboy haircut, who looked as if she'd never spent a night in the woods, handed me some forms to sign, along with a map. Her colleague, an older, heavyset woman, looked over disapprovingly. "I told whatsherface to make copies of the other map, the good one," she said. "She copied the wrong map!"

"I don't know anything about that," said the younger one. She showed me on the map where I could pick legally and where it was illegal. "That's Idaho over there," she said, pointing.

"You need to get a permit from them," said the older woman.

"They don't give permits," Faber corrected. And, besides, the route into the patch from the Idaho side was still under snow, while it was clear on the Montana side.

"You need a permit from them regardless."

"Drive all the way to Idaho for a permit that they don't sell?" I said.

"I guess so," said the younger clerk, not paying attention.

"That doesn't make any sense," her colleague agreed.

"All this bureaucracy for some mushroom picking?"

The younger clerk ignored my question and pressed on, explaining that I would need to cut each morel I found in half to make it clear I was harvesting only recreationally. Otherwise, I could buy a commercial permit.

"Cut in half? That's ridiculous. What if I want my morels intact?"

"Don't pay attention to him," Faber said. "He's just trying to ruffle your feathers."

"He's got a point," the older woman said in my defense. "These rules are stupid."

"I wouldn't know," said the young clerk on cue.

If Faber had his way, commercial pickers would buy a single permit each year, for perhaps a thousand dollars, which would be good for all the national forests. But as it was, individual district managers didn't want to deal with the pickers. While they bent over backward for big-game hunters, the mushroom pickers were too much hassle, in their minds. And it was true that in some cases the pickers had brought opprobrium upon themselves, notably the pickers who left dirty camps and garbage in the woods. These were not isolated events. Again and again, I would find the forest floor strewn with trash: bottles, cans, plastic wrappers, empty cigarette packs. Large concentrations of pickers posed concerns about garbage, sanitation, and campfires, concerns that required action and expenditure. One year, during a bonanza of morels, the Okanogan National Forest in Washington State was besieged with mushroom pickers. Even after taking precautions to funnel the pickers into two centralized camps, the district was then faced with a monumental cleanup and campground rehabilitation, not to mention the associated costs.

Still, the permit issue was a major headache for everyone in the wild-food business. One time, at Faber's place in Seattle, I met a picker named Bill, who was dropping off a few baskets of chanterelles on his way out to the coast. A short, compact man with a trim beard and clear blue eyes, Bill considered himself one of the last of a dying breed. "My mother calls me a free spirit," he said. We got to talking about permits, and he said he didn't bother with them. He didn't pay taxes either. Bill said he declined to play by the rules because he didn't trust the government. As someone who loved the wilderness, he saw the Forest Service as just another money-grubber trying to *get the cut out,* to the detriment of the woods and everything that lived there. "As a mushroom picker, I can go wherever I want. I'm free. I've been all over the mountains of Washington, Oregon, and Idaho," he said. "I know those ridges better than any Forest Service ranger." To illustrate his point, he told me a story about picking a morel patch near Idaho's Gospel-Hump Wilderness with Doug. The area was crawling with Forest Service personnel, county sheriffs, even the FBI. Why? Because of a controversial logging sale nearby that was pushing into a roadless area. Shop windows in town advertised unpleasant outcomes for environmentalists who had come to protest. "It got too hot," Bill said. "Earth First! was there, cutting hydraulic hoses and moving survey stakes. Folks in town were pissed. We didn't have permits. Me and Doug went our separate ways. I was driving a van that had *mushroom picker* all over it." It was white, with big patches of peeling paint that revealed slate-gray primer underneath. Christina Choi had dubbed it "Moo Cow Car." "I found a place to store Moo Cow and went down to Enterprise, got me a shiny new rental car, shaved my beard, cut my hair, and parked right at the trailhead, like a hiker." He spent the next week camped on the patch, hauling morels out at night. "I brought six hundred pounds of morels to Jeremy that first week. 'Just cut me a check for six thousand and we're square,'

I told him. I made thirty thousand dollars that season. Didn't pay a dime in taxes."

"That's a true story," Faber said to me later.

AFTER LEAVING THE RANGER station, we continued up the West Fork of the Bitterroot River. Faber was already thinking about picking illegally on the Idaho side of the border. He figured there was a good chance most of the Mexican pickers wouldn't risk it (because of INS), and the Southeast Asian pickers, though in the United States legally, were often too afraid of authority to stray. We turned a corner to see the trucks and conversion vans of mushroom pickers, dozens of them, parked alongside the creek, most with California plates. It had been a terrible year for spring porcini in the Sierras and Mount Shasta area, so Cambodians living in Redding, Sacramento, Stockton, and elsewhere had turned to the Rockies for morels. Farther up the road we came across a few Oregon plates and a smattering of Montana plates, the latter probably recreational pickers, or "local yokels" to Faber. We gained elevation, finally topping out at 7,200 feet on the pass between Montana and Idaho. We could see down into the Idaho side, and it looked good. A forest fire had blazed through the previous summer, torching thousands of acres. The burned forest had a strange beauty to it, with undulating patterns of colors—black, red, and green—that showed where the fire had burned hottest or not at all. Through binoculars, Faber sighted what appeared to be a hot springs, with several tents and cars in the vicinity. We drove on over the saddle. Almost immediately his theory—or hope—that the pickers were staying out of Idaho was popped. Battered rigs lined the road, many of them with Washington plates that he recognized. "It's getting hammered," he said glumly. The hot-springs camp turned out to be an illegal mushroom camp. We stopped to chat up an elderly woman driving a Rhino ATV that looked like a golf cart with knobby tires. "You need a vehicle like this for these roads," she said brightly, her white hair tied sensibly in a bun, before puttering off.

"I like her," Faber said. "I bet you back in the day she was feisty."
He didn't like the number of cars. "It's getting stomped," he said
again. This was the only game in town. A bad year for spring mushrooms had funneled every out-of-work mushroom picker into western Montana. With all these pickers walking through the patch, the
nearly invisible baby morels emerging from the ground were getting
stepped on by an army of heavy boots.

On our way out of the patch, we stopped for each picker we saw in
the road. Faber told them he had just arrived and would be paying
thirteen dollars per pound tonight. "Tell your friends," he said. On
the far side of the pass, we met an old Toyota pickup coming up the
road. The driver slowed and rolled down his window—a white man,
the first we'd seen, maybe mid-forties, with faded tattoos on both
arms, a curly dark beard, and thick eyebrows. Faber said hello. "I'm
from Illinois," the man started in without prompting. "Came out here
to get back together with the ex. You know, the kids and all that. Lost
my job six months ago, and one day she up and says, 'Get the fuck
out.' I'm just trying to scrounge enough money to fix my rig so I can
move on."

Without hesitation, Faber started to reel off the names of morel
patches all over western Montana and Idaho: drainages, Forest Service roads, mountain ranges. The man's eyes widened and seemed to
roll around in his head as he took this all in. They were worried eyes,
eyes with fear in them. "You're a white guy with Montana plates,"
Faber said finally, trying to reassure him. "Go pick illegally. And
don't worry about the woman. What are they good for anyway?" The
man made a crude gesture, and we left him there in the middle of a
dirt logging road, contemplating a dozen coordinates where he might
find enough mushrooms to keep the fear at bay.

. . .

THAT NIGHT FABER HAD a long line of pickers at his station. Word
had gotten out. One picker with a drooping mustache and a T-shirt

that said THAI ROYAL MARINES CARBINE GROUP brought his entire encampment over to get the extra dollar per pound that Faber was paying, even though they were camping with another buyer across the
street. Faber called him Fu Manchu. The picker drank a Coors tall-
boy and flashed gaudy rings as he negotiated with Faber for an extra
two dollars per pound for himself—a finder's fee, he called it—all the
while fingering an oversize silver belt buckle that he claimed was
won as second prize in the stampede rodeo. He looked like a character right out of the movies, and as he gripped that belt buckle with
one hand while gesturing with his beer, I was convinced that he'd
probably seen every Western ever made since he'd landed in America. He sucked a Marlboro down to the filter, and Faber gave him the
extra couple of bucks.

Mexican crews started to arrive by the vanload. "How you doing?"
Faber said to the boss man of one crew, giving him the soul shake.
Faber was suddenly in a good mood, giddy even. He was raking it in.
The boss man, surprisingly clean cut and wearing a white straw cow-
boy hat—he was probably the driver and translator—looked con-
fused. *Who is this crazy white guy?* "I'm okay . . ." he said tentatively.
"Do I know you?"

"What do you and your boys want? Sodas? Beers? I'll have a
cooler tomorrow."

The boss looked more confused.

"Ladies?" Faber went on.

"Ladies?"

"Women. You want some women?"

"Womens?" asked the man, starting to smile. His crew broke into
laughter.

"I'll be here tomorrow," Faber said, sealing the deal. "Price is
firm." Everyone nodded. That's what the Mexicans wanted to hear.
"I'm pissing off some buyers tonight," Faber added merrily.

Later, while continuing to weigh out basket after basket and pay
the pickers, Faber noticed the same truck drive by several times. It
was one of his competitors. He recognized the make. "Just wait, he'll

stop here eventually and talk to me. He can't resist. *Jeremy,* he'll say. *What's the matter, Jeremy? You don't need to pay so much.*" But paying a little more, besides ensuring a steady supply of mushrooms, also meant that he could turn away the less able pickers—the pickers with paltry, time-wasting amounts or dirty or old mushrooms. "I'll pay whatever it takes," he said, ignoring the truck as it drove by.

Faber was relieved to have mushrooms, though the quality wasn't great, and it was clear even after one night of buying that the Montana morel patches weren't going to produce the volume he needed for the next month. He called a picker in Raymond about his patch in Washington, the one where the Astro threw a rod, leaving a message on voice mail: "I've got a patch that'll be killer," he began, "if no one touches it. It's super tiny. Just the two of you. That's all it's good for. Bring one more and you won't make any money. It's a perfect hundred acres—if you farm it and take care of it. Don't say anything. I was saving it for myself. No one knows about it." The good morel pickers knew how to farm patches. They walked carefully through the patch, choosing their steps wisely to avoid stepping on babies. They covered up clusters of immature morels with evergreen boughs and other bundles of forest brush to shade and protect them. They picked the biggest, freshest mushrooms in intensive bouts of all-day picking, then rested the patch for a couple of days. The good morel pickers knew how to make money.

. . .

BACK AT CAMP, Faber built a fire and cooked dinner. With so many pickers, it had taken longer than planned to weigh all the baskets into even thirteen-pound shipments for tomorrow's run to the airport. The time was nearly midnight and Faber wasn't halfway through his meal when the rain started, just a few heavy drops at first and then a Rocky Mountain downpour. He sat in his camp chair beside the hissing fire and continued to eat his steak. A puddle collected on his plate. His legs and arms darkened with rain. When he was finished, he stood up, covered the mushroom baskets with a tarp, strung another tarp between a few trees above his hammock, got in the hammock in his wet clothes, and immediately fell asleep.

I got in my tent, feeling a bit guilty that I'd allowed Faber to helm the camp cooking on a night when he had already worked so many hours. Perhaps it was deference to his professional kitchen experience. The next night, I decided, would be different. My education as a home cook had begun in similar circumstances, after all, in rustic conditions with few implements at my disposal and a limited menu that could only be improved by the wild foods available. Learning how to perfectly pan-fry a trout from an alpine lake was a necessary skill in the backcountry. My first stuffed fish was on a Colorado backpacking trip, where I opened the cavity of a fat brookie and filled it with a stuffing made from aspen boletes and wild greens. Camped beside a glacial cirque in the North Cascades with Martha, I supplemented our pasta dinner with freshly sautéed fiddleheads. I learned how to catch bigger fish and in time acquired the skills to match: how to fillet a salmon, how to brine and smoke it, how to make a restaurant-quality presentation of roasted sockeye. I started reading cookbooks. My first red-wine reduction accompanied a fly-caught silver from the salt. I worked through the French sauces, making a beurre blanc for lingcod, poaching rockfish in court bouillon, and improvising a rich golden lobster sauce for halibut. It became tradition to welcome spring with a stinging nettle soup. I used nettles and other backyard weeds in ravioli, gnudi, and gnocchi. Every Memorial Day we camped in the mountains with friends, making elaborate camp dinners with the abundance of the season: spring chinook grilled over the fire with a sauce of Pinot Noir and morels; a salad course of miner's lettuce, wild wood sorrel, and dandelion greens; huckleberries from the previous fall for dessert.

With greater fluency came confidence. After a memorable Italian dinner to celebrate a friend's birthday, I called the restaurant the next day on the offhand chance that someone might be able to explain the pasta dish in greater detail. Spinasse's chef answered the phone. I was taken aback at first, then realized this was my chance. He kindly walked me through the dish, telling me how crucial it was to caramelize the diced porcini, how to make a quick butter-parsley sauce and then add the porcini back to the pan. Next came the chicken stock, which he advised me to reduce at least twice with the rest of the sauce before tossing it with fresh tagliolini. The result the second time around was nearly as good as the dish we'd paid for. The deeper I went, the more it seemed that good food could be achieved at home without bartering one's soul to the devil. The wild ingredients spurred me on. These foods I was bringing home on a regular basis commanded a hefty price tag in the market. They demanded respect and imagination. With a hard-won geoduck clam or a basket of shaggy parasols, I felt a responsibility to cook the ingredients in a manner that reflected their innate qualities, acquiring in time some basic cooking skills.

As the rain continued its loud parade on my tent, I fell asleep thinking about the next night's dinner. It would need to be quick yet hearty. Faber didn't eat pork, so I would buy some lamb sausages, which I had seen at the market in town. To these I would add a stew made with white beans, onions, kale, and morels. Simple, stick-to-the-ribs camp fare, the sort that could see you through a brief rain-soaked sleep in a hammock.

Three hours later Faber woke up and packed my Subaru with five hundred pounds of morels. By 3:45 A.M. we were on the road, arriving an hour later at the Missoula airport, where passengers and cargo shippers formed a line together. A family eyed the morels, trying to figure out what the peculiar-looking shipment was. Aaron, Faber's sole New York employee, called at dawn to see if any of the previous day's commerce was coming his way. It wasn't. Faber tried to reassure Aaron in his typically unreassuring way: "This place is a fucking zoo. Every buyer in North America is here fighting over a pittance of mushrooms. Don't worry. What I buy tonight is all going to New York. I'll have at least a couple hundred pounds to you by Friday."

The checker at the terminal had her hair pulled back with a

braided black headband. She was wearing running shoes and athletic socks that barely reached her ankles, showing off toned calves. She didn't give Faber a second thought. He tried to charm her colleague instead. "My job is to make your job easier," he said, offering to round up the poundage on a few baskets—and the cargo rate—because they had been improperly weighed in the haste to get back to camp. "You have to be friends with these people," he whispered to me. "Otherwise they can make your life hell." On that note, he asked me to remind him to deliver a gift of morels to the Darby ranger station.

Ahead of us in line was one of Faber's competitors, with about the same size load of morels. Jay, a field buyer, was from Coos Bay, Oregon, though he neglected to mention his employer. He was wearing camo-colored fleece and a trucker cap that said DUI TEST DRIVER. "This is a great industry," he said to me, the way people who have done a lot of different jobs will talk about their latest work in an upbeat way. "It's a rush," he went on. "All the buyers competing, the price wars. I love it." He said more buyers would be arriving in town later that day. "It's gonna get real interesting." He had the last of his baskets weighed and stacked on a dolly to head over to TSA. "Good luck, Hoss," he said to me as he wheeled his cargo away. Faber came back from the shipping desk and said the sexy clerk in the headband was warming to him. He planned to ask her out. Why not? He would be visiting this counter virtually every morning at five A.M. for the next month.

At a Starbucks down the road, Faber got an iced green tea and sat back in an armchair with a copy of *The Wall Street Journal,* one leg draped casually over the other. He waved the front page at me. "I'll be on here one day. First mushroom buyer to make a billion." He called Jonathan. "Dude, you wouldn't believe what a shitshow it is. I got lucky. Pickers everywhere. Suddenly they're all at my station. My phone is ringing off the hook. Spent five grand last night." Jonathan had some intel for Faber. Apparently one of their competitors, Portland-based Mikuni Wild Harvest, had undercut Faber's morel price by a suspicious one dollar, and they were charging even less for spring porcini. Faber was convinced they were making a play for the Seattle fresh market. Lately he'd received tip-offs from a few regular customers who had bought Mikuni products in a pinch, only to be dissatisfied. "Mikuni coming after me on my own turf," Faber mused. "Game on!"

Another call came in. Faber glanced at his phone and cursed. He had to take it. "Let me tell you," he said to the wholesaler, "this is not an easy mushroom year. Check back at the end of the week. I might have mushrooms at restaurant prices but not wholesale. I can't promise you anything. New York takes priority. You're second, that's just the way it is."

After a couple of hours of wading through the morning's emails, texts, and phone messages on his BlackBerry, it was time to scout again. It wasn't quite eight A.M. "I have a bad feeling about tonight's buy," he said, apropos of nothing.

We drove back into the mountains, this time following Lewis and Clark's route over Lolo Pass into Idaho, catching glimpses of the Lochsa River a thousand feet below thundering through its gorge with spring runoff. Faber had once used a raft to cross the Lochsa in similar high-water conditions to reach a patch inaccessible by foot. "Must have gone a mile before we made it to the other side," he said. His partner in that episode had not been thrilled. "Yeah, it was pretty hairy." Faber grinned. "But an epic pick." We turned left onto a logging road he'd never been on, noting patches along the way of fiddleheads ("maybe a hundred pounds"), miner's lettuce ("gas money"), and huckleberries ("I'll send a crew here"). We gained elevation, expecting a blockade of snow around each turn, until a large Engelmann spruce tree across the road brought our mission to a halt. We were at about seven thousand feet. "You don't have a Swedish saw?" he asked me, incredulous that I would bring assorted camping gear yet nothing that could cut through a two-foot-diameter log. We got out and began to walk, soon encountering heavy drifts of dirty, compacted snow. The morel patch, he figured, was just over the next ridge. Though still under snow, it looked good—the right mix of trees. "Two weeks and this is going *off*," he pronounced. The only problem was that it was in Idaho: illegal to pick commercially here.

UNLIKE MOST OF THE buyers in town, Faber tried to pick during the day as much as he could, in part out of financial necessity, in part because spending time in woods and mountains was one of the main reasons he got into the business in the first place, though he was careful not to sentimentalize this aspect of his work. Always there was the drudgery and the lack of money, the need for more product, the obtuseness of banks, while I was still stuck on the food itself. "It's just a mushroom," he'd say. But the romance of it didn't wear off easily for me. Seeing these foods on restaurant menus never failed to strike a nerve, reminding me of hours spent both in the field and at the table. Once, while Faber and I were picking a fall mushroom patch together on the Olympic Peninsula, he revealed a hint of why he did what he did. He called it his "oddball spot" because he always came away with bizarre, lesser-known species that only certain restaurants would buy. I followed him up and down steep ridges of old growth that had escaped the saw. This was classic ancient forest, the sort that environmentalists had waged pitched battles over: towering groves of moss-draped Douglas firs, western hemlocks, and red cedars. There were even some yew trees, a small, uncommon conifer that has cancer-fighting properties and was a favorite of T. S. Eliot. We picked a few matsutake and hedgehogs and then crested a wrinkle of topography to find a valley of strange-looking fungi that looked more like the inhabitants of a tropical reef. Bear's head mushrooms, a member of the *Hericium* genus, grew off stumps in basketball-sized clumps and resembled an unwieldy collection of tiny white icicles. At the foot of old fire-scarred Douglas firs, Faber found *Sparassis*—cauliflower mushrooms—some of them several pounds or more. Round and coral-like, with cream-colored ruffles, they looked like big skeins of egg noodles drained in a colander.

The cauliflower mushroom was an oddball, to be sure, and one of the best-tasting of all the wild mushrooms, with a rich, nutty flavor and a nearly crunchy texture that stood up well to bouts of extended cooking. I liked to braise cauliflower mushrooms in pot roasts and then serve the meat over the fungus, playing off its egg-noodle form. Most recreational hunters would be overjoyed to find a cauliflower. A single specimen made a trip worthwhile. In the space of an hour, Faber found seven or eight, for a total of thirty pounds or more. He would sell these to restaurants for ten dollars per pound. A three-hundred-dollar reward for a bushwhack among heart-stopping groves of ancient trees. "Matt will take most of these," he said, referring to his old friend Matt Dillon from the Herbfarm days. Our trip—gas, ferry, time—was already paid for. It was a rare sunny fall day on the peninsula, though even at the height of the day the sun barely penetrated the furrows and pleats of this rugged terrain. Horizontally filtered light swam through the old growth and lit up the tree trunks. Faber stopped in the middle of a mossy notch in the forest, his pack now full. "This is why we live here," he said, and I knew the equation in his mind had nothing to do with mushrooms.

On the way back to the ferry that day, we pulled over suddenly, having just passed by a green smudge at fifty miles an hour: watercress swelling around a spring. Faber reached into his pack and found a handful of garbage bags and two pairs of scissors, handing me one. In fifteen minutes we had nearly thirty pounds of the spicy wild mustard, a salad green that made its domesticated counterpart pale in comparison. At seven dollars per pound, this was another two hundred dollars in the bag.

A few nights later, on a whim, Martha and I stopped by Matt Dillon's place, Sitka & Spruce, just to look at the menu. We had planned to grab a quick bite nearby and see a movie. There on the menu were the cauliflower mushrooms, served with the wild watercress beneath a fillet of black cod, perhaps my favorite of all fish. Just seeing this dish written there in an elegant script, posted by the maroon-red door, I knew we had to stay for dinner. Martha frowned at me, then relented. She didn't need to sit in a dark movie theater anyway. The wait for a table would be an hour. We sat at the bar next door, eating oysters and sharing a glass of Muscadet. Suddenly it seemed like a night to celebrate. Once seated, we couldn't resist ordering both the black cod and the chanterelles, which came in a gratin with parsnips, celeriac, chard, and salted pork. "I'm sort of a mushroom geek," I apologized to the server. We stole glances at the table next to us: a family of four, the parents older than we were, with two grown boys in their twenties. They all shared plates and talked excitedly about the coming election. On the other side of us, two men eagerly discussed the stock market. Colorful gourds and squashes lined the windowsills. Mason jars of spices filled a cabinet. The low strumming of delta blues drifted down from hidden speakers above. "Look at the rose hips and heather," Martha said, admiring our table's odd flower arrangement. The night had taken on a new, unexpected feeling. Our server presented a plate of locally caught smelt in a simple lemon–parsley dressing. We pulled off hunks of house-baked sourdough and alternated stacking pieces of tender fish and spoonsful of the gratin on the bread. The server poured glasses of Grüner Veltliner. What had started as a last-minute date night was turning into a feast of surprises. Martha teased a slice of chanterelle and a cube of parsnip out of the ramekin and topped them with some of the creamy sauce and bread crumbs. "Take another bite," she pleaded, "before I demolish this whole thing." She called the babysitter from the bathroom to explain our tardiness. We finished with a wedge of gateau Basque covered in poached pear and candied almonds. "He never eats dessert!" Martha told our server, as she signed the slip in a hurry so we wouldn't keep the sitter any later than we already had.

. . .

ON THE WAY BACK DOWN into Montana after scouting, Faber spied a bull moose in a bank of willows by Lolo Creek. Its antlers were just coming in, their smooth velvet visible to the naked eye. He had me pull over. "That might be my favorite animal," he said, looking through binoculars. "Bears are too common." The prehistoric beast looked at us dumbly. It approached the car at first, seemingly curious, then spooked all at once, as if some terrible knowledge had just been revealed, and ran off in a flurry of gangling limbs. "So cute," said Faber. He admitted to owning three stuffed toy moose. This was a good sign; it countered the wolf clipping at the auto-repair shop. Now he felt better about tonight's prospects at the buy station, but moments later, after seeing another hold come in from Chase on his BlackBerry, he retracted his change of heart and reverted to his original pessimism. What he needed to do was sell his business. "I don't plan to be a mushroom buyer the rest of my life," he said to me, as if even the thought of such a plan was sheer lunacy. The only problem was finding a qualified buyer. His competitors didn't need to spend the kind of money he wanted just to secure a new client list, and anyone without the requisite experience would surely go under in no time. This severely limited the possibilities for attracting a buyer. Faber concluded that the only way to sell would be to include himself in the deal: a year of full-time help without pay before he vanished off into the mountains. "I want a briefcase with 1.2 million dollars in cash," he said, imagining the high-stakes horse trading with some former foe, "and his wife on a silver platter, wearing a thong." Then he'd disappear into the British Columbia wilderness.

"Seriously, if I sold the business, you probably wouldn't see me for a few years. I'd be skiing."

AT HONEY ENTERPRISES, the van was still not ready. The brothers explained that NAPA had sent the wrong radiator over. "So get the right one," Faber fumed to me back in the car. "How difficult is it to go across the street and get the right part?" Incompetence all around. He grabbed some more things out of his van, including a bunch of maps and a bright hunter-orange hat, which he perched on the top of his head, redneck style. "It's wartime," he said gravely, then collapsed into fits of strung-out laughter. Here he was, in just the first week of a monthlong stay in Montana, and already he was a jangled bundle of nerves. He needed to ask out the girl at the airport.

That night at the buy station, a Cambodian woman reported that a white pickup with Montana plates had been cruising the patch, yelling at any Asians on the road, saying the mushroom hunters would be the ones to be hunted next. And the worst thing? she asked us. The worst thing about it was that he had his kids with him. Faber shook his head. He heard this sort of thing all the time from his Asian pickers. A call came in from Kahne up in Alaska. His patch up there was finally starting to produce. Faber had been paying him to scout for the last two weeks. He'd been dropped off by helicopter. It was serious backcountry. Now they had to decide whether to float the morels out fresh by whitewater raft or set up a drying operation on site and copter everything out. While Faber strategized on the phone, a picker named Mario from Guatemala took me aside. Chain-smoking his way through a pack of Camels, Mario sported a long braided ponytail, safari hat, and blue bandanna neckerchief. He was one of the unofficial mayors of the patch, keeping an eye on what went down and an ear open to any injustices. For a moment I thought he was going to chew me out for being here. After all, what skin did I have in the game? I held on to the camera that dangled from my neck. "What your friend is doing for the pickers," Mario said seriously, taking a long drag off his cigarette, "is a very good thing. He's paying a fair price. I wanted you to know that."

By the end of the week, Faber figured he was in the two-thousand-pound range. That was good. That would keep his business humming along. Another thousand pounds on top of that would be profit. But he didn't want to get greedy. He hunkered down and got to work, knowing that he'd be hanging his hunting cap in Montana for many nights to come.

CHAPTER 6

Autumn Aroma

...

WHEN THE MOUNTAIN BLEW ITS TOP, a mile-wide plume of pumice-studded ash sprayed ten miles into the air at twice the speed of sound. A twelve-thousand-foot stratovolcano before the eruption, Mount Mazama blasted itself into smithereens, an annihilation of rock and magma. You could hear the explosion for hundreds of miles. Lava flowed freely while ash and pumice rained down upon five hundred thousand square miles of the Pacific Northwest, covering scorched hillsides in some places with as much as two hundred fifty feet of volcanic debris. The blast flattened surrounding forest. Mudslides picked up mountain lakes by the scruff and dropped them elsewhere, miles away in some cases. This was 7,700 years ago, more or less, in central Oregon's Cascade Mountains. Soon after, the magma began to falter under its own weight and then slip back into the hole that remained, an implosion of colossal proportions that left behind a perfect anti-mountain, the submerged mirror of a peak: a deep caldera that would, in time, fill with the most pristine and clearest of spring-fed mountain waters, Crater Lake. Just shy of two thousand feet deep, the lake is a deep ultramarine color. Klamath Indians who inhabit the area have a myth to explain the circumstances. Skell, the sky god, was not pleased with his colleague Llao, god of the underworld. Their battle sealed the fate of the mountain.

Eventually, the forests recovered, as they will when left alone. First came the forbs and grasses, gaudy-colored things like pink fireweed and purple lupine. Then saplings—lodgepole pine, yellow pine, firs, and spruces. As the forests matured, so, too, did the surviving network of mycelial fibers beneath the volcanic soil. In particular, one species of fungus living among the conifers thrived in the sand-like soils prevalent along the volcanic spine of the Cascades, nowhere more so than along these pumice-laden shores lapping up against the extinct Mount Mazama. The Japanese, also members of the Pacific "ring of fire" club, on the far side of the ocean, had a name for this Vulcan fungus: *matsutake*.

If ever there was an Elysium in the lore of the mushroom trail, a time and a place in which the veteran picker thought he had finally found that great patch in the sky, it was during the Oregon Cascades matsutake pick of the late 1980s and early 1990s. But that was so long ago that few on the trail could even speak of it firsthand. It was legend.

. . .

SOMPHONE NHAMNHOUANE GENEROUSLY SPLIT his earnings with his partner, Forrest Cook, then tossed his receipt into the fire. Orange flames lit up Forrest's face and hands as he fanned a stack of fresh twenties. Someone went to the cooler for another round of Coors. Som arched his back and said it was a good day despite getting a late start. They had picked matsutake mushrooms today, as they had for more than a month since arriving at camp, and though theirs was a partnership down the middle, with gas, food, and camping equipment all in the mix, it was Som who had committed the mushroom patches to memory and Som who possessed the experience to line their wallets and Som who would determine where they'd pick tomorrow. He had first picked matsutake—usually called matsi or pines by the pickers—in these forests as a teenager with his mother, then later on his own, and now he had taken on his carpenter friend Forrest as an apprentice of sorts, since the shriveling of the construction business in the Great Recession.

Standing together by flickering firelight, they looked like an odd pairing: Som, Laotian by birth, short and squat, with a cherubic face and easy smile; Forrest, white, tall, and skinny, with a mouthful of broken or missing teeth where he'd taken a fastball a decade earlier. Twenty years ago this partnership would have seemed unlikely at best, but much had changed in central Oregon's famed matsutake patches. Another buddy of theirs, named Todd, sat on a stump by the fire, roasting hawkwings he had found that day. The hawkwing (*Sarcodon imbricatum*) is a type of toothed fungi related to hedgehogs, a dark mushroom with beautiful, intricately patterned shingles on the cap that resemble the fine etchings of a hawk's feather. Though some pickers call it a chocolate hedgehog, the name is misleading; if anything, hawkwings taste bitter rather than sweet, which is why Todd was passing these low-rent mushrooms around now to eat. Behind us, the three hundred pounds of matsutake mushrooms stacked beneath the canopy of the buy station were way too valuable to even think about as a small fireside snack.

Matsutake means "pine mushroom" in Japanese, a reference to that country's dwindling red pine forests where it was formerly abundant. These white, gilled mushrooms with dense stems and tannish, sometimes even brown scales on the cap are the most cherished fungi in Japan. Wealthy captains of industry will give presents of matsutake to their business associates for the holidays: carefully gift-wrapped boxes with number-one buttons nestled among ferns and orange blossoms. Ideally, the buttons will be so immature as to still have intact veils covering their gills—a mushroom that looks surprisingly like an uncircumcised penis, and maybe that's the point. This youthful shape is something of a fetish among well-heeled Japanese, though it is ultimately the aroma of the matsutake that is most important, a scent memorably described by mycologist David Arora in his eccentric

field guide, *Mushrooms Demystified,* as a "provocative compromise between 'red hots' and dirty socks." This spicy yet funky smell, known
in Japan as "autumn aroma," can suffuse a kitchen in no time when
the mushrooms are fresh.

Matsutake (*Tricholoma matsutake*) have been in decline in Japan
for half a century or longer, a result of many unforeseen social and
environmental factors. Formerly, the mushrooms thrived in the open
park-like settings of the country's highly managed pine forests, in
which the red pines (*Pinus densiflora*) flourished while broadleaf trees
were continually cut back for fuel, a process called coppicing. Even
the leaves of the broadleaf trees got raked up, leaving an open-
canopied pine forest with a bare, pine-needly ground—the perfect
habitat for matsutake, which prefer nutrient-starved soils with little
competing underbrush. These woodlands were called *satoyama,* or
village forests, a term that connotes a balanced civilizing of the wild.
It was said that a woman could walk through such woods in high
heels with an open parasol. Modernity caught up to the satoyama,
though. The rise of fossil fuels obviated the need to cut down broadleaf trees, which in turn began to crowd out the red pines. Meanwhile, a pine-wilt disease hitchhiked from North America and
attacked the remaining red pines, while pollution took its own toll.
Today the matsutake harvest in Japan is a fraction of what it was even
a few decades ago, a fact that many people equate with the vanishing
of rural Japanese culture.

Enter the North American matsutake (*Tricholoma magnivelare*),
like a superhero to the rescue. This very similar species with an
equally pungent aroma can be found from Maine to California, and
especially in the forests of the Pacific Northwest, where it fruits, often
in profusion, in poor, sandy soils along the backbone of the Cascades.
Japanese Americans found matsutake in the years before World
War II in suburban California and even right in the Green Lake
neighborhood of Seattle, before the big trees were cut. Legend has it
that rumors of great matsutake patches in the New World filtered
back to Japan, whereupon Japanese mushroom scouts traveled to the

States to see for themselves. Supposedly, they found part-time mush-room pickers gathering morels and spring porcini in the dry pine for-ests of central Oregon. Liking what they saw, they told the pickers to check back in the fall for a white, aromatic gilled mushroom. By the mid-1980s, local pickers were cashing in, and then the Southeast Asian immigrants caught wind of the Oregon matsutake pick. By the early nineties they had mastered it, much to the consternation of the whites. And then the market went haywire.

The year 1993 was the high point, economically speaking, for mat-sutake pickers in North America. Throughout the 1980s Japan had gone on an economic winning streak, and though the nineties would later become known as "The Lost Decade," the Japanese didn't know it yet. Wealthy Japanese wanted their matsutake—and they had to look abroad. Demand went up and buyers started bidding wars. Prices went off the rails, briefly topping six hundred dollars per pound for number-one buttons. A gold-rush atmosphere took hold, and the fact that many of the Southeast Asians carried guns was not lost on anyone, notably the media. Newspapers reported sensational stories of running gun battles in the woods, social ills in overcrowded camps, and a general Wild West ethos more appropriate to the O.K. Corral than to Crescent Lake Junction.

Crescent Lake is in central Oregon, in the Deschutes National Forest, two hours from Eugene across the Cascade Mountains. Maybe at one time, in the late 1800s, it might have been a tough cowpoke sort of place, when cattle drives passed through on the way to summer pasture. These days it was part of a vast recreational playground of fishing lakes, hiking trails, and snowmobile routes. The lake itself, named for its crescent-moon shape, is five miles long and four miles across and famed for its trophy mackinaw, a few of which hang on the walls of the local watering holes in unincorporated Crescent Lake Junction. Most of the mushroom pickers used to stay at a revolving series of seasonal camps nearby, until opportunistic landowners in the small community of Chemult, twenty miles to the south, started to offer cheaper rents. When I visited the area, I found several dozen harvesters in the nearly defunct Crescent Lake camp. The rest were in Chemult. They lived in tents and shanties constructed from lodge-pole stringers cut, peeled, and erected on site and covered with tarps. Propane gas fueled their stoves and heaters. The district's commercial matsutake season opened the day after Labor Day and was scheduled to continue until November 6—two months of intensive picking that would determine future prospects and decisions for a thousand or more itinerant pickers.

It's not an exaggeration that many of the pickers carried guns in the early years, which they used for communicating in the woods (one shot to let your picking partners know where you were; three shots if you were in trouble) and, in a few cases, because they were afraid of wild animals. Many of them had had military careers in their former countries. A longtime white picker told me the guns had nothing to do with claiming patches. But the idea of armed mushroom hunters with little or no English scared recreationists, and soon rumors spread that ethnic tribalism, territorial pickers, gunplay, and a frontier men-tality had taken hold on public land. A few tawdry incidents over the years—nothing that would surprise a city-dweller—confirmed in the minds of many that the mushroom trade was a violent free-for-all in the long tradition of frontier capitalism. Newspapers carried head-lines like this one in the Sunday, October 6, 1996, edition of *The Seattle Times:* BOOZE, MONEY, GUNS COMBINE TO FUEL RISKS OF MUSHROOM-PICKING. The article leads: "It didn't take long for the other mush-room pickers to move out of the campground loop after one of them was arrested for shooting his wife in a drunken rage." Note that the crime occurred in a densely populated camp, not in the bush. As is common with violent crime in America, the participants knew each other and the assault sprang from drugs, alcohol, money, relationship woes, or a combination thereof. The U.S. Forest Service responded to this and a few other well-publicized conflicts—few of which actually happened while picking mushrooms in the patches—by imposing regulations to keep the peace, and ever since a truce of sorts has been in effect.

These days, pickers and buyers will mostly dismiss the stories of shoot-outs in the woods. It's not good for business, and certainly much of it was overblown in the media. But Doug told me himself that he'd packed heat around Crescent Lake "back in the day," and his account suggested that the tales of territorial pickers in the press had at least a ring of truth. "It's all intimidation," he told me, "firing over your head. It happens with people who pick around other people. I had an SKS, a Chinese version of an AK-47. We all had assault rifles. They were ninety dollars apiece back then, in the early nineties." I had pictured something more along the lines of a smallish pistol tucked into the waistband. "No, we had rifles. Look, it's not my style. When in Rome, do as the Romans, right? They were talking about jacking this guy or jacking that guy, and I was like, 'Don't talk to me about that.' It's all games. I won't take a penny from anybody, won't jack anybody. It's like a little combat game. These guys shot at us—not me but guys who were with us—and we were going to retaliate. Their camp was over the hill. We broke camp, got our stuff together, and started shooting overhead. We shot probably a thousand rounds. They thought it was Vietnam all over again, those poor Cambodians. At the time it was a lot of talk and the guys got a kick out of it. Not me. Them guys really love shooting guns, the Romans."

. . .

TWO DAYS EARLIER, Som and Forrest had missed a day of picking because Forrest needed to be back home in Weed for a palimony hearing. Som drove him, and they managed to eke out a half day of picking on their return the following day. On a full day—and a good day—they might have picked more than a thousand dollars' worth between them, which they would dutifully sell to a buyer named Joy Thavisick, another Laotian, who bought their harvest for a wholesaler and was now listening to a superior through his earpiece by the fire.

Lissome in a neat ponytail, leather sandals, and a navy-blue sweat

suit with white racing stripes, Joy championed this declining mushroom settlement in the woods. As the last buyer left in camp, he convinced the campground management to lower its prices or fold
altogether in the face of a diminishing clientele. (Rumor had it they
would close next year anyway.) The lure of lower rates, not to mention electricity, was too much for most pickers, who had decamped
for Chemult in recent years. Only three dozen sites remained in this
wooded outpost twenty miles up the road, and most of the inhabitants
sold to Joy. For him it was a no-brainer. You don't camp in town. Joy
had wanted to be an architect once. The mushroom trail beckoned
while he was in high school. Though it probably had been a mistake
to skip out on his education, he had no regrets about working in the
wild-mushroom trade. But camp in town? Might as well become an
architect.

With Joy as a mentor, Som was doing his own sort of apprenticeship
—just as he was apprenticing Forrest—as a buyer-in-training. After
selling his mushrooms to Joy, Som took over the buy station and Joy
took a seat by the fire. Som said that each season he would visit all the
buyers before choosing which one to sell to, to see who had the gen-
tlest hands. A good buyer could squeeze the matsutake and know
whether it was wormy inside. This was a necessary skill, since, unlike
porcini, the mushrooms couldn't be sliced in half and then sold to
picky Japanese consumers. Too-soft hands might miss a few ques-
tionable mushrooms, meaning more money for the picker. Now he
was on the other side of the deal and trying to perfect his own touch.
Spend too much time squeezing the mushrooms and you potentially
bruise them and scare off the seller; go too easy and you hear about it
from the boss, who doesn't like finding a bunch of wormed-out mushrooms in a shipment.

Robert, another Southeast Asian picker, sat by the fire next to Joy.
He was acerbic and sleepy-eyed, with the slouched posture of someone who was impressed by little. Next to him was Todd—white, a
strapping elk hunter dressed in a camo jacket and black cargo pants.
He was married to a Laotian woman and owned a Thai–Lao restau-

rant in Klamath Falls, where he worked as chef. The restaurant offered the usual Thai fare so in demand these days—curries, stir-fries,
and soups—plus a few Laotian favorites, such as the minced-meat
dish known as larb (pronounced "lop") served with leaves of cabbage
or lettuce. Todd handed me an amply charcoaled hawkwing mushroom. Tomorrow night there would be a Buddhist celebration in
town, and Todd, Joy, Som, and Robert all planned to be there after
the day's picking and selling was complete. I planned to go as well.
Anyone was welcome.

"You've got a good nose," Robert said to me. "You smell free food."
A cow would be sacrificed and butchered for the event, with plenty of
meat to go around. Buddhists considered the death of a single large
animal for food preferable to that of many smaller animals. Todd said
he would let his wife go to the party in his place so he could do some
midnight picking.

"He'll camp up there on the patch," Som laughed. "Crazy white
guy."

"I like two-day picks," Todd explained. "You don't waste gas."

"The party don't start 'til we get there," Som said with mock brag-
gadocio.

"We gotta make money first."

"Yeah, we gotta make money," agreed Som, who was probably the
best equipped among the pickers to do just that—and the most modest. "Beer's not free," he added. Everyone roared at this. Som didn't
even drink beer—unusual among pickers, and even more so among
the Lao, who loved their cheap American lagers.

I asked Forrest what his biggest day had been so far.

"His biggest day is just getting out of bed," said Som. "We take
him because he's scared of Asian people." This got the biggest laugh
of the night. It was well understood that the Asians were extra careful
around the local white population. Tensions had been high in the
early years, back in the early nineties, and they were still cautious two
decades on. At a café in Chemult, I asked the waitress if she had any
Asian customers. "They don't eat this kind of food," she said dismis-

sively. "They eat squirrel and whatever else is running around. That's fine with me. They're dirty people, dragging pine needles behind them wherever they go. They use the bathroom as a shower, wash their clothes in the sink, flush paper towels down the toilet." She made a skeevy face and walked off. Many other white-run businesses felt differently; the Asian-born mushroom pickers brought a much-needed economic boost to Chemult and neighboring communities each fall, a boost that was hard to deny.

Todd wanted me to know how he'd fallen in among these Asians—besides being married to one. It was 1993. "I'm tracking a bull across the flats out here below the butte. I had no idea about mushrooms. Killed a lot of elk, that's all I know. I'd seen all these damn Asians running around. I'm walking along and I see a mushroom where the elk had ate it. Pulled three more of 'em out. I'm walking down the road with these mushrooms and my rifle over my shoulder, and an Asian comes along in his truck. Asian stops"—Todd made the sharp sound of screeching brakes—" 'Where'd you get those?' 'Well, I dunno. Back there. Are these the mushrooms you guys are looking for?' 'Yeah, I'll give you a hundred dollar right now.' And I was, like, jackpot! I hand 'em to him and he gives me a hundred-dollar bill." Todd pauses. The pickers all know the punch line. "The guy took me for, like, two hundred fifty bucks! That's when I got into mushrooming. I said, 'Never will an Asian take me for two hundred fifty dollars again.'"

"Yeah, right. He married one."

It was nearly ten P.M. when the refrigerated truck pulled in. The driver jumped out and started loading baskets of graded matsutake into the back. Another year and the entire cargo area might be stacked with mushrooms, but not this year. For whatever reason—and every picker had his own theory—the pick was small. Even so, a refrigerated truck was a necessity. The mushrooms needed to be kept cold and escorted quickly to the airport so they could be on their way to Japan. Each basket got tagged with its grade and weight. Joy called his boss and told him the evening's commerce was officially over and then went over the numbers. That was it. Someone carried an arm-load of beers back to the fire and the storytelling began again. I asked about gunplay. *Talk to Joy,* they all said. He'd gotten in a little trouble in Montana one year during the morel pick. Joy didn't really want to discuss it. Some shots had been fired, he admitted. There might have been a few nights spent in jail. "But it wasn't about the mushrooms," he stressed. "It was personal."

The pickers were still talking around the fire when I said good night an hour later and went to find my tent in the campground. The night was moonless and cold, and I got into my sleeping bag fully dressed.

. . .

A PIECE OF PUMICE looks like a small rock. Pick it up and you im-mediately realize the difference: It's half the weight of a typical stone of the same size. Find a nice piece of palm-sized yellow pumice for the first time and you'll almost certainly roll it around in your grip and toss it up and down a few times, admiring its surprising lightness, before slipping it into a pocket for later examination. Pumice de-mands scrutiny.

Crater Lake, the site of ancient Mount Mazama, is about an hour's drive south of Crescent Lake Junction. In between is the town of Che-mult, where Dana Van Pelt owns a pumice mine. The pumice—a whole mountain of it, which rises to the west of town—is mixed with dirt to produce what he calls a "supercharged soil." The prop-erty also includes a run-down motel, the former Whispering Pines, that's closed ten months out of the year. Come matsutake season, though, the worn-out place is given an exemption by the authorities and books up with pickers and buyers. Eighty-eight other ad hoc sea-sonal structures, most of them constructed from the usual stringers and tarps, form a dense rabbit warren of a neighborhood around the motel, complete with cul-de-sacs, blind alleyways, and even a restau-rant, known simply as the Noodle House. It's the sort of shantytown you might expect to see in a place like Mumbai: colorful tarps, fires burning out of garbage cans, people wandering back and forth with armloads of wood and beer or just huddled by the fire to keep warm. Big pots of soup boiled on a dozen different camp stoves around me. Nearly everyone in this camp was picking matsutake mushrooms in the dry woodlands of central Oregon, and those who weren't actually picking were supporting the pickers in some way, either by keeping camp, cooking food, or doing laundry or some other necessary chore. One researcher studying the Oregon matsutake harvest reported, "When I look at the material culture, the food, the music, the arrangement of village sociality, it's sometimes hard to believe I'm not in rural Southeast Asia." This same researcher also encountered pickers less enchanted with the scene, even if it was a facsimile of their former lives. "Buddha doesn't find mushrooms," one of them said.

When I called Jeremy Faber and left him a message about my plans to visit this largest of the matsutake camps and maybe even attend a Buddhist ceremony involving the slaughter of a steer, I could imagine him blinking with indifference. "Sounds really boring," he texted me later, "except the cow thing." All these mushrooms were bound for Japan, after all. His allegiance was to American restaurants. In fact, Faber's business would need to be completely retooled to serve the Japanese market. Besides, American restaurants weren't about to pay the prices that Japanese consumers willingly shelled out. When Faber dealt with matsutake at all, he dealt with pickers who gathered it as an incidental and mostly outside the usual matsi hot spots. Still, he would need to come close in price for those pickers. Doug told me Faber had paid him 20/20 (twenty dollars for both number ones and twos) for a basket just the other day, a figure that Faber scoffed at. He called it a favor, "out of the goodness of my heart." Many of the pickers I had met in the past year had forsaken matsutake. It was a mushroom, they said, that had caused problems.

I found Dana Van Pelt sitting back in a ripped-up easy chair on the porch of the former Whispering Pines motel, drinking a Heineken. Wearing a black ball cap and a lime-green Tommy Bahama polo shirt that said RELAX on the breast pocket, he was talking business with a compact, well-dressed Lao man who had a manila folder under his arm. Van Pelt shifted his belly as he talked from the easy chair; he had a ruddy complexion and was slightly walleyed. Van Pelt's son, strawberry-haired with bright white teeth, stood nearby, leaning on a post, a Corona in his hand. Van Pelt told the Lao man that he would have room number one reserved for him, and they both laughed as the man walked back to his truck. He turned to me. "I love these people, I really do. The Hmong and Mien are straight as can be, but the Lao are connivers. Just try to do business with them. Whatever you agree, they'll do the opposite." We talked about some of the controversies that had dogged his mushroom camp, the accusations of gambling, prostitution, even a murder or two. Van Pelt blamed it on those dickheads in the media for blowing it out of proportion. He said he'd retained some very expensive lawyers to get up the ass of *The New Yorker* for a story they'd done. These are nice people, he said again. The people that scared him, those were always white people— tweakers, Aryans, and so on. He turned to his son. "What did they call me, anyway? Red-faced and chubby?"

"Hilarious," said his son. "Mom cut it out and saved it."

"What a bunch of dickheads."

Everyone agreed that there were quite a few new pickers in camp this year. I found one of them, Seng Fo, by a fire outside a buy station, with his wife. They had just sold their day's labor of about five pounds. This was vacation, he explained somewhat sheepishly, adding, "The most benefit for me is exercise." Fo was a social worker from Portland, where he'd lived for the past thirty-three years. Before that he had grown up in Laos, where he fought against the communists as a machine gunner, then fled across the Mekong River in 1975 to a refugee camp in Thailand. "I had no choice," he said. "If I stayed, I would be killed for sure." His second child was born in the refugee camp before they found asylum in the United States. Their lives had been full of tumult and also good fortune. Fo's wife agreed without speaking, bobbing her Tar Heels stocking cap up and down vigorously as her husband did all the talking. At last he put his arm around her. "Thirty years ago my wife was young, energetic, and beautiful," he said.

"Thirty years ago my husband was young and skinny."

"And very handsome!" he added.

A dozen buyers operated out of Van Pelt's camp. Across the street were another five buyers at the Cascade Inn. Several more had tent stations a few blocks to the north, and one buyer was even set up in an empty shipping container deposited on the roadside. I found Leo Wells working out of a defunct filling station on the west side of the street; STUBBY's was stenciled in small black letters above the door. Inside, a propane heater glowed bright orange and a wall of cigarette smoke hit me like exhaust from a cold-morning tailpipe. A white long-haired picker named Rick sucked on a Camel 99 while Leo filled his Styrofoam cup with another shot of coffee. The letters L-O-V-E were tattooed on the back of his fingers. "I was thirteen and stupid," he said, giving his hand a little shake. Both Rick and Leo had been in the mushroom business for more than thirty years.

"We weren't too friendly with the Asians at first," Rick admitted.

"We didn't tell them nothing," Leo agreed. "They mostly picked fives and sixes the first couple years. They figured it out eventually. That's when the raking started. Everywhere you looked it was roto-tilled."

Matsutake can grow into large mushrooms if the conditions are right, yet the most prized specimens are usually found beneath the duff or moss that covers them during their initial phase of growth. For a number of years, pickers resorted to rakes and other garden tools to unearth the matsutake. These days, raking was prohibited, and most pickers prided themselves on being able to find the buttons simply by locating a crack in the ground, though areas with intensive harvesting still suffered from an inordinate amount of soil distur-bance where pickers probed with sticks and other legal instruments.

And what about all the guns? Rick said the Asians were always firing their weapons in the air but not to claim patches. "For fun," he said. One time an Asian came up to him in the woods all friendly and asked him a question. "I didn't give him the time of day. The guy turned around and squeezed off five shots. Scared me half to death. I grabbed the kid by his shirt and shook him good. I yelled all kinds of mean things. 'There's all sorts of people around here,' I said. What goes up must come down. It might be a one-in-a-million shot, but I've heard about a million shots fired in the last three or four days." After that the kid gave it some thought and then thanked him. "He thanked me!"

These days, Leo said, most of the conflicts were not between the whites and Asians but between Asians of different ethnicities, or even the same, sometimes. One murder was over a cheating spouse. Neither Leo nor Rick could remember who cheated on whom. They thought the murder weapon was a knife, or maybe a machete. "Asian divorce court," Leo called it. In another case that made headlines, a man was killed over a gambling debt. His ring finger had been cut off to get a flashy diamond band, and then his body was dumped in the patch. By the following day, every Asian had left town. They thought it was a hate killing. Leo wasn't sure whether anyone had ever been charged. Whoever killed the man must have known him, because only one shoe had been removed—the shoe where he kept his money. Friends and relatives left burning candles in the patch, where the body was found. For years, Leo said, no one picked that patch.

"Yeah, things happen over at the Pit," Rick said, referring to Van Pelt's camp. "Things happen."

. . .

THE NEXT MORNING, I joined Som, Forrest, Robert, and Todd for breakfast at the Odell Sportsman Center in Crescent Lake Junction, where we took advantage of the morning special: a paper plate of biscuits and gravy with a sixteen-ounce cup of coffee for three dollars. The pickers broke the news that I wouldn't be welcome on today's pick. It was the height of the season, with the most pickers and the highest prices, and they needed to make money. Today's pick, they said, might take them into territories that were technically off-limits. Competition was fierce, and they couldn't abide by what they viewed as silly rules. My presence would slow them down. This was disappointing, since the pickers had promised to take me along. I wasn't sure what I felt about the illegality, which they didn't even try to hide. Had these been salmon fishermen or big-game hunters, I would have been outraged. That was poaching. Mushroom picking, however, wasn't the same. The pickers felt they knew much more about the mushrooms than those who created the regulations. In many cases, they did. Unlike fish and game, mushrooms didn't require a certain level of "escapement"—the term for breeding-age animals that manage to reproduce—in order to maintain their population. If anything, the regulations were meant to impact the mushroom hunters (to contain them) rather than the mushrooms. The other part of the equation was the land itself, how it got scoured and probed by the pickers, though no one seemed too concerned about the many deer and elk hunters who often brought a heavier footprint to the forest each fall. There were plenty of harvesters, old-timers, who had cleaned their hands of Crescent Lake altogether. One of them, a well-known white picker from the Oregon coast who was venerated for his matsutake-sleuthing abilities, told me he had abandoned the area years earlier because it was overrun with pickers. He deplored the trash and crowded camps and gold-rush atmosphere, explaining how his own business ventures with the Japanese had fallen apart because of strong-arm tactics and threats made by competitors. "That's not why I do this," he said. He went to the woods for peace and quiet.

I said goodbye and took my coffee outside to sit on a bench and feel the rising sun on my face. Though it was still cold out, in the low forties, it would get hot by afternoon. There was a wistful message on my phone from Doug. He wanted a report. Doug's two biggest paydays as a mushroom picker had come back-to-back during the matsutake boom. He was picking with a crew from the Shoalwater Bay Indian Reservation in '93. One of the early mushroom dealers had put the crew together to exploit a little-known patch over the border in California. A member of the Klamath Indian tribe had gotten in touch with the Shoalwater Bay tribe, who in turn invited Doug because they knew he was familiar with the territory. Though most of the action was centered on the national forest surrounding Crescent Lake, this crew was driving down into California, to an area called Medicine Lake and Glass Mountain, where there was little pressure. Maybe not so surprisingly, Forest Service officials in California didn't know what to make of these knockabout mushroom pickers. "We went in to get permits at Glass Mountain and they said, 'We don't have any mushrooms in our district.' 'Yes, you do.' They said come back Monday and we'll have permits for you." It was Friday and the pickers were eager to start scouting. The next day the rangers were waiting for them when they came out of the woods with their buckets full of matsutake. "That fuckin' cop that was sitting in that office was writing tickets," Doug told me. "I turned around and headed right back for the woods. The cop is *Hey, HEY!* I stashed every mushroom I had and came back the long way. I started giving the guy hell. *You knew we were picking up permits on Monday.*" The ranger wanted Doug's mushrooms. "I said, 'You're not getting mine.' He wrote those other guys tickets, but he wouldn't write me one because I was going off." Later, Doug confronted his fellow pickers, wanting to know why they hadn't backed him up and raised hell with the rangers. The answer was simple: They all had warrants out.

The men quietly paid their fines and got their permits. The pick was on, and a few hundred dollars was small change now. "It was so cool, man," said Doug. "We were going there and it was secret. We had a group of ten people and we were sneaking down there and picking all day and then driving all the way to Crescent Junction. It was a three-hundred-fifty-mile round-trip. Every day. They had a price war." The buyers around Crescent Lake Junction started trying to outbid one another. On one day Doug got paid more than five hundred dollars per pound for number-one matsutake buttons. He made nearly six thousand dollars in two days. "For over a week it was more than three hundred dollars, for ten days or more, so there was a long period of time when a lot of money was made. Two days in a row I picked six buckets of mixed grade, a hundred pounds. I had to split with these other guys. I agreed to that. I just went down to have some fun with it, never knew the price would go crazy. I figured I'd go down and make a couple hundred a day and share it with these guys, camp, smoke up, and tell stories and stuff. All of a sudden we made some real money. There was a handful who would work hard and a handful who would pick for a few hours and then sit in the rig. We had to split it all the way around. We were carrying quite a few people. I never once regretted having to share, because I signed on." The crew boss took his cut too.

Even so, the secret didn't last. "We had some guys who were drinking in our crew and they couldn't be tight, you know. They either sold the information or let people follow them, one of the two. I think it was the former. It was worth at least ten grand, but they probably got a cheap two thousand dollars for it. We were making over that in a day." Doug went back the next year, but word was out. He was stopped at a road-construction site and started chatting up the flagger. "Here's a hot tip for you," she said, noticing the mushroom baskets in the back. "Go down to Glass Mountain." The sign lady was giving his patch away!

AFTER TRYING TO CALL Doug a couple of times, I drove back to camp to find Joy, who agreed to take me picking along with his two kids, a boy of nine and a girl of seven. His wife and children were visiting for the weekend from their home near Springfield, on the other side of the mountains. Though they had all slept in a tent last night, they planned to get a motel room in town tonight for the celebration. We drove up the Crescent Lake Cutoff, turned on a dirt logging road, and parked in a turnout. Thin lodgepole pines dominated the forest, with a smattering of larger ponderosa pines ("pondos") and the occasional ice-green noble fir rising above the canopy with

Christmas-tree grandeur and all its cones clustered at the top. The air was thin and resinous here at five thousand feet, with a crispness that persisted even as the day warmed up. The sun sat above the trees in a cloudless blue sky and everything looked slightly washed out, like a photograph with blown highlights. Joy said not too many people knew about this patch. We roamed among the saplings and hopped over windfall. Joy's son wandered off, eating a package of peanut butter cookies, to explore by himself. His sister, in her pink fleece jacket and a wool hat with a kitten's face, reminded me of my own little girl. At the first stop, by a downed log, Joy asked her to find the mushroom. She bent down with a tool shaped like a tire iron and poked around. As far as I could see, there was nothing here, not even the telltale rise of a mushroom forming below. Joy guided her closer. She scraped a little forest debris next to the log to reveal the white cap of a button.

"Oh, oh!"

Joy bent down to pick it, a cigarette now pinched between his fingers. It was a smallish button, though still a number one. "This is a three-dollar mushroom," he said.

"How did you know that was there?"

"You just know. A little crack in the earth." I hadn't seen anything resembling a crack. In a mixed pine forest such as this one, it was a good idea to search out the larger pondos, Joy said. The mushrooms would fruit off the underground root systems, sometimes in an arc that followed the roots far from the tree. With experience, you could find a likely host tree and know where to look. Frequently the mushrooms clustered on one side or the other, depending on the slope aspect and the way the ground broke around the tree. Probably there was science behind it, but, for Joy and other pickers, the knowledge came from experience, from millions of hours in the woods, when you could just look at a piece of ground and *know*.

At the next spot, fifty yards away, Joy found a half-exposed mushroom pushing up through the pine-needle litter. On my hands and knees I could see a fine network of lacy gills. This was a mature mushroom, maybe a five, and it was also a sign. Joy scraped away nearby duff to find two more perfect buttons. He was up to three number-one buttons of about the same size and one heavier five, or an average of about a dollar a minute so far. But the patch had already petered out. "Last year this place was covered with mushrooms. Not so much this year." Joy had some business in town and we parted ways. It was still light out, so I decided to poke around the woods on my own, walking until the shadows grew long, an empty bucket at my side.

. . .

MORE THAN 90 PERCENT OF the North American matsutake harvest goes to Japan, where the mushrooms are cooked in traditional ways. Gohan is a simple rice dish that shows off the matsutake aroma for anyone within a city block of the rice cooker. The mushrooms, along with a handful of diced vegetables such as carrots, are chopped up and added to the cooker once the water has been mostly absorbed, whereupon they are delicately steamed. As steam issues from the rice cooker, the aroma, too, escapes to fill the household. Another classic recipe is sukiyaki. Matsutake buttons are thinly sliced and sautéed with shredded cabbage, green onions, and bok choy before being added to a kettle of soup made from beef stock, sake, and soy sauce. The spicy flavor of the mushrooms permeates the sukiyaki. In China, too, the mushrooms are frequently used to flavor broths, and upwardly mobile Chinese pay exorbitant sums for prime buttons to show off their new wealth.

My own appreciation of matsutake had taken years to form. At first I didn't get what all the fuss was about. The more I used the mushrooms, though, the more I fell for their unique flavor. Cooking matsi at home was like attending an experimental theater class. It was an excuse to do all kinds of improvisations in the kitchen. I particularly liked wok-frying the mushrooms in Chinese preparations, with hot chili peppers and lip-numbing Sichuan peppercorns. The Chinese have evocative names for their ancient flavor combinations. One is called "fish-fragrant flavor" for its use of ingredients that conjure the fish cookery of olden times, even if there isn't a single element from the sea, while another is called "strange flavor" for its complex marriage of multiple tastes. A favorite of mine was an adaptation of a typical velvet-chicken recipe, which I supplemented with matsutake. The original preparation relies on black vinegar and pickled chilies to create a sweet-and-sour flavor; the matsutake adds a spicy dimension that takes the dish into new territory. When I served it to friends of mine who had lived all over Asia, they said they'd never tasted such a thing anywhere, and then asked for seconds. I called it "provocative-flavor chicken."

What I did not care for, however, were the typical Western preparations that relied on dairy ingredients such as butter, cream, or cheese. It turns out that the flavors in matsutake mushrooms are water-soluble as opposed to fat-soluble. This, in part, is why they pair so well with sake, soy sauce, and rice vinegar. They are mushrooms seemingly made for Asian cookery. Yet no one in the mushroom camps of central Oregon cooked with matsutake. They were too valuable.

BACK AT THE PIT at dusk, the sounds of chain saws mingled with loud Laotian pop music from a car stereo. The smoke of fifty fires gathered into a blue haze that settled over the camp. Residents were preparing for a party. Behind the Noodle House, a Buddhist monk—resplendent in orange garb, red socks, and sandals—ducked into the alleyway briefly for a smoke. A woman named Candy introduced me around. Though Candy lived in South Carolina now, she returned every year for matsutake season, to help her mother with the restaurant. She filled a shot glass from a plastic liquor bottle and handed it to me, calling it "medicine." I hesitated. The handmade label was in a language I couldn't read. "Oh, it just means something like *bear bile bark*," she explained. It was vodka that had been infused with a medicinal plant from Laos. "Drink it. It's good for you."

Though seasonal, the Noodle House was a more substantial structure than any of the camps. Rather than tarps, salvaged two-by-fours and plywood covered most of its walls. Rubber mats lined the floor. In the back of the room were a TV, stereo components, and a pair of Peavey amplifiers for karaoke. A bowl of pho was two dollars. On most nights, diners took their meals at foldout tables with rainbow-colored tablecloths and plastic chairs; tonight the pickers sat on the floor around woven straw tables. A stone Buddha with a golden silk scarf draped over his shoulders stared down from a shelf.

I took a seat on the floor next to Joy's father, Phet. Like most of the men in Joy's family, Phet had pursued a military career in Laos before fleeing to the United States. Now he was a mushroom picker, a skill he had learned from his son. Phet handed me a bowl of sticky rice and pointed to the different plates of meat on the low-slung table. Earlier that morning, a cow donated by Van Pelt had been slaughtered right on the premises for tonight's feast. Candy's uncle, a jovial man with wide, red-rimmed eyes, was barbecuing slabs of beef ribs outside. I ate from a bowl of beef tripe soup and wrapped a handful of beef larb in a lettuce leaf. Phet directed me to the "tiger meat," raw sliced beef mixed with diced hot peppers and other spices. He said it was very good for the health—and the libido. I folded up a piece of lettuce with a dollop of tiger meat.

"Very fresh," someone said. It certainly was.

In the back of the room, several elderly men and women busied themselves with donations, taping dollar bills to a plastic ornamental tree. A monk came through and accepted my donation with a blessing. On the other side of the alley, a special tent was set up with a sound system. A Laotian pop star on tour in the States had been commandeered for the evening. With a karaoke backbeat and additional help from a bongo drummer, guitarist, and keyboardist, the diminutive, slightly effeminate singer cracked jokes and sang weirdly mesmerizing songs that seemed to blend Eastern and Western musical traditions. Candy's sister hustled beers and shots to the crowd, and her uncle, the grillmaster, took a break from his duties outside the tent to forcibly matchmake dancing couples. Someone gave me a shot of a sweet liqueur. My head was swimming.

I took a breather outside the tent by the fire, where I found Som and Forrest, back from the day's picking. Som said there had been an incident.

Forrest sighed. "Todd's still on the mountain."

"Which mountain?"

"I dunno. The mountain we were picking. Somewhere by Crescent Lake."

"You left him?"

"He left us," Forrest said. "He saw Som put some of his mushrooms in my bucket to lighten his load. I guess he didn't know we were partners. He was like, 'Am I picking all alone?' Me and Som have been partners since the first day. We were like, 'Yeah, you're on your own, bud.' He got mad and took off."

"So he's up there right now?" It was in the mid-thirties and pitch black.

"Yup, unless he got down."

"How far from camp?"

"Long way. He does this sort of thing all the time. He's an elk hunter."

"You couldn't find him and take him back?"

"If someone doesn't want to be found in the woods," Forrest said, "they won't be found. Especially someone like Todd."

Som just shook his head knowingly. I got the feeling this sort of misunderstanding had happened before with Todd. He didn't seem like the sort to take anything too lightly.

Som was the only one without a drink in his hand. "I like to maintain control," he said. "All it takes is one beer and I'm like . . ." He made a cuckoo gesture. "My girlfriend calls me a cheap date." A fire felt good on a clear, starry night like tonight. The temperature was dropping. Soon it would snow in the high country. Som had a lot to think about. He was trying to decide whether to continue on to the next big mushroom pick on the trail, Cave Junction, southwest of Grants Pass, where pickers would continue to gather matsutake and chanterelles in the Siskiyous. After that, the action would move closer to the California border, to Brookings, Oregon, and the beginning of winter pick: black trumpets, yellowfoot chanterelles, and hedgehogs. Som wasn't sure whether he would go to either Cave Junction or Brookings. His regular job back in Weed was arc welding. Already his boss had been flexible enough to give him two months' leave to pick matsutake at Crescent Lake. If Som wanted to keep picking—and learn how to buy—he would need to choose between the two jobs. Welding meant regular, if monotonous, work near his family. Mushroom picking, on the other hand, took him away from home, with unpredictable payouts. Still, there was the chance to work out-doors and potentially make a windfall profit if the pick was good. And now that Som was learning the buying end of the business, he could move up the food chain, rest his body, and still pick a little on the side.

The crowd was getting rowdy. Som said nights like this almost always ended in a fight. "You need to know when to walk away," he said, quoting the old Kenny Rogers gambling anthem.

John, a twenty-something Laotian picker from Red Bluff, sat in a lawn chair beside the fire with a can of beer in his hand. He asked me what I was doing here. The fire jumped and lit up his face. Staring at the flames, he emptied his beer, crushed the can in his grip, and tossed it in a cardboard box. "I don't pick for money," he said finally, turning to face me. He was wearing just a T-shirt with baggy jeans. He re-garded me with a stony expression. "I pick for survival. We all do. This is survival." I told him I understood, collected my things, and left.

. . .

NOT LONG AFTER THE BOOM years of the early nineties, matsutake was "discovered" in other parts of the world: China, Korea, and even Ontario. David Arora, who has studied the commerce all over the globe, suggests that it was more a case of the emerging infrastructure in these places—roads, bridges, towns—that allowed the matsutake harvest to occur where it hadn't in the past. With a glut on the market, the price quickly crashed. While pickers traded conspiracy theories and aimed accusations of collusion at buyers, the real culprit seems to have been globalization. As in so many other markets, the workers at the bottom—without whom the entire market would be unthinkable—now earn a relatively small piece of the action. If it's a conspiracy, it's the same old conspiracy that has plagued workers from the beginning. One British Columbia mushroom buyer, infuriated by the low prices he had to pay his pickers in order to compete, made a YouTube video called "The World's Most Expensive Mushroom Stomp," in which he destroyed his entire inventory in protest, one bootheel at a time.

Some years it was hardly worth picking matsutake. The year before my visit to Crescent Lake, while fishing for steelhead in British Columbia, I stopped in at a mushroom-buying station north of Terrace in the crossroads community of Kitwanga, just off Highway 37 (only 700 miles to Alaska, said the sign), where I found a buyer named Ave. He was having a terrible time trying to convince anyone to bring in matsutake, since the price was hovering between a dollar and two dollars per pound, thanks to a boom of mushrooms down in Washington and Oregon. His station was the usual wall tent with a woodstove, set up on a friend's gravel lot just outside town. Two Indian men were leaving as I pulled in. "I don't know if I'll see them again," Ave said, showing me back into his tent, where the transactions took place. Dealings with Indians (Native Americans in the United States, First Peoples in Canada) were complicated, he said. In many cases, the Indians owned land with good mushroom patches; in other cases, they didn't own the land but it was understood to be part of their traditional territory. In recent years Indians had picked more mushrooms, though many buyers considered them inconsistent pickers who might let a good flush go to waste because something else came up—a potlatch with another tribe, or maybe nothing at all. Ave said the Indians were deeply ambivalent about the mushroom harvest. It was hard to let a potential moneymaking operation go to waste on your own land, and it was even harder to cede it to non-native interlopers, yet their culture didn't have a place for many of these mushrooms, particularly matsutake. This was in contrast to the Indians of northern California, who had eaten matsutake for as long as anyone could remember, calling them oak mushrooms instead of pines, because they grew among the tanoak rather than the conifers.

"They'll have their revenge," Ave said. "They'll lease their lands to the Chinese, the Chinese will rape it for all it's worth, and the white man will go crazy." Even though he figured he'd have a bunch of pickers pulling in later that afternoon with mushrooms to sell, he wasn't too enthusiastic about the season's prospects. He planned to head south to Vancouver Island in a few weeks to buy chanterelles, and then on to southern Oregon and northern California for the black trumpet pick come winter. The gig was mostly up, he said. The Chinese were busy buying up British Columbia timber leases—not just from the natives but from the crown as well—and he expected most of the good remaining matsutake patches to be logged out before long. "You can go up to Cranberry Junction if you want," he said. "Not much to see up there anymore." I'd heard of Cranberry Junction. Locals called it "the Zoo." It was British Columbia's answer to Crescent Lake—the biggest matsutake mushroom camp in the province. Or, at least, it had been once. I found it mostly deserted.

Adventure writer and mycologist Lawrence Millman filed a colorful dispatch from Cranberry Junction for *The Atlantic* in 2001, interviewing pickers and buyers with names like Wormy Pete, Alberta Al, and the Iron Maiden. In Cranberry Junction's heyday, well over a thousand itinerant mushroom hunters combed the nearby hills by day and camped at the Zoo at night, where a canteen sold booze and "you might see a few punches exchanged, or someone who's imbibed not wisely but too well sleeping it off in a rain puddle." Those days looked long gone. A dirt turnoff led to a bleak gravel lot, perhaps the size of a football field, with a network of smaller lots tucked into the woods, most of them empty. The Cranberry River meandered nearby, slow and muddy. In the entire sprawling encampment I found maybe a half dozen forlorn-looking holdouts living in tents, trailers, or temporary shanties made with plastic sheeting nailed over wooden stringers. There were a few burned-out cars and an outhouse in pieces on the ground. The B. S. Mushroom Depot, a combination trailer and shanty, looked abandoned, with just a few rotting chanterelles on the floor beneath a plastic foldout table. Across the gravel lot, a ruined tent listed in the wind. The only living soul around was Grace, who had run the mobile general store here for years. She came to the door of her silver Airstream with two yapping dogs in her arms. Grace had never seen the camp so desolate, and she didn't expect it to get any better. At two dollars per pound, there was little incentive—even poverty, it would seem—for a picker to hump mushrooms out of the bush all day. Grace explained that expenses (gas, food, auto repairs) could be as much as a hundred dollars a day, meaning that fifty pounds of matsutake hardly covered your overhead when the price was that low.

One picker, going by the name Cranberrydawg, reminisced online about the old days: "You could be from Mars and you would be accepted along that stretch of highway and truth be known, many were. You remember how the zoo was back in the day; it was a hodgepodge of ethnicities—Russians, Czechs, Poles, Yugoslavians, Swedes, Hungarians, Vietnamese, heck, there was even the odd Englishman . . . it was great . . . that is what made that place so damn interesting—the people! That is what kept us coming back year after year too. It wasn't so much the mushrooms, although of course that was huge, it was more the people. And when it was time to do it all again the next season what was the first thing we did when we got back to the zoo? It wasn't rush around to the buying stations to see what the price was, it was drive around and see who was in camp."

...

ON MY WAY OUT of Crescent Lake, I scouted a known matsutake patch in the hills overlooking Davis Lake. I passed trucks pulled over in several turnouts and even saw pickers through the woods with their buckets. Stopping at a likely spot, where large firs grew alongside ponderosa and lodgepole pines without too much ground cover, I started walking around, looking for the telltale cracks in the earth. Though I had found plenty of matsutake closer to home in past years, this most famous of North American matsi picks was proving to be difficult ground, especially in a poor year such as this, and skilled pickers were keeping their patches clean—that is, they were careful to pick regularly so that nothing was allowed to burst through the duff, where it would be seen by less-skilled pickers. Even old wormy mushrooms got cleaned (stomped or otherwise buried) to keep the patch looking barren. Clues were few. My heart raced momentarily when I found a bump in the duff with a white mushroom poking out—just a white chanterelle. After a couple hours of searching in vain, I had to admit defeat and continue north. When you cut out all the gossip and nonsense and hurt feelings and racism and poverty and shots fired and all the rest, you were left with the simple fact that picking matsutake—and picking it well—was an art form.

DOUG SAID HE WAS a reformed matsi picker. Whenever I saw him, he always had mushrooms of one variety or another for me—except for matsutake. He said he actually enjoyed the hell out of picking pines—those big, meaty buttons hiding under duff and moss—but the price fluctuations were too much to keep up with. He preferred to make his money with other, more dependable species. One time, though, he had a basket of matsutake for me, about ten pounds. "Keep it," he said, pushing the basket at me. "I can't do anything with these." Doug had driven over the mountains to Yakima the previous day to visit his brother. On his way home, he couldn't help but stop at one of his favorite patches, just to take a peek. The mushrooms were up all over the place, conical white buttons pushing through the moss and duff, acres of them. The price had dropped once again to around $1.50 a pound for number-one buttons. He was wasting his time, and he knew it. Still, he couldn't resist. He picked for an hour, filling his bucket, before summoning the strength to get out. His mixed basket of ones, twos, and threes might have been worth ten dollars.

I thanked Doug and took the basket home, leaving it on my front porch to keep cool. The next day the UPS man delivered a package to our door. I saw him eyeing the mushrooms. "Take a few," I said. "I've got more than I know what to do with."

"Really? Are you sure? I've seen what these cost at the market." Sealed in little packages with a piece of fake greenery, they were fetching between thirty and fifty dollars a pound at my local Asian market. I grabbed a bunch of nice mushrooms and put them in his hands before he could object.

"Thank you, thank you. My wife is Japanese. She'll flip."

I went back inside with a few buttons of my own. I had the ingredients for sukiyaki arranged on the kitchen counter. Sometimes, when hunting in known matsutake areas, I see Japanese pickers pulled off on the roadside in the afternoon, squatting around a hibachi as they grill matsutake and make a one-pot sukiyaki stew. Even outdoors, the autumn aroma hangs in the air like a beguiling cloud, hinting at marvelous rewards to come.

CHAPTER 7

Winging It All the Way

. . .

MATT DILLON CAN REMEMBER when he actually had a day or two off and could go picking. He remembers getting his tires slashed while picking matsutake with Jeremy Faber near Mount Rainier. Or the feeling of driving up to a gray and misted ferry terminal with a carload of wild mushrooms after spending a couple of days on the Olympic Peninsula. "I'd have hedgehogs, a few matsutake, some chanterelles, some yellowfeet, maybe a couple cauliflower mushrooms, all sitting in the trunk of my car in mushroom baskets I'd borrowed from Jeremy. It's raining, it's mid- to late October. It's cold out. I'm in my rain gear, drinking hot cocoa, my dog in the back."

Dillon took a sip of Chardonnay. We were sitting at Bar Ferd'nand—his bar—in Seattle, next door to his restaurant, Sitka & Spruce. He swirled his wineglass and looked up at me. "I fucking miss that shit. It was an epic feeling." This was fifteen years ago. "I'd come back to the restaurant"—the Herbfarm, where he worked as sous chef—"and sell the mushrooms to myself or give them to Jeremy to sell. It was that feeling of *I just went on a two-day adventure in the middle of the woods and slept in my car or stayed in this horrible motel in Port Angeles called the Chinook, where I walked in and there was blood*

*on the ground and the shower was dirty and the sheets smelled like three-
day-old sex from who knows what, a bunch of meth heads, and I was like,
'This is cool! It's fun!'"*

Dillon remembers a trip to Lake Ozette, picking hedgehogs—
"monster spreaders." There was a Huskies game on TV and he
needed to get up early to pick his cauliflower spots on the Dungeness.
He asked for a wake-up call. "There was this huge South African
woman in a sweater with a wolf on it, and she's drunk. She opened up
this cabinet and hands me like seven alarm clocks. 'Put 'em all over
the room!'" Dillon remembers going out to the coast with Faber and
picking coastal boletes, remembers all the Russians out there picking
saffron milk caps, one of his favorite mushrooms, a member of the
Lactarius genus, so named because it bleeds a milky latex.

Matt Dillon and Jeremy Faber were best friends now, but it wasn't
always like that. "We hated each other at the Herbfarm," Dillon told
me matter-of-factly. It's not hard to see why. Dillon was second-in-
command under the acclaimed chef Jerry Traunfeld, and though
Faber saw himself as Dillon's equal, technically Dillon was his boss.
"Jerry was writing his book at the time, so I was running the show. I
was, like, 'This sonofabitch. I work here every day from seven in the
morning until two in the morning. I'm the first one in and the last to
leave, and you come in and cop this attitude.' I was like, 'Fuck this
guy.'" Then, one day, while making dessert in the restaurant, they
came to terms. "We bonded," Dillon laughs, "while scooping ice
cream. We both love ice cream more than just about anything in the
world. He took me skiing, and he says, 'What are you doing tomorrow, let's go pick morels.'" It was too early for morels, so they ended
up picking spring beauties instead. This was a watershed moment for
Dillon. It didn't matter what time of year it was. So what if it was too
early for morels? "There was food all over the forest floor."

Meanwhile, back at the Herbfarm, Dillon was taking a crash
course in wild foods and seasonality from owner Ron Zimmerman.
The Herbfarm in the mid-nineties was an incubator for a new generation of Northwest chefs. Though Dillon had picked stinging net-

tles and watercress and maple blossoms before, Zimmerman opened up a wider menu for him. "Forget Noma in Copenhagen, even though I love that restaurant. The Herbfarm was doing that twenty-five years ago. Beyond the whole Alice Waters local-food-movement thing. Anything you could stick in your mouth and eat—if it was local and didn't kill you, Ron was all about it. I would sit and talk to Ron late at night. We would all make something to eat after dinner and sit around and bullshit about food, and Ron would say, 'Go look for this, look for that.' I met Jon Rowley [another Northwest food guru, called the 'disciple of flavor' by *Saveur* magazine] by doing classes, taking fifty Dungeness crabs and cooking them fifty different ways to find out which way really tasted better. He's the first guy to teach me about umami. The guy's a badass."

Zimmerman gave Dillon a copy of a book, *The Auberge of the Flowering Hearth,* by Roy Andries de Groot. "It's about this guy who's looking for the secrets of Chartreuse, a liqueur that's made from a hundred and forty wild herbs by monks in an Alps valley, and he ends up finding this little inn to stay at, with these two sisters who cook just because some guy arrives at the back door with trout or wild thyme or wild oregano or all these other things that grow out there. It's the same book that influenced the Herbfarm. It's so simple and so beautiful. Whenever I smell fresh rosemary, I remember what it was like being at the Herbfarm, baking the rolls, making the cookies, being there early in the morning, feeding the llamas, feeding the crazy geese that were attacking me, being alone at seven in the morning before anyone got there."

In time, Dillon and Faber would each leave the Herbfarm to pursue their own businesses—Dillon to open Sitka & Spruce, and Faber to launch Foraged and Found Edibles—but that time together forged a lasting friendship. "Take a look at the tree," Dillon said to me. He was speaking of the Sitka spruce that is the namesake of his restaurant. Its image, in silhouette, graced the smoked-glass front of the restaurant. I got up from the bar and walked over. At the base of the tree, virtually invisible to anyone without a magnifying glass, was a tiny king bolete—two iconic species of the Pacific Northwest, wedded in mutual symbiosis.

Dillon opened the first iteration of Sitka & Spruce in 2006, in a tiny strip mall in Seattle's Eastlake neighborhood. It could serve maybe twenty customers at a time, max. Even so, it was a neighborhood joint that aspired to be much more, serving dishes like angel hair pasta with Oregon black truffles and a truly wild green salad with miner's lettuce and wood sorrel. A couple of years later, Dillon bought a charming turn-of-the-century building in the industrial neighborhood of Georgetown in South Seattle, complete with gardens and period details. It was a little oasis beside the train tracks and the raised deck of I-5. The Corson Building served festive family-style meals and hosted events like pig roasts and wine tastings. Next, moving steadily westward, he hopped the Fauntleroy ferry to move from the city to a twenty-acre plot on Vashon Island in Puget Sound, the Old Chaser Farm, where he started growing all his own produce, raising animals, and foraging for the local bounty. Faber, who tends to cast a very critical eye on most restaurateurs, told me he thought his friend was the real deal, making some of the best food anywhere. "No BS," he said. "Matt's food tastes the way it should." Dillon didn't use fancy sauces or techniques. As at the Herbfarm, he relied on fresh herbs and spices, whatever was local and in season, and arresting combinations of ingredients.

Sitka & Spruce had since moved to its present location, strategically located between Capitol Hill and downtown Seattle, inside the spacious Melrose Market, where it comingled easily with a butcher, flower shop, Bar Ferd'nand, and Taylor Shellfish, the biggest shellfish purveyor on the West Coast. Jeremy Faber felt lucky to have such a knowledgeable clientele when it came to chefs and their mushroom chops; none was more knowledgeable than Matt Dillon. Dillon had roamed the coastal scrub for beach porcini with the throngs of Cambodians. He'd cooked with matsutake before most white guys even knew what it was. He'd traversed the mountains and the rain forests for oddball species of fungi that only mycological geeks could identify. You didn't become a first-rate chef by hiding in the kitchen.

One time Dillon was out on the coast, picking chanterelles. He made one run through a patch, circled back, and was just starting his second run when he heard a roar through the woods: "Who's picking my spot?" The antagonist was out of sight on the other side of a densely wooded hump. "I'm gonna cut you!" the guy yelled. Dillon, who had lived in Washington State since he was three, had run into these types before. He figured it was some hard-up tweaker, a dangerous, strung-out wild card. There was no sense in running away. "The coast is a scary place. I flipped open my knife and started walking. If that guy comes at me, I'll cut his throat." Still, he was freaked out and not at all sure he had what it took to go military. "I popped over that hill and there's those two sonsofbitches laughing their asses off." It was Doug and Faber.

Dillon shook his head and finished off his glass of wine. He was as surprised as anyone by his friendship with Faber. "Here's this brash, shit-talking, bigheaded New Yorker. I was going through my divorce and he was there for me." These days, both Dillon and Faber were working so much that they hardly saw each other; when they did, they fell back into the same easy rhythm. "He's essentially family to me at this point," Dillon said of Faber. "I don't know any other two people in our peer group that work like we do. We don't take days off. We work morning 'til night. We put everything we have— emotionally and physically—into our business, and we keep branching out. It's a lifestyle thing for the two of us, and it's really difficult for me to give up. I woke up at four-thirty this morning because I have animals to feed. When I'm not here, I have to be doing something at Corson, or doing some private event somewhere else. Feeding the goats and cows and sheep and pigs and chickens. I'm hoping that in the next few years I'll actually make a little bit of money."

Like Faber, Dillon is a stubborn perfectionist. He serves generous quantities of extraordinary foods because he refuses to do anything else. "If I was smart I'd just open bars. Sell shitty food and make a bunch of money. At bars people are paying seven dollars for fifty cents' worth of product." At Sitka & Spruce, he figures, customers are paying more like thirty-five for thirty dollars' worth of product. "I want to serve porcini and spot prawns because they're perfect together. Those porcini are nineteen dollars a pound, and spot prawns are fourteen dollars a pound. It's absolutely the perfect combination. We'll roast the porcini and shave a bunch raw over the top." I told him about a meal I'd recently had with friends at his other restaurant, the Corson Building, how a platter of marbled king salmon from Neah Bay came smothered in the most morels I had ever seen on a restaurant plate. "When you're taking a wonderful piece of Pacific-coast wild king salmon," he explained, "and you stick it in front of somebody with morels, caraway seed, and fava beans sautéed in a bunch of butter . . ." For Dillon, there was no other way to operate.

"I'm not serving a morel just because it's a morel," he went on. "I want a good morel." For instance, he refused to serve California orchard morels, even though these were generally the first morels of the season on the West Coast and therefore in demand. The orchard morels were flawed. They were sandy. And because they fruited among the olive groves of the Central Valley, they were probably loaded with chemicals. Faber had stopped selling them as well. No, Dillon was partial to the morels that he could find himself in Washington State, such as the stately cottonwood morel, which was among the first to fruit in the Pacific Northwest. "Seeing it, finding it, knowing what it is. Your eyes popping open. That's what I want to serve on the plate."

. . .

AS IN VOGUE AS WILD FOODS and foraging had become in recent years, the real action in the culinary scene remained in the kitchen. Chefs were the new rock stars. Thanks to reality TV's cooking-as-competition sensibility (*Iron Chef, Top Chef,* et al.) and Anthony Bourdain's tell-all *Kitchen Confidential,* which launched a cottage industry of hot-stove memoirs, a young, camera-ready food elite was busy tearing down the gates of fusty old-school cookery. The new generation brought a globetrotting mix of exotic ingredients with them and a penchant for saucy language, controlled substances, and walk-in fornication. And they knew food. They lived it—tattooed it all over their bodies: images of frying pans, goats, pigs, oysters, a cow dissected by the needle artist into individual and carefully labeled cuts of beef across a human shoulder. Amid the elevation of new ingredients and styles, an attitude reigned. Chefs weren't content to be unseen in the back. They had opinions—and appetites. Suddenly, as if getting a transfusion from Keith Richards, bad behavior and haute cuisine went together, and the combo was as necessary and irresistible as steak frites. For his part, Faber kept a foot in this world by catering events from time to time. Recently a magazine had named a long list of influential culinary trendsetters in the Seattle area; Faber hadn't made the list. "WTF?" he texted me. "Molly Moon ice cream?" Dillon was near the top.

At first glimpse, you might lump Matt Dillon in with the other rock-star-chef types out all night partying after closing. Week-old stubble, evil grin, tattoos up and down thick arms, including a blurry inkblot of Washington State that might mask an ill-advised earlier work of skin art. But then he opens his mouth and you think you're talking to a bodhisattva.

"He talks that way to impress girls," quips Faber.

Though I had eaten Dillon's food on numerous occasions, the first time I got to watch him in action closely was at an event he catered with Faber. It was a dinner for some auction winners who were helping to support volunteer work in Ghana. Faber and Dillon had agreed to donate their time. On an overcast Saturday, I joined them at a farm in Snohomish, Washington. Tall and barrel-chested, Dillon exuded a surprisingly soft-spoken manner that was in deep contrast to the hotheaded egos stalking the Michelin-starred kitchens of the popular imagination. He showed up at the charity event in a black button-down shirt and jeans, chef whites nowhere in sight, carrying a thread-worn canvas knife bag. "We shouldn't tell our ingredients what to do," he said to me quietly while unpacking his things. "We should listen." Bill Gates's personal chef happened to be on hand, and though he was a guest at the dinner, he was also familiar with the kitchen setup and offered his help. He wheeled out a Weber grill the size of a bumper car and started a fire with some chunks of alder so Dillon could smoke a few chickens. Dillon grabbed plastic bins from his pickup, filled with ingredients he might use: lamb, halibut, duck eggs, king salmon lox, harissa, a spice called za'atar. Faber had brought a few of his own ingredients. He had sea beans and goosetongue—wild seaside greens gathered by Sang somewhere near Willapa Bay—and a variety of spring mushrooms: morels, porcini, and two types of coral, yellow and pink.

Earlier that day, as part of the auction prize, Faber had taken the winners mushroom hunting on the eastern slopes of the Cascades. He was a gracious tour guide, despite having worked a string of busy days with little sleep, and even brought beer and cold cuts for the group. As he had previously done with me, he led everyone through the woods, stopping here and there at trees he knew personally to uncover their annual crop of wild mushrooms: spring porcini, puff-balls, yellow coral, and, near the end of the trip, a patch of pink coral that he had been picking for years. Though coral mushrooms weren't widely used in restaurant kitchens, Faber had several clients, includ-ing Dillon, who would take whatever he found. With its warm shade of rose that darkened at the tips, the pink variety, *Ramaria botrytis,* was the more flavorful of the two corals. Both yellow and pink had hundreds of branchlike stems rising off a wide base, which gave them a look identical to sea coral. They brightened the forest floor and made a walk in the woods seem like a slightly surreal safari through an animated landscape.

Dillon looked over the haphazard array of foodstuffs spread out on the island. I asked him if he had a menu in mind or was just planning to wing it. "Winging it all the way," he replied with a wink, the picture of calmness. This might have been his motto.

Faber offered to toss together blanched sea beans and goosetongue. That sounded good to Dillon. He would use the wild greens with wet-pressed king salmon. Dillon started to slice local asparagus on the bias and asked me to cut up the porcini buttons, slicing them as thinly as possible. He handed me a huge knife that felt like a deadly weapon in my hands. The boletes, dense as unripe pears, had a surprisingly floral quality. This was one of the few mushrooms that could impress in its uncooked state. When I finished (with fingers miraculously intact), Dillon tossed the raw porcini together with the asparagus and a medley of homegrown herbs, to which he would later add a simple dressing of sherry vinegar and olive oil.

Faber and Dillon next looked at the halibut. It was a beautiful slab, translucent white, a few inches thick, and maybe three pounds. Give Jeremy Faber a cut of fish—except salmon, *anything* but that—and he was happy. A fillet of striped bass was good, sablefish even better. That was one thing he missed about the Atlantic coast: more varieties of finned fish. While the Northwest won hands down for shellfish, he missed all the weird and wonderful sea creatures hauled up by the day boats off Cape Cod, Montauk, and elsewhere in the Northeast. This Pacific halibut, however, was as good as anything. An idea crept across Dillon's face. "How about halibut with cream and spring onions?" he thought out loud, leaving room for argument. Faber considered this. He had two roasting pans of morel medallions and pink coral already caramelized and ready to go. He'd add the mushrooms to the cream and onions, along with a healthy squeeze of lemon to brighten the flavor and a generous sprinkling of sea salt. This was what you did with such extraordinary ingredients. Keep it simple. "Yeah," Faber said, warming quickly to the idea. "Yeah."

Dillon and Faber hardly had to speak to each other. They moved through the kitchen as if they'd worked together in it for years, their movements never crossing, an invisible control tower monitoring

their flight paths. It was better appointed than many restaurant kitchens: eight-burner Montague, stainless-steel island with refrigerator
compartments, walk-in cooler filled with hanging smoked hams and
other charcuterie. Nothing was written down. No menu, no list of
ingredients. They pulled items out of the plastic bins, held them up to
the light, tossed them up and down while pondering their virtues—
and into the food these things went. Dillon braised cardoons from his
garden while walking around the island with a large saucer cradled
in his arms like an infant. The saucer was full of golf ball–sized tomatoes, fire-engine red with dark green stems, bobbing up and down
in water. Glistening droplets ran down the tops of their tight skins.
He stopped. Faber nodded. The tomatoes would go under the broiler,
a colorful and acidic finishing touch to the smoked chicken tossed
with harissa. Faber pried open wooden boxes of Montrachet and
Châteauneuf-du-Pape. Everyone had a glass of Peyrassol rosé in
hand. The ten guests mingled in the next room, coming into the
kitchen in small groups to watch the dinner take shape. Dillon chatted amiably, looking the guests in the eye as he sliced onions.

Once the appetizers were served, Dillon came out of the kitchen to
give a quick spiel about the dishes on the table. One of his ingredients,
argan oil, he explained, was from Morocco. Village goats climbed the
argan trees to eat their fruit and then passed out the seeds. The villag-
ers collected the excrement, dried it over a fire, crumbled it to dust,
and separated out the now-tenderized seeds, which were then washed,
pounded, and made into oil. The goat-shit oil accompanied a platter
of seven-minute duck eggs sprinkled with the succulent, slightly sour
crunch of wild purslane. "Give me some more of that!" cried one of
the guests, holding out her hands to receive the platter. Faber raised
an eyebrow at me. Maybe his friend was taking the Middle Eastern
bit just a tad too far.

After the halibut and chicken, dessert was a simple plating of
sliced strawberries and rhubarb over crème fraîche, with a drizzle of
Dillon's own homemade honey and rose-petal vinegar. A few of those

plates came back half finished. Later Faber would suggest that dessert was his friend's one weak spot. "He punted," said Faber.

From start to finish the meal took about four hours, though it felt more like two, tops. Dillon wiped down his knives and returned them to their beat-up satchel while Faber dried wineglasses. It wasn't even ten P.M. Dillon had a ferry to catch, and Faber, going back to a bed he was actually relieved would be empty, needed to get home so he could sleep for the first time in days. Driving all over creation in recent weeks to procure morels had taken its toll. He confessed that to stay awake he'd daydreamed about U.S. ski racer and Olympic gold medalist Lindsey Vonn. "Best athlete in the world," he said, his eyelids heavy. Neither Faber nor Dillon had broken a sweat.

CHAPTER 8

The Discreet Charm of the Golden Chanterelle

...

IF THE HEDGEHOG IS THE UNDERDOG of wild mushrooms, the matsutake an exotic foreigner, and the king bolete royalty, the chanterelle is a preening starlet on the red carpet, hoping—praying—for one more *People* cover. Despite its romantic twirl off the tongue, you'd think the chanterelle was practically domesticated—an off-the-shelf French floozy Halloween costume. Is there an A-list wild mushroom that gets less respect among the mycoscenti, after all, than the chanty? Like an overexposed model, it has the faint whiff of "been there, done that" among connoisseurs. Well, I for one wouldn't kick a golden chanterelle out of the kitchen for getting around, and apparently I'm not alone.

More than any other fungi, including even morels, the chanterelle is the wild mushroom most likely encountered by the average restaurant patron. This is in part because of its abundance the world over—and its cheapness. Known as *girolle* in France and *pfifferling* in Germany, with its signature egg-yolk color and fluted shape—a golden goblet of the woods—the chanterelle cuts a striking figure on the plate, even if it sometimes gets bloated and soggy after heavy rains. It has a slightly fruity aroma and a flavor that is reminiscent, some will tell you, of apricots. Chefs love it for that warm color and singular taste. Combined with a salty cut of pig, it's irresistible.

The temperate forests of the world are flush with chanterelles. They fruit on every continent except Antarctica. Recent estimates of global chanterelle commerce put the total annual crop at more than 400 million pounds, worth $1.25 to $1.4 billion. Their many common names are an indication of their ubiquity. The Japanese call them *an-zutake* (apricot mushroom); the Portuguese *canarinhos* (canary bird chicken); *crête de coq* (cock's crest) is just one of many French common names; Hungarian is *csirke gomba* (chicken mushroom); Dutch *dooierzwam* (egg yolk mushroom); Chinese *jiyou-jun* (chicken fat mushroom); Turkish *yumurta mantasi;* Icelandic *kantarella;* Swahili *wisogolo*. They're mentioned in literature as early as 1581 by Dutch herbalist Lobelius. Linnaeus chose the name *Agaricus chantarellus* for the common European golden chanterelle in 1747, and Elias Magnus Fries, the Swedish father of mycology, updated it to *Cantharellus cibarius* in his *Systema Mycologicum,* published in three volumes between 1821 and 1832; that name persists today in both the Old World and the New. The Greek *kantharos* means cup or goblet; *cibarius* is Latin for food. The family *Cantharellaceae* contains more than ninety species and, at last count, five genera, including the closely related *Cantharellus* and *Craterellus,* which, between them, account for many edible species harvested on the mushroom trail, all of them distinguished by their goblet-like form and hint of stone-fruit aroma.

Picking chanterelles in coastal Washington and Oregon is nearly a cliché. Doug apologized at the outset for what he figured would be a boring day—the closest thing there is to industrial mushroom picking. And he was right: Chanterelles are a bread-and-butter pick for harvesters. The money only gets good with volume, meaning a long, repetitive day of "grinding it out." Still, this was a backyard pick, and a famous one at that. To not pick chanterelles here would be like passing on a ride up the Eiffel Tower in Paris. After negotiating a maze of logging roads, we arrived at our destination: a skid road along a ridgetop, where several fallen trees brought us to a sudden halt. Doug and Jeff worked either side of the road, plunging down into dense commercial forest with their buckets and knives, returning to the car every so often to dump a bucketful into baskets in the trunk, take a break (and a drink of cold coffee for Doug), and then go back for more. The work was hard. We traversed a steep slope, perhaps thirty degrees, with thick concentrations of slippery salal that made each step potentially hazardous. There were holes in the ground where stumps had burned into nothing after the last timber harvest, holes that could swallow a leg whole. At one point, while gangplanking along a keeled-over log, I snagged my bucket on a branch and got spun around in a pirouette before tumbling backward into a net of salal. The brush broke my fall. I felt like a turtle capsized on its back, struggling to flip over, my mushrooms scattered on the ground among the prickly confines of Oregon grape. At the bottom of a narrow defile, a creek slipped through a dense thicket of alder. "A place only a bear could love," Doug said. We worked our way methodically down the slope and back up in a zigzag pattern, starting a half mile away from the car for our first pass and gradually making our way closer, so that each trip back to the rig with a full bucket was shorter than the last. By the second pass I had shed my layers down to a T-shirt. My face was dripping.

While chanterelles are harvested all over the world, the Pacific Northwest is one of their strongholds—for paradoxical reasons, I would soon learn. Rumors of great flushes in outer Siberia surface from time to time, as do whisperings of wall-to-wall Saskatchewan forests and Maine woods overflowing with yellow, not to mention great flushes in Africa, Asia, and elsewhere. Within a thin band of rain-washed territory along the West Coast that stretches roughly from Santa Cruz, California, north through British Columbia, several varieties of chanterelle flourish, and in the coastal ranges of Washington and Oregon they are often one of the more prolific mushrooms in the woods. The most common variety is the Pacific golden chanterelle (*Cantharellus formosus*), with the white chanterelle

(*Cantharellus subalbidus*) a distant second. As with mushroom classification in general, there is plenty of taxonomical work yet to be done. Recently added to the group is a distinct species called *Cantharellus cascadensis,* which looks like a cross between the two most prevalent Northwest species and has long been known to commercial harvesters as "the hybrid." Another edible species, called the blue chanterelle (*Polyozellus multiplex*), is now thought to be part of a different family entirely.

When recreational mushroomers from the Northwest say they are going pot hunting, they are often specifically after golden chanterelles. With its bright yellow coloration, fluted cap, and blunt ridges rather than gills, the chanterelle is one of the easiest mushrooms for a novice to identify, and it's also among the most accessible of the top-tier edibles to find, often loitering around hiking trails and even city parks, an attention-getter starved for footlights. Chanterelles are ectomycorrhizal fungi, which means that they not only have symbiotic relationships with plants but they do so by forming a sort of protective sheath around the underground root tips. This cements the union in a truly physical manner, a shotgun wedding of sorts, and while chanterelles build such bonds with countless members of the plant kingdom across the globe, there is one tree in particular that is favored in the Pacific Northwest.

North of California's redwood belt, the king of the conifers is the Douglas fir. It is the tallest and most numerous tree from the Cascade Crest to the Pacific Ocean. Though it grows across a good swath of the West, it is in the hills and valleys of the coastal Northwest that it truly thrives, reaching heights of well over two hundred feet and dominating other trees such as hemlock and spruce with its ability to grow higher and live longer. The tree is the namesake of nineteenth-century botanist David Douglas, who called it "one of the most striking and truly graceful objects of Nature." It would also become the most commercially important tree in western North America.

There are still a few groves of ancient, uncut Douglas fir left that

give a picture of what these forests looked like before white settlement: thousand-year-old trees with trunks as wide as VW buses that
reach for the sky with that stock-straight posture loggers adore, some of
them a hundred feet tall before the first branch knot. Most of these trees
were cut down during the go-go years of industrial logging. Take a
flight over the Northwest and you'll see a mosaic of clear-cuts below—
intrusions into the formerly vast Douglas fir ecosystem. Where once
stood primeval forests of towering Douglas firs, we now have tree farms
packed cheek by jowl with planted firs that are cut on short rotations.
Some of these farms have been cut three or more times since the old
growth was first removed, and rarely are the trees allowed to age more
than forty years. The timberlands are treated like crops. Such highly
managed forests are dense and dark. But sometimes the lugubrious setting is brightened by jaunty dabs of yellow.

It turns out that the Pacific golden chanterelle is attracted to young
Douglas firs. This is why the Olympic Peninsula and Oregon Coast
Range are such chanterelle factories. They were once home to the
world's greatest Douglas fir forests, forests that have been cut down
and replaced with fast-growing monocrops, the timber industry in
the Northwest having unwittingly created a boom in chanterelles that
commercial foragers have learned to exploit. The average recreational
hunter, however, might not be inclined to trouble with such hunting
grounds, no matter how productive. For one thing, it's not a simple
walk in the woods, as Doug would point out. Timberlands in western
Washington and Oregon are usually rugged and trail-less, the going
slow. For another, it's dark inside these places, and biodiversity is substantially lower than in an untouched forest. Trudging up and down
the sunless folds and draws of a Douglas fir tree farm is a reminder of
why the forest is a setting for fairy tales about heedless little boys and
girls. Gloom abounds, along with a reptilian sense of impending
doom. Commercial pickers know this rough terrain is where your
chances of a hundred-pound day are best, even if some of these plan-
tations are posted. *All the king's deer.*

———

NEAR THE TOP OF A KNOLL, Doug called out to me. He was excited, had found what he called a demijohn: an antique glass carboy,
maybe gallon-sized, that might have been used to make home brew
or wine. As Doug pried it out of the clay-like earth, he found that the
neck was broken off, making it worthless. A good one might fetch
twenty dollars on eBay, he figured. Over the years he's found quite a
few in the old cuts, some of them dating back to the days when these
woods were still old growth, as far back as the turn of the previous
century. At one point he had amassed quite a collection. His ex-
wife—the third one, that is—reduced most of it to shards. "The Destroyer," he calls her.

"Yeah, she had an anger problem."

We drove to another patch, following a byzantine network of dirt
logging roads to a little spur choked with saplings. A stacked pile of
dead salal gave Doug pause. Mexican brush cutters had been combing
the woods in recent years for greenery used in floral displays. The fact
that chanterelles are often found in company with salal is not lost on
the brush crews. We started into the woods anyway. Not too far in we
came across the first cut stems—little yellow protuberances from the
moss. "They found it," Doug said. With that we headed for the next
patch. Doug reeled off dozens of numbers—"there's the fifty-two
hundred, the fifty-three thirty, the twenty-two oh-one"—the coded
names of other logging roads and spurs nearby. The cutover forests
for as far as you could see on a clear day were all loaded with chanterelles. You could find one or two mushrooms not far from the road
virtually anywhere in the district. The skill was in finding the honey-
holes, places where the tree and soil composition acted in perfect har-
mony to produce bucketloads of mushrooms. Other factors came into
play as well: elevation, slope aspect, topography. The real skill was not
so much in the picking—although tricks in efficiency paid off there,
like using your shirt as a bag when the bucket was out of reach—but
in locating new patches when old ones got found out or logged.

Lately, logging had been as much of a problem as competing pickers. Driving to another spot deep within the tangle of industrial forest, Doug was momentarily confused about our whereabouts—until he realized the area we had been seeking was now a sea of gray stumps, his former landmarks reduced to two-by-fours. "They're clobbering my hedgehog spot," he said with resignation. An empty potato-chip bag at the next spot boded poorly too. Jeff walked into the woods ahead of us and found the forest floor littered with more trash and discarded mushrooms. Another brush crew had blazed through.

After four buckets apiece—about sixty pounds of chanterelles for each picker, with a value of two dollars per pound—it was getting late. Doug and Jeff considered this a slow day on the whole, mainly because the buyer—Jeremy Faber—had made a special request of the pickers. He wanted what he referred to as "curled cap" chanterelles— that is, he wanted smaller mushrooms with firm, quarter-sized caps that were still youthfully curled under rather than fully open. "Jeremy's particular about his product," Doug said. "Maybe that's why he's always got woman problems."

As chefs have become savvier about their wild-food offerings, they have also become pickier about what they buy. Late in the season, many of the chanterelles are large, with ragged edges and cracked caps. Pickers call them flowers. They lack the firm texture of the less-mature specimens and don't look as good on the plate. For Doug and Jeff, this means bypassing pounds and pounds of mushrooms in the woods that don't fit the criteria. Faber will make this up to them by paying an extra fifty cents per pound (the going rate at the buy station in Aberdeen is $1.50) and through other promised perks that had yet to reveal themselves.

We pulled over at one last spot before dark. The pickers split up, working either side of a ridge. I asked Doug if he knew who was buying the curled-cap chanterelles from Faber. "That's Jeremy's business," he said a little gruffly, sitting back on his haunches in the moss to take a rest; this high-grading was tiring. "I can understand why he wants to diversify. Chefs always want something new. I bet Matt takes as many curled-caps as he can get. He knows a good product."

"Have you eaten at his restaurant?"

"Let me tell you something. One time I visited Seattle when Jeremy's dad was in town. We went to some fancier 'n shit place. Not Sitka, someplace else." Doug cupped his hands and pretended to look inside, as if through a peephole. "These tiny little portions come out. It was like a week's pay. Jeremy's dad picked up the tab."

"Was the food good?"

"Sure, if you're one of those food-this and food-that types, not to be disrespectful. I got a burger at Dick's afterward." Doug stood up, hefted his bucket, and started across the slope, then paused. He wiped his brow. "I'll tell you who knows how to cook a chanterelle. Christina. I bet you she does hardly nothing at all to it, just puts it in the pan and cooks it up. There you go: chanterelle. See, this is what I'm talking about. All the tricks in the world don't do jack unless you truly love the product."

I saw Doug's point. Recently I had brought a class of high school students to Christina Choi's restaurant. We'd been foraging as part of a weeklong "experiential" class. I'd taken them to the mountains and the shore, to tranquil woods and a busy city park. The final exam was to join together to cook a feast at school with the foraged bounty. On Thursday afternoon, the day before the meal, we all went to Nettletown to celebrate our week together and get inspiration. I warned Choi ahead of time. She had a long table ready for us. The small lunch spot was packed with professionals eating foods normally seen on the dinner menus of the nicest restaurants, in modest preparations that showed off the ingredients' intrinsic attributes and character: soups, salads, and sandwiches, all loaded with wild greens and mushrooms that might have been gathered just a few miles away in a quiet foothill forest. Every day there was a variation of chow mein that seemed to combine all these things: fiddleheads perched on top, with hen-of-the-woods mushrooms and strands of lamb's-quarters or watercress intertwined with the noodles, the accents of garlic and ginger tying it all together. Whatever was in season, Choi would have it on the menu, prepared with a simplicity that was startling in its effect. Wild foods brightened virtually every dish, and I wondered how many of the customers recognized the exceptional spirit of this place. Christina came out of the kitchen to meet the kids. They warmed to her immediately—she could have been one of them. She talked about the ingredients in her pantry as if they were personal friends and said a few words about how the natural world had influenced her cooking style, how she wasn't trying to improve on nature, just allowing it to shine. Afterward, on the bus ride back to campus, one of the students paid Choi the ultimate compliment. "She's rad," he said.

"If any of these mushrooms end up in Christina's hands," Doug went on, examining his bucket, "then all this kowtowing to Jeremy was worth it." He made a loud, owl-like hoot that echoed through the industrial timber. A moment later a distant hoot answered back. It was time to go. Jeff met us at the car. With a trunk loaded to the top with the prettiest chanterelles in the woods, we piled back into the Blue Pig and drove out of the forest.

. . .

CHANTERELLES ARE VERSATILE MUSHROOMS in the kitchen. Larger specimens will expel a fair amount of liquid during cooking, which can be concentrated into a flavorful stock. They make a good cream sauce. Button-sized chanterelles caramelize easily in the pan and, when scattered on the plate, make an attractive adornment to cuts of meat and fish. Because of their fruitiness, they can be used in ways that differ from typical mushroom cookery—yet they're still fungi and complement any pizza, pasta, risotto, stuffing, or meat sauce. Cream of chanterelle soup is one of my favorite fall dishes, as is a mess of chanterelles cooked with pancetta, butter, cream, and a sprinkling of nutmeg, which can be eaten on toast or with a shaped pasta such as farfalle, orecchiette, or radiatori. Once sautéed, they keep well in the freezer. I have bags and bags of vacuum-sealed, frozen chanterelles year-round. One method of preservation I don't use with chanterelles is drying. After rehydration they're leathery and tough, without the depth of flavor that enlivens other dried mushrooms such as porcini. Interestingly, in a region famed for its vitamin D deficiency, chanterelles are second only to cod-liver oil in this necessary nutrient. They contain beta-carotene, which may explain why Chinese herbalists use them to treat night blindness, and antioxidants similar to those found in salmon. They also seem to concentrate heavy metals and radiation less than other mushrooms, a characteristic discovered in the aftermath of Chernobyl.

One of my favorite recipes for chanterelles comes from Suzanne Goin and her restaurant Lucques in Los Angeles. It's a tribute to fall, with its crisp golden colors. The mushrooms are sautéed and tossed with ricotta gnocchi in a sage brown-butter sauce with fresh corn off the cob and toasted parsley bread crumbs. The dish is sweet and savory, with a little crunch, the mushrooms acting as a balance between the counterweights of flavors and textures. Sometimes I'll give chanterelle buttons a quick sauté almost as an afterthought to accompany a grilled or seared cut of meat—a chicken breast, say, or a pork chop. Having frozen chanterelles on hand year-round is a simple way to energize an everyday dish, and they're more festive and flavorful than grocery-store buttons.

But no one gets rich picking or selling chanterelles. They're just too common. It seemed to me that the chanterelle harvest was a time when everyone was a little on edge. They required work: baskets upon baskets of mushrooms hauled out of the woods, cleaned, sorted, packed into trucks, re-sorted, boxed up, and delivered. The sheer volume of work surrounding chanterelles was astronomical. Yet they paid little—and you couldn't really avoid them. Back in Seattle, while visiting Faber's basement warehouse one afternoon and watching chanterelles get dusted off and packaged for delivery, I could see that the harvest was wearing on Faber and his employees. They'd been pulling long shifts, and Faber was on the road all the time. Delivery boxes littered the floor. Columns of baskets stacked to the ceiling presented an obstacle course. A homemade dryer over in one corner rattled incessantly, its screens loaded with ugly, oversize mushrooms that would be added to packages labeled WILD MIX. Faber's employees, busy cleaning and weighing yet another thousand pounds of chanterelles, didn't have time to look up from their tasks. Pictures on the wall of swimsuit beauties frolicking improbably with tumescent fungi hardly lightened the mood. Faber looked over a basket of curled-cap goldens that was destined for New York. Apropos of nothing, he told me he wouldn't be surprised if he woke up one morning to read about Doug Carnell in *The Seattle Times*.

"Doug's harmless as a fly," I protested.

"You don't know Doug," he said.

Whenever I've spent some time with somebody only to be told by a mutual acquaintance later that I don't know the person, well, I'm a little irked. I'd ridden around in Doug's Buick, listened to his stories, picked mushrooms with him. Each time, he sent me home with a basket, despite my refusals. *Doug,* I'd say, *this is your living, let me pay for this.* One time I tried to press gas money into his hand. He waved me off and drove away. "Okay," I granted Faber, "maybe you don't want to be on his bad side."

"Did he tell you about the trial?"

Yes, he had. After the Destroyer broke all his keepsakes and left him for another man, Doug had to defend himself in court against her accusations. The prosecutor called him to the stand. "Did you call your wife . . . a cunt?" he asked Doug before the judge.

Doug composed himself and, without raising his voice, he responded, "No, your honor, in truth I called her a *fucking* cunt."

"You didn't?" I said to Doug.

"Yes, I did."

"No."

"God's truth."

"Well, that wasn't very smart."

"To hell it wasn't. I got off."

Faber sneered. He'd heard the story a million times. "Is it true?" I asked him.

"You never know with Doug. Probably. He didn't hit his wife, I'm pretty sure about that."

"So why might I read about him in the paper one day?"

It wasn't just Doug, Faber tried to explain to me. It was the whole scene out there, the whole scene out on the Pacific coast, from Forks, Washington, all the way down to Fort Bragg, California. "It's miserable. It rains constantly. When it's not raining, it's foggy. The woods have been hammered by clear-cuts." Rural poverty, methamphetamine, petty crime, poaching—the cycle repeated itself endlessly, a backwoods version of inner-city despair. Most people in places like Seattle or San Francisco didn't give even a moment's thought to what was happening in the coastal communities that once provided the country with so much of its natural wealth. They figured the people out there were, in a word, resourceful. Meanwhile, the woods filled up with garbage, catalytic converters went missing, and smoldering resentment grew. "I could never live there," Faber said. "I'd go postal too."

. . .

IT WAS IMPOSSIBLE TO overstate Faber's devotion to honest physical labor. Hard work was his mantra, and he was always quick to puncture any romantic notions I might have entertained about the happy-go-lucky forager at play in a bucolic idyll. One time I met him at a pub after work. Earlier that day he'd picked two hundred pounds of wild watercress from a spring on the far side of the mountains, about two hours east of Seattle. Over pitchers of beer, he wolfed down a burger and fries with a side order of fish sandwich, then decided he was still hungry and ordered the Reuben. Another time, when I told him I would be scouting morel patches that day, he asked me to pick four garbage bags' worth of vanilla leaf for him; he dries the native green and uses it in teas along with rose hips, wild mint, and other aromatics. "It'll give you something to do," he snickered.

Later that day, after scouting up and down some of my favorite morel patches with less than a pound to show for my efforts, I understood his amusement. I was a week too early. So I switched to vanilla leaf. Two hours later, after filling the second bag, I called it quits. My lower back was in open rebellion and I'd managed to cut myself in three places with my dull kitchen shears. That night, picking up the vanilla leaf, Faber tried to comprehend my rate of one bag per hour and shook his head in disbelief. He usually did three times that.

Sometimes I wondered whether this was all talk—bravado from the professional forager to maintain his mystique. But then I'd get a text at ten P.M., saying he couldn't make our arranged meet-up because he was just now arriving at his fiddlehead patch after picking miner's lettuce in the Columbia River Gorge that afternoon—in other words, after an eight-hour round-trip drive to harvest a couple hundred pounds of wild salad greens the size of half-dollars, he was now strapping on a headlamp to liberate an ungodly amount of barely emerged fern shoots from some dark hollow.

How Faber balanced his social life in the city with a working life spent mostly among the rural poor remained a mystery to me, though I started to get an inkling on a November trip to the Olympic Peninsula to pick the last of the Washington chanterelle crop near the old port town of Shelton. This was a late-producing patch first shared with him by two other pickers, one named Joe and another named Gerry. Nowadays, Joe mostly raked truffles and Gerry was in jail.

"You'll want to meet Joe," Faber said to me on my front stoop as I gathered up my things. Though he had pickers and buyers up and down the West Coast that I had to meet, Joe was near the top of the list. When I asked him why, he just murmured something about how I needed to understand what he was dealing with on a daily basis. Apparently, Joe had harvested part of the patch with a picker named Red Dog the day before.

One picker we would not be meeting on this trip was Doug Carnell. During a routine traffic stop, the police had run his license and discovered he owed back child support. His license was suspended. Doug argued that he'd never gotten the letter saying he was delinquent, but Faber wasn't buying it. He called this new development a "Dougism." "How do you claim you forgot to pay child support? Because you didn't open some letter from the state? Typical Dougism." I was concerned this might mean Doug was out for the winter. "He'll make it to California," Faber assured me. "I'll do all the driving and he won't have any gas money, but he'll make it."

We debated which vehicle to take, mine or his. Initially Faber had wanted to take my car. In a text message he wrote: "I need an incognito car. Interested?" I replied back right away that I wanted to go and could supply the vehicle. Instead, we settled on his latest Astro van, a seventeen-year-old model with tinted windows that had cost him two thousand dollars and came with an aftermarket cassette player. The cassette player was a nice touch. He figured no one would recognize him, because it was mainly an around-town delivery vehicle, tinted windows and all.

I slid into the passenger seat. Used Chevrolet Astro vans had been his vehicle of choice for several years running, and this one was the newest in a fleet of three. Faber burns through an Astro every eighteen months or so, averaging about a hundred thousand miles per year. Though he covets the Dodge Sprinter favored by other delivery businesses, such an expensive, tricked-out van, as Faber put it, makes boneheaded economic sense. Astro vans have four-wheel drive and a large cargo area (once the backseats are removed) that can be easily chilled with the rear air conditioner on full blast. An hour down I-5, we pulled into a Shell station just north of Olympia, where gas was twenty-five cents less than the competition. "I always score the cheapest gas," he crowed.

It was the height of the fall mushroom season in the Pacific Northwest, and Faber's BlackBerry was ringing incessantly. The chef at Crush wanted five pounds of lobsters and five pounds of watercress. The Harvest Vine needed chanterelles. Lark wanted porcini. He took orders and tried to encourage callers to dial his employees back in Seattle instead. When we got to the patch, Joe was nowhere to be seen, and Faber seemed a little miffed. "I don't know what he does all day. It's not like he spends time cleaning his trailer." We pulled over just past an intersection with a gravel logging road, careful not to park on the logging road itself, even though the gate was open. "It's red-dotted. Simpson Lumber doesn't think twice about handing out tickets or locking you behind the gate."

I told Faber about Doug's "all the king's deer" theory, how the timber companies were getting tax breaks and still keeping the public out.

"That's a Dougism."

"Aren't more roads red-dotted than ever before?"

"They're closed because of garbage and illegal dumping. I've called the timber companies about this."

"What about elk hunters?"

"Have you ever seen an elk while mushroom picking on private timberlands?"

I admitted I had not, though Doug had told me more than once that he gets an elk every year around here.

"Another Dougism. There are no elk in the second growth. Maybe you see them crossing a clear-cut every now and then, but think about where you see the elk. They're in the old growth. Second growth is too dense. Would you want to walk through that shit all day?"

"We do."

Faber pulled on a pair of heavy-duty Helly Hansen rain pants and big boots, strapped on his backpack, and grabbed a seven-gallon bucket that would hold close to twenty pounds of mushrooms. He'd sawed the lid in half and put it back together with a duct-tape hinge, so he could keep the lid on at all times in the needle-shedding forest. We walked into wet woods, pushing through saplings and under-brush, passing empty beer cans in the first hundred yards before coming to dense thickets of salal. White and golden chanterelles hid among the moss and brush wherever I looked.

An hour later we were back at the van, dumping our first load into baskets, when I heard the squeal of a car veering off the road. I jumped out of the way. "You're all under arrest!" a man yelled through his open window as he skidded to a stop in the grass. Joe. He was driving an old Toyota pickup, primer gray, with two other passengers sardined into the cab. He stepped out and brushed himself off. His ponytail was pulled tightly behind his head, his tan canvas jacket zipped over a trim yet muscular frame. Though clearly fit, he showed deep fissures in his face and the yellowed complexion of an inveterate smoker. He might have been retirement age or half that—it was impossible to tell.

"Who are these two?" Faber said, nodding toward a man and a woman still sitting in the cab and arguing over a pack of cigarettes. They didn't make any attempt to answer.

"Sorry," Joe said, "that's . . ." And his voice trailed off as he mumbled something. They might as well have been nameless. Neither could be bothered to make introductions, and their distant expressions told me it didn't matter. Whoever they were, they were lingering around today because of some misunderstanding or a liaison that had already exhausted itself well beyond any usefulness. Joe might have picked them up hitchhiking—who cared?

The man got out and slammed the door, with the woman still sitting in the car. Pulling his hoodie off, he got all tangled up with a garish neck chain and had to unwind himself. The woman slid across the seat, gripped the roof, and pulled herself out the open window as if exiting a race car. She looked Native American. Her dark face was slightly acne-scarred, with black stringy hair falling across it in clumps; her eyes were mere slits. She felt around in her pockets for some missing item, her face utterly expressionless. Then she found the lighter, cupped her hands, and lit a cigarette. Her friend took the lighter and kept it. She looked as if she'd had a hard life, more animal than woman, yet when she opened her mouth her voice was soft and feminine and nearly musical, a voice that didn't square with her outward appearance at all. They both wore cotton jeans and sweatshirts, hardly the right material for such wet conditions.

Joe made a little small talk, during which it was agreed that he would go to the back end of the patch. He grinned at me. "Go deep or go home." Then, before the next car could round the bend, the three hurried into the woods, out of sight, as if running from the law.

"See what I mean?" Faber said after they had disappeared behind the tree cover.

I was confused. "Their truck is right here on the roadside, visible to anyone who drives by. It's not like they're fooling anyone by sneaking into the woods like that."

"Paranoia," said Faber. "Their natural state."

"And those other two?"

"Now you're getting it. A shitshow. I guarantee you, by the end of the day I will have picked more than those bozos combined."

"Why would Joe share a valuable patch close to town with those two?"

"It doesn't make any sense. It never does out here."

I made a quick inventory of the trash piled in the pickup's bed: motor oil, gasoline, banana peels, an industrial-sized jar of peanut butter ("Jif!" Faber snorted), and several twenty-four-ounce empties of Hurricane High Gravity lager ("8.1 percent alcohol," bragged the label). Alcohol, though, seemed like only part of the problem. I wondered aloud whether the two guests needed some quick cash for drugs.

"Probably," Faber said.

Or maybe they owed Joe money and this way they could work it off.

"There's a good theory."

Mushroom hunting is sometimes viewed as a speedy way to make some extra walking-around money, this despite the handful of inexperienced pickers who succumb to exposure in the bush every year. Meth-heads in particular had started picking mushrooms to fund their habits. Users were easy to spot: emaciated, hollow-cheeked, teeth rotted out. In his rental room in Westport, Doug had a row of T-shirts tacked up on the wall: METH = DEATH; TWEAKERS SUCK; GOT TEETH? He saw the drug's devastation every day. There was no point buying a new catalytic converter for his Buick, he said, because the crystal-meth addicts, prowling for cash, would just steal it again.

I followed Faber back into the woods. With Joe and his friends here, we would need to give them some room and find a different spot. "I'll never take a check from the government," Faber was telling me as we dodged salmonberry briars. "They can keep my Social Security." An hour later, making our way back to the van with full buckets, we came upon the nameless woman. She was soaking wet and holding an armload of mushrooms. "I lost my bucket," she said in nearly a whisper. "I put it down back there and now it's gone. Is this a chanterelle?" She held up a large, decomposing gilled mushroom of some sort.

"No," Faber said.

"How about this?"

"No. This is a chanterelle." He held one up by its stem.

"Are there hedgehogs here?" But Faber was already moving off through the woods. He didn't have time for this. I explained how the hedgehogs had teeth under the cap instead of gills—*like a hedgehog*.

"Oh, I get it. How about this?"

"Not edible." She showed me her pile of mushrooms that she'd been keeping in a bundle of newspaper since losing her bucket. The newspaper was darkening with moisture and would soon fall apart. We went through the pile and she tossed the non-edibles. "If I were you, I'd try to find the bucket before looking for any more mushrooms."

"It's around here somewhere."

"Which direction?"

"Back there. I don't really know." She bent down to look at the chanterelles, admitting quietly that she had lost her knife too. It was somewhere else in the woods.

A few minutes later we came upon her again. This time she was empty-handed. "Have you seen my mushrooms? I put them down somewhere."

FABER HAS WORKED WITH dope growers, meth-heads, illegals, and all other manner of social castoffs who do their bidding in the unpoliced corners of rural timber country. He's had a knife pulled on him in the bush and been chased by a bear. It all goes with the territory. Like cleaning houses or punching in a late-night shift on the factory floor, though, trading in wild edibles is primarily a path for those looking to get a leg up. After leaving Joe and company, we continued west toward the coast. Faber's main goal today, it turned out, had nothing to do with picking. He needed to buy a thousand or more pounds of mushrooms from his network of Southeast Asian pickers who worked the southern end of the Olympic Peninsula. In Aberdeen, he checked in with an employee to make sure payments had been collected and deposited, then withdrew a few thousand dollars from his account. Next we pulled into Sang and Srey's Raymond home, finding the Durango up on blocks and waiting for a new transmission—an affront to Faber. "I own it," he explained. When the family had first tried to buy a new truck, every loan office in town turned them down, so Faber stepped in and bought the car himself. Now they paid him in monthly installments. He had tried to steer them away from the Durango, but Sang was adamant. He wanted an American truck. Faber said he would probably buy them a new transmission too.

On the porch, the older generation of Cambodian immigrants sat in chairs or on buckets, cleaning freshly picked chanterelles with little pieces of foam. We went into the kitchen and found Sang and Srey, both of them busy readying their kitchen for the evening's commerce, a pot of rice on the stove and the children kneeling in the glow of a giant TV, a framed Buddha looking down.

———

SOMETIME AFTER ELEVEN P.M., the grading was complete, all the pickers paid. Sang helped Faber load baskets of porcini, lobsters, chanterelles, and a few cauliflower mushrooms into his van. Though Sang could go to bed now, Faber still wasn't finished. Our final stop was in Elma, a small logging town on the southern peninsula. "This will be a different scene," he warned me as we pulled into the driveway. Before stepping out of the van, he told me a quick story about one of the couples we might meet inside. After a day of drinking and arguing with her husband, the wife had jumped in her car and roared off. Faber got a call in the middle of the night warning him that she was on her way. She had decided that Faber, seen as the most eligible bachelor around, should be the one to take her in so she could be done with her abusive husband once and for all.

"Take her in in what sense?" I asked.

"What do you think?" Apparently this episode was old history now, forgiven and forgotten. "She's pretty cute," he allowed as we got out.

Several Cambodians stood around in the cool garage, a few of them drinking cans of beer and smoking cigarettes. A short, slender woman in tight jeans and makeup stubbed out her Parliament and gave Faber a shy hug before disappearing into the house. The older women were seated beside mushroom baskets, laboriously cleaning away forest debris. Nearly the entire floor of the two-car garage was covered with golden chanterelles, with baskets stacked haphazardly against the walls. It was hard to tell which crates were cleaned, weighed, and ready to go. Faber wasn't happy. "Which ones?" he wanted to know, a little testily. A middle-aged woman pointed with her cigarette to several stacks against one wall, maybe sixty crates of mushrooms in all, each one weighing twelve to fifteen pounds. The day before, Faber had left off eighty baskets so he could collect the thousand pounds he needed for an overseas shipment. We started carrying three at a time out to the van. I could hear the men laughing inside as we moved the product. More baskets got piled up by the door.

"*A thousand pounds,*" he finally shouted, exasperated.

The pickers nodded in agreement.

"This is fifteen hundred, at least," he said to me outside.

"What will you do?"

"Pay for the thousand. If they can't keep track, that's their problem. I hate dealing with drunk people."

Loading and unloading a thousand or more pounds of chanterelles in a day is nothing special. When he's exhausted, Faber thinks about the skiing he'll do during his monthlong midwinter vacation and about spearfishing in the Bahamas. We drove north through a light drizzle. "Every extra hour this time of year," he sang aloud as a reminder, "means two hours on the slopes." He clapped his hands. *Shit yeah!*

It was well past midnight when Faber dropped me off at home. His day wasn't done. He still had to drive crosstown and unload two thousand pounds of mushrooms, after which he would drive to Sea-Tac Airport to airmail a few hundred pounds to clients in California, charging down the wet tarmac of a nearly empty I-5 in the dark, visualizing narrow chutes, dropouts, and a foot of fresh powder.

CHAPTER 9

Ingredients as Art

...

FORAGED AND FOUND EDIBLES epitomized a DIY approach to business. There wasn't much of a blueprint to begin with when it came to wild foods, and Faber was clearly bent on doing things his own way. This included conducting business on either side of the country. His operating philosophy in the New York expansion, as in everything else, was personal diligence. "Hard work is more important than intelligence," he told me. "If you're a hard worker, you'll succeed at whatever you do. Just because you're smart doesn't mean you'll succeed." It was never "business as usual" at Foraged and Found, and even though he loved the feel of cold hard cash, Faber loved the woods even more, meaning his frequent travels took him away from the day-to-day management. This was a quandary. Though loath to cede control, he was finally compelled to give Jonathan just enough leeway to make a few adjustments to their routine, the sort of changes that would be taken for granted anywhere else. Jonathan started a more organized filing system. He boosted weekly email sales by harvesting addresses. He researched other markets and cities. It was Faber, though, who kept the books and did most of the purchasing, and it didn't take a lot of horse sense to see that New York was a stress on the business.

A few weeks before Christmas, while visiting relatives on the East Coast, I caught up with Faber in Manhattan, with an aim to see what the country's biggest restaurant scene had in store for his products. "I don't know why you want to come here now," he said. "This is the most boring time of year. It's dead."

This wasn't entirely true. Though winter mushrooms such as black trumpets, hedgehogs, and yellowfeet were late this year and had yet to arrive on menus, the harvest of golden chanterelles was still in full swing on the Oregon coast. Faber had been driving from Seattle down to Eugene and Springfield a few times a week to buy from a family of Laotians and their network of pickers. For a month now, ever since the end of the porcini beach pick, chanterelles had been the only game in town, and Faber was sick of them. Usually when he made trips to New York, he liked to drum up new business with cold calls to an ever-changing list of restaurants, which he maintained by vigilant study of *The New York Times* dining section and *New York* magazine's capsule reviews. He brought along a stack of brochures and samples of various mushrooms that he handed out free of charge. "Like a crack dealer," he said. He tried to educate the chefs on the variety of wild mushrooms available, with their unique flavor profiles and textures. New York chefs, however, were harder to turn than their West Coast counterparts, for reasons that weren't entirely clear. And, anyway, this shtick wasn't possible with a basket of oversize chanterelles at the end of November, when the rains had performed their sodden duty. Everyone knew about chanties already, knew them well, and after a month of dealing almost exclusively in chanterelles, a certain fatigue had set in. Besides, the first of December was just a day away and restaurants would be drawing up new menus, menus that most likely would not include a signature food of fall.

No, this trip would be different. Though he didn't say as much, I gathered that this was a mission of sorts to buck up his sole employee at the East Coast outpost. Aaron had been sending SOS messages from their Brooklyn warehouse for weeks. New York wasn't performing as well as planned. He needed more product, more resources to get the job done. Break-even required a minimum of five hundred pounds of wild mushrooms a week; their best week to date was 496 pounds, and most weeks it was more like three or four hundred. Faber figured it would take a thousand pounds before long if the expansion was going to flourish.

The New York operation was causing problems back in Seattle as well. Just before leaving for the East Coast, I ran into Jonathan in the parking lot behind Poppy restaurant, where he was making a delivery. Jonathan suggested we get a beer sometime so he could fill me in. The slumping economy plus the expansion were taking a toll. His colleague Shane was now on reduced hours and had taken a second job as a bartender at the Four Seasons three or four nights a week, riding a bus home at one in the morning. Jonathan said that in the three years he'd worked for Faber he'd met or exceeded all of his performance goals, yet his paycheck had been frozen in place for a year. Faber's belt-tightening was expressing itself in other ways. "I'll buy a sheaf of printer paper at Walgreens," Jonathan said to me with frustration, "and a month later I'll hear about it from Jeremy when he's doing the books. I'll get a text that says, 'How come you didn't use that coupon to get thirty cents off?' Or maybe I'll be coming back from the coast with a load and I'll buy gas at the wrong gas station. 'Why didn't you go to the one next to the Indian casino and save fifteen cents a gallon?'" Jonathan said that Aaron still didn't have his own business cards, because Faber hadn't gotten in touch with his friend who printed discount cards. He thought there was what he called a "kink in the system," because they weren't fulfilling all the potential demand in Seattle either. "I love this business, I really do," he said, even if he wasn't sure what future he had at Foraged and Found.

AT 5:30 A.M., I MET FABER and Aaron outside a coffee shop on Canal Street, a block from the Lexington Avenue subway. Steam bil-

lowed from vents, and the damp asphalt gleamed under bright
streetlamps with an Edward Hopper loneliness. It was still dark, and
most of the vehicles on the streets were white delivery vans like Faber's, which presently idled in a loading zone, the small initials F.F.E.
glued on the side in violation of municipal law, which required a
more definitive stenciled identification. Aaron was at the wheel. Tall
and thin, he wore a voluminous black knit cap tilted back on his
head, Rasta-style. His demeanor was laid-back, reserved. (Later,
Faber would tell me he was worried about his friend: "He's got no
swagger about him. He used to have swagger. He dressed nice. I go to
New York for, like, five days and I come back with New York swagger. Yesterday at the farmers' market I was on it, dressed good. I
asked out two girls.")

I sat in the passenger seat while Faber, sounding hoarse, rode in
the back with empty baskets and a scale. He was in high spirits. They
had gone to the hockey game at Madison Square Garden that night
and slept only a few hours. "The Rangers suck, but there was a fight
within four seconds of the opening face-off," he said cheerfully. He
reminisced briefly about a Canadian woman he had known (or imagined, it was hard to tell) wearing nothing but a hockey jersey and a
Labatt's ball cap. We set off through the bumpy streets of lower Manhattan and hadn't gone a block before Faber's eyes alighted on something that displeased him. "How long has that check-engine light
been on, Aaron?"

"You knew about it. You said it didn't matter."

"That was last time. Has it been blinking?"

"It's fine. It doesn't mean anything."

"We need to take it in."

Aaron shrugged and steered toward the Holland Tunnel. We
drove under the Hudson River and resurfaced in New Jersey, a landscape of tired tenement buildings spreading out before us. Aaron
mentioned approvingly that the mayor of Newark had made a point
of living in one of these bleak apartments. Faber rolled his eyes. Big

deal. The mean streets of Newark were still filled with foreign pros-
titutes. They got shipped over at the age of sixteen. "Into the meat
grinder," Aaron agreed.

We exited at the Newark International Airport cargo terminal. At
the cargo desk, a clerk admitted that someone had misplaced the paperwork. Steely-eyed, with an Eastern European accent and a prim
bun that contrasted with her short skirt and sheer pantyhose, she
looked the part of a double agent, glancing behind her at all the other
clerks at their desks, then back at us, deflecting any blame with that
simple gesture. Faber had to smile. The incompetence at cargo termi-
nals was laughable. "Every time. They find a way to screw it up *every
time*." Now shaking her head in assent, the clerk went off to deal with
the problem, and Faber and Aaron watched her go, admiring both
her toughness and good looks. "Get with her and she'd have all your
money before dawn," Aaron whispered.

A moment later she came back, waving the paperwork, and we
followed a hard hat into the storage facility, where a guy driving a
forklift was already maneuvering two pallets of mushrooms toward
the bay. The door went up to reveal sunrise over Manhattan. Faber
and Aaron loaded three hundred pounds of Oregon chanterelles into
the back of a van that could hold more like two thousand pounds. Just
the same, Faber was visibly excited. They had product, unlike the day
before, when one of the employees back in Seattle had failed to ship
priority. Though a day late, the mushrooms looked good. Faber handled a few, moving them around in their baskets, mounding up the
nicest caps with their fine ridge-like gills exposed to the light. Aaron
looked relieved to see his boss smiling. Faber slid the last basket into
the back and closed the van doors. Manhattan glimmered in the distance, its skyscrapers tinged with gold. He stretched his arms. "I need
to make some money. Get me a little apartment in Williamsburg."

We drove back into the city. The traffic was light at this hour.
Gulls wheeled over the Hudson, and a black cormorant motored by
with single-minded purpose. "Be nice to keep a boat down there,"
Aaron said. "Take it out fishing." The mushroom purveyors talked

about the good qualities of stripers, their beauty and white flaky flesh. Faber said a lot of the oysters being sold as local were actually from the Pacific Northwest. "Willapa Bay, Puget Sound. They've got a shit-ton of oysters up in British Columbia. You're telling me this oyster is from Long Island? I don't think so." It's easy to tell an Atlantic, I argued. They're brinier, with a different look to the shell. Faber laughed at my naïveté. "You have no idea what goes on." I tried to stump him with mushroom varieties that he had yet to sell. "I. Know. Every. Single. Commercially. Viable. Species," he said slowly. Shrimp russulas? "They deliquesce right away." Pig's ears? "Wormier than shit. Mikuni sells wormy pig's ears for four or five dollars a pound. I don't want to sell wormy shit. It's not my M.O. Ever been to Eataly? They have dried porcini there for ridiculously cheap prices. They look like brown, shriveled-up scrotums." Eataly was Mario Batali's latest venture, a complex of shops and restaurants devoted to Italian culinary traditions.

"It's pretty cheesy," Faber decided.

Aaron agreed. "But it would be a banging account."

"I can understand why businesspeople go there for lunch, or for a drink. It's easy, all these options in one little place. Hot business-women everywhere."

"That's the damn truth."

Soon it was high commute, the hour of smart suits piling up at intersections. Faber, always on the road or in the woods, had gone a long time without a girlfriend, and it was becoming increasingly clear that, despite his patience and his entreaties, he wouldn't be getting back together with Allison. Now he saw eligible women wherever he looked: well-dressed put-together women who were ready to rule the world. This was New York, after all, not the coffeehouses of Seattle or the mountains of the Pacific Northwest. Fleece was nowhere in evidence, or—*thank God*—the deadly socks-and-Birkenstocks combo. He bemoaned the frumpiness of Northwest women. "Fucking in the tent is overrated. I've gotta move out of Seattle. I want a girl who looks good in a suit. I've got standards these days. I went out with this doctor. I was really excited about it. I was, like, yeah, a doctor."

"Your parents must have been so proud."

"She was a Jewish doctor!"

"Grandma's dreams finally coming true."

"She was the worst kisser on the planet, and she sweated a lot. I'm not a sweater." He did some quick arithmetic. "There are eight million people in New York, four million females. There are probably two million beautiful women in this city." All the while he weighed out deliveries in the back. At this point it was hard to even look at a chanterelle. "You *will* have black trumpets and yellowfeet next week," he said to Aaron. "I don't care if it's the only ones I have." He had a buyer named Soun who was setting up shop in Brookings, Oregon, right near the California border, where pickers camped in the national forest every winter. "He'll be set up to buy Thursday or Friday and I'll be paying big. Fuck those other buyers. They're only paying eight or nine bucks for trumpets down there. I told Soun, 'You're paying eleven.' I don't give a shit." Shipping was a problem, though. He could load only as many as the van would hold and drive them up to Portland or Seattle. "You used to be able to fly them out of Coos Bay. If there's no volume in Brookings, it sucks. When there's no volume, you have an empty truck. It all depends on how many Cambos are in camp."

Aaron, showing he'd left behind his Seattle roots, yanked the van into the right lane despite the best attempts of a cabbie to keep him pinned in the left. "Some hippie chick in the coffee shop was asking me the other day what I did. She said, 'Don't environmentalists get upset about what you guys are doing?' 'What do you think we're doing exactly?' She's like, 'Aren't they worried about you guys taking things out of the woods?' She's a vegan pastry chef. Her name's Sunshine."

Faber reminded Aaron that he lived in New York now. Vegans named Sunshine weren't the only action in town.

We turned off the West Side Highway onto Fourteenth Street.

Just the week before, the Occupy Wall Street protesters had been evicted from Zuccotti Park, near the southern tip of Manhattan. Splintered factions remained all over the city, picketing corporate headquarters and others deemed complicit in the financial meltdown of the Great Recession. We passed a collection of picketers near the Meatpacking District, a place of former squalor that had been transformed into a bustling center of nightlife and that was now undergoing another transformation, into a high-end district for boutique retailers and restaurants. New glass and steel gleamed in hard geometrical patterns. The picketers, in classic big-tent style, carried a disparate collection of signs airing grievances from corporate malfeasance to endless war. Faber yelled a few insults out his closed window. "Look at that guy with the banana. He's eating global capitalism. That banana came from five thousand miles away, funded by agribusiness." Aaron tightened up behind the wheel and hurried through an intersection, despite the motions of a traffic cop who might have been trying to stop him.

"Was that guy holding up his hand?" He looked in the rearview and stepped on the gas and we left the protesters behind, with their clatter of cymbals and high-pitched whistles. "I think he saw you back there," he said to Faber, who was unbelted in the rear of a delivery van with no backseat, flagrantly breaking the law. As Aaron hustled us away from the protest and police, his employer complained about the ridiculousness of the regulations. Not only did you have to take the seats out of these delivery vans, you had to cover up the bolt holes so no one would be tempted to put the seats back in. "Even if it's just a bunch of cardboard," Faber scoffed. New York was killing him.

Signs near the Manhattan Bridge warned of gridlock later in the day. President Obama was due in town to light the Christmas tree in Rockefeller Center. Faber and Aaron agreed that their early-morning pickup and deliveries had been a good call; the city would grind to a halt before lunch. Brooklyn promised an escape from all that. They had only a few more deliveries to make before returning to the warehouse.

As we drove through the relatively quiet streets of Brooklyn's Cobble Hill neighborhood, I found myself asking Faber the same question over and over, rephrasing it each time in hopes of getting a different answer: *How are you going to do a thousand pounds of wild mushrooms a week in New York City and fulfill demand in Seattle without loosening the reins and delegating more?* With each new version of the same question, I could see Faber get more and more irritated, until he had finally had enough. "This is a stupid conversation," he said, putting an end to any discussion of his ceding control.

Moments later, inside a rustic Brooklyn restaurant while his old friend and boss waited outside, Aaron turned to me. "See what I'm dealing with?"

Back in the van, a call came in on Faber's BlackBerry. It was Matt Dillon. Faber gave a series of yes and no answers, looking a little vexed, finally begging off without so much as confirming an order. "I don't know why he suddenly needs all this hand-holding," he said. Dillon was making plans for a new restaurant—a wood-oven pizza place of all things. This would be his third restaurant. Soon the word *empire* would get trotted out. I could see the calculations forming in Faber's head.

"He's showing deference to the New Yorker," I suggested.

"Matt knows good pizza. He's just bored or something. Needs reassurance."

"Maybe you should go in on it."

"He asked me. I thought about it." Faber started to jot down figures in a notebook. "I'm too busy."

In the Bushwick neighborhood they gave me a tour of the New York warehouse, a single room in a six-floor building that mostly housed hipsters, artists, and start-up companies. For $2,100 a month they got nine hundred square feet—and an apartment for Aaron. His mattress was in a corner, a milk-crate night table beside it with a paperback copy of *Henderson the Rain King* next to a tiny desk lamp. Across the room, a stainless-steel industrial table stood near a large double-door cooler and a dehydrator. "Mixing a foodstuff with living quarters?" said Faber. "That can't be legal." Aaron's shirts and jackets hung neatly from the exposed sprinkler line.

. . .

DURING MY STAY IN NEW YORK, I made a point of eating at restaurants that bought from Faber. At the Spotted Pig in the West Village, I ate a dish called bath chap—"Basically, pig face," said my server. The hockey puck of savory cheeks and jowls was deep-fried and served with strands of braised garlic mustard and sautéed chanterelles. It was meaty, fatty, crispy—and yet tempered by the slightly sweet fruitiness of chanterelle mushrooms. It was delicious. The pan-fried skate also came with big slices of sautéed chanterelles that brightened the plate. At Roberta's in Brooklyn, they used the chanterelles on wood-fired pizza. Momofuku Ssäm paired them with pickled quail eggs, bone marrow, and green juniper berries. The list went on, too many for me to visit: Bouley, Bucatino, Brooklyn Kitchen, the new restaurant at Lincoln Center. And yet many of these restaurants insisted on placing impossibly small orders, a couple of pounds here and there, the sort of orders that would never fly in Seattle, and Faber was forced to play along, at least for now, because he needed the business.

My last night I ate dinner at Faber's most high-profile client, Del Posto, with my sister and brother. Opened in 2005 by Mario Batali, Joe Bastianich, and Lidia Bastianich, and helmed by chef Mark Ladner since its inception, Del Posto is one of a handful of New York restaurants to earn four stars from *The New York Times,* in 2010 from restaurant critic Sam Sifton, who reported that "brilliant technique renders incredible ingredients as art." In a more reserved review for the same paper, critic Frank Bruni said Del Posto challenges patrons "to accept Italian cuisine presented with fastidious rituals and opulent trappings usually reserved for French fare." *Opulence* is a fair description. You enter through heavy doors to broad marble stairs that take you to the lounge and restaurant. High ceilings, dark wood, polished brass. A tuxedoed piano player coaxes tasteful notes from his grand, not too loudly.

After sitting down, I buttonholed our server. Could we share plates? "Yes, sir." Were the white Alba truffles perfectly ripe? "Yes, sir." Could we see one? "Yes, sir." Are the porcini fresh? "Yes, sir."

"Do you usually get these sorts of questions?" interjected my brother.

"No, sir."

The orecchiette came with a lamb-neck ragu, sage bread crumbs, and carrot puree. Fusilli was tossed with lobster. A type of pasta known as agnolotti—"little envelopes with something good inside," remarked the waiter—was served with a filling of Grana Padano and Tyrolean speck and a broth punched up by black truffles. And those were just the first courses, or *primi*. For the *secondi* I ate a perfectly cooked veal chop, sliced into medallions and garnished with caramelized chanterelles. The meal was rich, surprising, abounding in flavors—and much, much more money than any of us was accustomed to spending. In a word, decadent.

When we emerged back into the night through the double doors, seeing our breath in the air, I didn't think about the bundled-up protesters picketing nearby or the mushroom hunters on the other side of the country, who, at that hour, were just starting to ponder their own dinners after a day in the woods. I didn't think about much of anything. I was full, slightly drunk from the wine, lighter in the wallet, and wondering whether to take the subway or just let it ride and get a cab. The meal had been a once-in-a-great-while luxury, and I was determined to enjoy it without regret.

. . .

A WEEK LATER I joined Faber for an Oregon buying mission, to see where the mushrooms I had eaten in New York City originated. He was in a good mood. The night before he'd gone on a date to Linda's Tavern with a Cherokee Indian woman. Her résumé was perfect:

"super toned" downtown hipster rock climber with a high-paying professional job. "Listen to this. She said to me, I swear to God, 'If we have sex—and I'm not saying that will happen—but if we do, you need to know I'm bi.'" He couldn't wait for their next date. He was playing it cool. Not even a good-night kiss. Not yet. "I'm actually sort of a prude and play hard to get."

We drove south on I-5. It was a chilly morning and the side window of his Astro van kept flapping in the wind, both its latches broken off, siphoning a feeble current of warm air straight out. The cold had no effect on him. Faber hated this drive, called it the most boring stretch of road in the Pacific Northwest. He passed the time taking orders on his BlackBerry and quizzing me on my meal at Del Posto. Was it good? Worth the bill? After a lengthy discussion, during which I broke down the entire meal plate by plate at his request, I couldn't help but admit that it was one of the five best meals I'd ever eaten. Did this prove my lack of worldliness? The shortcomings of my palate?

Faber thought about it for a moment. "The five best meals I've eaten in my life," he said finally, "I've cooked by myself in the woods."

By this time of year the chanterelle and porcini pick is finished in Washington, with knowledgeable local pickers eking out a living with hedgehogs and yellowfeet. Most of the action turns to areas south of Eugene, where the tree composition begins to change from mostly Douglas fir to mixed deciduous and coniferous woodlands. Pure stands of Douglas fir in places such as Cottage Grove still continue to produce golden chanterelles, but these mushrooms can be large and unattractive this late in the season (those farther north, by contrast, have turned to mush after hard frosts and drenching rains). Despite their unsightliness, end-of-the-season chanterelles command some of the highest prices of the season. In some years there can be a decent matsutake pick around Cave Junction as well and farther to the south in the oak woodlands of northern California. The rest of the pick is focused on the beginning of the winter mushroom season— the yellowfeet, hedgehogs, and black trumpets that fruit in mixed coastal forests. Pickers converge on areas such as Roseburg and Brookings throughout December, with some moving south into California in the New Year.

Doug was taking time off from mushroom picking. He had killed a deer and a young bull elk that would keep him in meat for months. I asked Faber whether Doug would join us later that winter. "He doesn't want to work," he said flatly. "I've worked double, triple, what he has this year. He's happy with a government check." Faber thought the coast had taken its toll on Doug. "If I lived out there, I wouldn't care what it took to get out. I'd work two hundred hours a week. Do you see yoga studios on the coast? Gyms? Do you see anyone biking? All you see are fat whales driving two blocks to the convenience store to buy Doritos." Like many self-made entrepreneurs, Faber had a bootstrap mentality that expressed itself in a crazy-quilt pattern of beliefs. His politics were almost impossible to predict, and though his own financial well-being was predicated on consumers buying what was largely perceived as a luxury food item, he was adamantly anti-consumerist and considered the shopping curse the downfall of Western civilization. "I haven't been to Target in three years. Last time I went there, I bought twenty pairs of underwear. What do people need all the time? Especially if you don't do anything. You have a sedate lifestyle, you don't ever leave your house or your car. How many pairs of shoes do you need? To the average person, walking around Discovery Park is bizarre. You go to Target and there's five million people there. On a beautiful sunny day like yesterday, I bet you Target was packed. Groceries are the only thing you need on a regular basis. You need to eat. Skis are my single vice . . . and clothing a little bit. I only dress nice because women like it."

On the other side of the equation was poverty. "People are poor for a reason," he said. "There are exceptions. I don't think we're a very hardworking society. If you take most people in poverty, I'd say half of them don't want to work. That's a safe bet. Half don't want to work and that's why they're poor. There's nothing you can do. People with no drive are going to be poor. Don't help them out. Welfare is a big money flush. A healthy thirty-five-year-old male does *not* need help. I don't care if he's not that bright. If he has two hands and is capable of using them, he doesn't need help. If he comes back from the war and has mental problems or lost an arm—yeah, he needs help. A healthy thirty-five-year-old woman does *not* need help. A woman has three kids and her husband leaves—she needs help. But most of the money is going to these morons who don't want to work. You've got to change your lifestyle a little bit. Your latte every morning and your *Dancing with the Stars* every night? Sorry, no. It's an ugly world."

The period between the fall and winter seasons is a slow time for Faber, and he finds himself in the unenviable position of moving farther abroad to keep business humming, often making three trips a week down to the Eugene area to buy chanterelles as well as early-winter mushrooms if they're available. It's a ten-hour round-trip from Seattle to Eugene, before adding on the hours it takes to sort, weigh, and load mushrooms into the van and pay his pickers. Because the pickers don't return from the woods until dark, it doesn't make sense for him to leave Seattle much before noon, meaning he won't arrive back home until at least midnight. On this day he wanted to get going before eleven because he had to stop in Kelso, Washington, on the banks of the Cowlitz River near its confluence with the Columbia, to pick up a load from one of his regular pickers.

"Everyone loves Elifonso," Faber said. "He's got like thirteen kids." Right now Elifonso was living across from the Burlington Northern train tracks in a one-story ranch house with a woman named Summer, whom he used to babysit. He had a large vegetable garden in the back and—a curiosity to the neighbors, who liked to take pictures of it in high summer—a tiny grove of banana trees, which he had recently wrapped in plastic against the cold in hopes they might bear their first fruit next year. Most of his family was in the United States now, though he still had some left in Mexico. A brother had been killed in the drug wars just two years earlier. Faber said Elifonso was a good matsutake picker, that he picked a ton of yellowfeet until his patch got logged. He was a good morel picker too. "He always outpicks me," Faber admitted. This was the first time I'd ever heard him say another picker could rival him.

We parked in a driveway cluttered with stuff that looked like it was destined for the dump. Elifonso had his baskets waiting outside. He was short and stocky and looked a little bit like a cowboy, in his brown Dickies jacket with its fake wool lining and a Ford Mustang cap pulled low and shading his eyes. He had picked more than two hundred pounds of chanterelles in the past three days, along with half baskets of yellowfeet and hedgehogs. This time of year he did most of his picking a couple of hours south, near Cottage Grove. Somewhat impertinently, I asked Elifonso if he was in the States legally. "Sometimes," he laughed. Actually, he had married a Texas woman once and now he was shacked up with Summer, with whom he had three children. He said the union of "brown and white" wasn't easy and left it at that. Still, he didn't plan to leave the country (for instance, to pick morels in Canada), for fear of not being allowed back. He showed me pictures of his boys. The thirteen-year-old posed alongside a bull elk he had killed the week before.

Elifonso hunted mostly morels in the spring and then chanterelles and lobsters in the fall. He traveled south in the winter to pick black trumpets. Like most pickers, he hadn't set out to be a full-time mushroom hunter, yet somehow in the past decade the mushrooms had found him. He hunted game, too, and tended his garden. Mostly, he said, he was a stay-at-home dad while his girlfriend worked as a nurse, though the lure of the mushroom trail kept him in the woods for long stretches. An Amtrak passenger train whistled by. Faber badgered Elifonso about the dirty appearance of the belly-button hedgehogs, which were bound for a charity event in New York, free of charge. "Dirty like a Mexican . . ." Elifonso sang on cue, a skillful bit of comic relief that mollified the buyer. He turned to me with a word of warning. Recently the picker had learned a lesson about sharing patches, even among family. "You never take nobody," he lectured me. "I take my brother and just the other day I find him in my patch. With a new woman!"

In Springfield, next door to Eugene, we made our final stop, at Van Pon Ratthanaphosy's home, where twelve hundred pounds of chanterelles were stacked in the garage, awaiting transport back to Seattle. Pon was mostly a mushroom picker and broker these days, though before his house burned down—and his tools with it—he had also worked as a mechanic. Pon came to the United States in 1987 from a Thai refugee camp, where he had lived since 1979, another casualty of the war in Laos. His father was killed in the conflict and his mother died of illness. Pon, too, had fought in the war ("They take you at fifteen," he said) and later he worked as a policeman, during which time he illegally helped many Laotian families escape to Thailand. When he fled Southeast Asia in his early twenties, he left his first child behind, a son whom he hadn't seen in more than two decades. He had five other children in the States.

We found Pon in his garage, stacking baskets filled with mushrooms. He had just returned from the woods after picking thirteen baskets of golden chanterelles—about a hundred fifty pounds' worth—which his wife, Daeng, was sorting and cleaning in the kitchen. "How's life?" Faber greeted him genially. Pon, in camouflage pants and sweatshirt, didn't answer. Faber apologized for a check-cashing issue that had occurred earlier in the week. Daeng had tried to cash a check for $1,900 that Faber had written against his business account at Chase Bank. The bank demanded four pieces of ID. She rummaged through her car's glove box, coming up with only a proof-of-insurance card in addition to her driver's license and credit card. Daeng called Faber in tears. Faber called Chase and told the teller to pay out the check, that he had written it. The teller balked. Faber, unbidden, started yelling out the answers to various hypothetical questions—his mother's maiden name, his place of birth, favorite color, first pet's name—before finally demanding an audience with the manager, who also refused to pay out the check. This incensed him, though it wasn't anything he hadn't seen before. He screamed at the man to stop being such a racist pig and pay the money. In the end, the bank paid up.

Standard-issue bigotry, Faber said to me. "Change the Asian name on the check to Joe Blow and it gets paid, no questions asked." He tried to lighten the mood. "Three-fifty a pound, right, Pon?"

For a second Pon fell for it, then he caught himself. Faber was paying five dollars, the same price paid to Elifonso. In town, the other buyers were paying four-fifty. The extra fifty cents was worth nearly six hundred dollars to Pon, though Faber wasn't exactly thrilled by the quality he was seeing. The chanterelles were huge, many of them larger than a head of Bibb lettuce, and dirty. Pon explained that this was the work of six pickers, some of whom weren't as knowledgeable about the tenets of clean picking. "And they don't have air compressor," he said.

Faber wasn't surprised. "It's Springfield," he grumbled. "I hate Oregon this time of year. No one picks clean around here, because they don't have to." This was virtually the last large-scale commercial pick anywhere in the world for fall chanterelles, and the buyers were going to need their product no matter what. Faber was also distressed by his shortage of baskets. He was seriously considering going in on a deal with another buyer to purchase an entire container of baskets from Taiwan—forty thousand dollars' worth. "My baskets are disappearing like crazy. I don't know where they're going. I leave for ten minutes and all my baskets are gone. We shipped some to Soun in Brookings. New York has a bunch. If I give ten to Elifonso, I get maybe half back. And Doug! If I get one in ten back I'm lucky."

It was cold in Pon's garage. For a week the entire Pacific Northwest had been experiencing record-high barometric pressure. The winter mushrooms needed moisture. Faber dumped the full baskets into cardboard boxes that held twenty-five pounds apiece. This was a new development due to the basket shortage, and he was careful to explain the situation to Pon. "Each holds twenty-five pounds, *capiche*?" Pon nodded, unconvinced. He watched the digital readout on the scale before going back to his sorting. Pon's daughter came out and briefly spoke Lao with her father. "Thank you," she said finally in English, closing her fingers around his car keys. "Bye-bye."

"What, I don't get a bye-bye? What am I, chopped liver?" The daughter tilted her head at Faber and left.

"Seven kids?"

Pon corrected him: six, but one was still in Laos. "I never see him. The police come and knock on my door."

"Only for you, right?"

"Only me." The police were onto him. That was when Pon had made his getaway, leaving his former life behind. I could see him thinking about his first son. He stood resolute, looking away, and then his iPhone rang. "They give me two phones for free," he said proudly. Pon was always buying and selling something. He had multiple phones and lines. Unlike the bank, his cell-phone provider understood how to keep a good customer happy. When Pon got off the phone, I asked him if he ate chanterelles. Barbecued, he said, and wrapped in rice paper with rice and fish sauce. Just the flowers. All the buttons got sold.

Meanwhile, Faber pulled out the largest and dirtiest of the water-logged chanterelles and tossed them aside to be dried. Some looked like baseball mitts and could easily hold a hardball in their pockets. Inexperienced recreational pickers and members of mycological societies often get excited about such humongous finds and circulate pictures for their fellow members to ogle. "Mushroom dorks," Faber called them. He pulled out another giant. "Welcome to Eugene, where anything yellow ends up in the bucket. If the pickers were decent down here, it would be okay, but they're just complete slobs. It's pathetic. There are seven buyers in Springfield–Eugene, and they won't even blink. They take everything. For example"—he held up one of the prettier chanterelles—"not a bad mushroom, but they don't even try to clean it up." Pine needles decorated its cap, and a dirt smudge ran down the stem. "This is the end, the lowest common denominator of the year. The recreationals would brag about this shit."

Faber didn't think much of mycological societies. He told a story about how he had volunteered to do a cooking demo at a mushroom show one year. Right in the middle of his presentation, the president of the club called him out for something he had said about matsutake picking, how the raking wasn't as bad as it was made out to be. "I can't remember what I said exactly. First of all, raking doesn't really happen that much, and, second, it doesn't have a long-term effect. If anything is a major problem, it's logging and hunters. Hunters cause tons of damage in the woods, just by sheer numbers and all the garbage they leave around. I'm there doing a cooking demo; everyone loved me. I had a room full of people; everyone's taking notes. I was by far the most entertaining person they'd ever had cook. I'm telling everyone where to pick mushrooms and how to cook them. They loved me. And here comes this guy calling me out. Has he ever been to Randle? Seen raking? He doesn't even go outside."

IT WAS NEARLY TEN P.M. when we pulled into the Acropolis Club in East Portland for something to eat. Seattle was still three hours away. Faber assured me I would love this place. You could buy a sixteen-ounce T-bone steak for about ten bucks and dispatch it with a beautiful naked woman dancing on your table. "They're not skanky," he said. "More like hipster girls. It's Portland. You'll see. Just avoid the salad bar." Faber paid our nominal cover charge at the door. Inside, a smattering of mostly older men sat at the bar and a few tables. Two younger guys in backward ball caps tipped a dancer bent over crabwise beside their plates of fried shrimp. She lifted one stilettoed heel high in the air, then the other. Faber was encouraged by the sight of a familiar face coming down the stairs behind the bar. Actually, it was the accent more than anything else that he recognized. "She's Polish or Russian or something," he said. "She's the best." We ordered a round of beers.

"Will you tell Martha about this place?" he asked me.

"Sure," I said. "Why not?"

"I guess so. But it must be different when you're married."

"She's not threatened by strippers at a steakhouse."

"A good egg," he said before taking a long sip of his beer. "Never let go of the good ones."

The waitress came back and suggested sautéed mushrooms for our steaks. Faber and I looked at each other momentarily before declining in unison, and then we settled in for a brief respite before getting back on the road.

CHAPTER 10

Sex, Love, and Truffles

. . .

I SUPPOSE THE DOGS TIPPED ME OFF that this wouldn't be a typical food festival. They were everywhere: in the hotel lobby, riding the elevators, practicing in a park across the street. Terriers, dachshunds, poodles, retrievers, even a Chihuahua. Their handlers guided them proudly, these truffle hounds that could sniff out an aromatic tuber hiding underground at fifty paces. The most serious among the handlers led Lagotto Romagnolos, an Italian hunting breed with tight curly hair. The Lagotto had originally been bred for retrieving prey from lakes and was now considered as the top truffle dog. While the canines came from ancient lineages, their owners were mostly a new breed: American truffle hunters. Even more fascinating were the truffle growers. To be a New World truffle farmer was to have a job description that barely existed a decade ago. The Oregon Truffle Festival, held in late January, was a chance for these pioneers, dogs and all, to compare notes.

Truffles are hypogeous ectomycorrhizal fungi—that is, fungi that live their entire lives underground and form symbiotic relationships with certain species of plants, mostly trees. This we know. In some quarters, truffles are also believed to be powerful aphrodisiacs. How else do you explain the intense passions generated by these otherwise unattractive lumps of what one mycologist at the conference called squirrel food? Scientists think that truffles evolved their potent aromas as a reproductive strategy: Small rodents such as voles and flying squirrels dig up and eat the truffles and, in turn, spread the reproductive spores in their droppings. For centuries, human beings, most famously those along the Mediterranean in Italy and southern France, have imitated the rodents to find their own truffles, sometimes using pigs to root out the tuberous delicacies. Roman senators enjoyed truffles, as did Renaissance nobles. French lawyer and gourmand Jean Anthelme Brillat-Savarin enthused over truffles in his *Physiology of Taste,* published two months before his death in 1825. Regarding their amorous properties, he concluded: "The truffle is not a positive aphrodisiac, but it can upon occasion make women tenderer and men more apt to love." Even today truffles are associated with romance and cuisine of the hautest sort.

There are hundreds of species of truffles, with only a handful worth foraging by humans. The most coveted and expensive of all— indeed, one of the single most expensive foods on the planet—is the Italian white truffle, *Tuber magnatum;* it is sometimes called the Alba truffle, for the Piedmont village in northern Italy where white truffles are auctioned before export worldwide. The starting price in the United States is about three thousand dollars per pound, though one weighing nearly three pounds sold at a charity auction for three hundred thirty thousand in 2010. The black Périgord truffle, *Tuber melanosporum,* of southwestern France is the second-most-valuable species of truffle and the preferred variety for cultivation. It usually sells for about half the price of the Italian white, or even less outside France. After that, the truffle rankings become more muddled. There's a summer truffle, sometimes called the Burgundy truffle (*Tuber aestivum*) and a widely maligned Chinese truffle (*Tuber indicum*), which is frequently unmasked as an imposter among shipments of more-valuable varieties. Other edible species include winter truffles (*Tuber brumale*) and desert truffles (*Terfezia sp.*). Somewhere in the middle of the hierarchy are North American truffles, the new kids on the block, principally the winter Oregon white truffle (*Tuber oregonense*), the spring Oregon white truffle (*Tuber gibbosum*), and the Oregon black truffle (*Leucangium carthusianum*). The names are slightly misleading; all three species of "Oregon truffle" can be found from northern California to southern British Columbia, in low-elevation Douglas fir forests west of the Cascade Mountains.

For centuries, truffles were harvested only in the wild. More recently, truffle farmers have learned how to inoculate tree seedlings with the fungi's spores before planting. Orchards now account for the majority of the world's annual truffle harvest. This comes at a time when the wild harvest, due to climate change, pollution, changes in forest management, and shifting patterns of human settlement, is on a precipitous decline. Edible European truffles prefer human company. They especially like to colonize woodlots that have been planted in old agricultural fields. This proclivity, along with their value in the marketplace, has made them an obvious candidate for cultivation. North American truffles, on the other hand, are strictly wild, though some landowners have discovered that they can encourage natural truffle production by planting Douglas fir Christmas-tree farms or timber plots.

I AM AN EAVESDROPPER. I have always had a tendency to listen when people with unusual occupations talk shop. The language of work can be a portal into otherwise hidden realms. When I first moved to Seattle, I would sometimes frequent the sort of taverns on the edge of town where commercial fishermen might gather and exchange carefully guarded accounts of the latest catch. I've always been drawn to stockbroker patter, even though I'm hopeless when it comes to matters of finance and rarely understand anything involving equities or taxes or dividends. The conversations of carpenters—with their bevels, load-bearing walls, miter cuts, and joists—have always fascinated me. As a corollary, there have been numerous times in my working life when I threw myself into a job that I knew almost nothing about, a job that frequently demanded skills that I had yet to possess. It seemed important that I learn how to tarpaper a roof or saddle a horse or polyurethane a freshly sanded wood floor without leaving a seam. But starting a truffle orchard from scratch?

On the first day of the Oregon Truffle Festival, I caught up with a bunch of truffle growers just as the day's speaker series was winding down. Most of them, exhausted from hours of lectures and reeling from the realization of the work yet ahead, were flooding out of the conference room (and probably heading straight to the hotel bar), while a few tarried around the hallway to commiserate. I sidled up to listen. A sociable blond-haired woman was riffling through a binder of photocopies and passing out pictures of her orchard. She didn't exactly look like a farmer. Business casual in herringbone slacks, lavender blouse, and a sapphire necklace that complemented her eyes, Margaret flashed a nervous smile at two men from Idaho who seemed to know what they were talking about. She still had a sense of humor, she said, even if she didn't know entirely what she was doing. Certainly predator control hadn't figured into her initial calculations. "I can handle a gun," she insisted. "You should see me out there riding around with my rifle." She was a Kentucky gal, after all, who knew the difference between bolt action and lever action, not to mention Booker's and Basil Hayden's, as I would discover later. She'd even pulled the trigger on an angry snapping turtle—an irrigation hazard, by her reckoning.

"You killed it?"

"Absolutely. It's a varmint."

"I've got a badger," the first Idaho man said, a white-haired dog curled up quietly at his feet. "Mean son of a you-know-what."

"Yeah, but he'll take care of the gophers," said the second Idahoan, a giant of a man in a plaid work shirt, who might have passed for a ranch hand or an alligator wrestler. Just a few minutes earlier they had all listened to the travails of a young Oregonian who had spent a year doing battle with an army of gophers. By year's end he had personally trapped and dispatched two hundred of the ruinous rodents. "I had a pack of coyotes doing the gopher work for me," the second Idahoan went on in a gravelly voice. "Until the wolves arrived."

By now a small crowd had gathered around Margaret to hear her story. She pulled out color copies of her two ponds, the used irrigation gun she was planning to buy, even the turtle. One of the ponds was substantial. "Man, let's go ice-skating," someone said over her shoulder.

"Keeping up the electric fence will be one of the highest maintenance costs," she explained.

"I used to raise hogs. You can't keep the deer out."

"You said you had a son. Ship him back there and put him to work."

"Putting college kids to work mending fence and digging weeds?" said a bystander, with a knowing shake of his head. "Really successful—good plan."

"Boy, I tell you what," Margaret said, "they thought I was doing drugs. I told my son—he's in the fencing club at school—I said, 'That's great. . . .' And he looked at me like, 'Mom, that is not the kind of fencing we do.'"

"Is this a hobby or a business?"

Margaret burst into more uncomfortable laughter, those ice-blue eyes flashing again with a humbled combination of fret and hunger.

"We hope it's a business," said the second Idahoan, voicing both their desires.

"Right now it's a diversion!"

"Yeah, diverting money from here to there."

Margaret figured she was a hundred grand into the project, and the trees weren't even in the ground. The Idahoans nodded. That seemed about right for the size of her orchard, twenty-four acres. Bringing the soil pH up with an application of lime had cost ten thousand alone, and she needed to do a second application. She had excavated two ponds and now needed to settle on an irrigation strategy.

"I've got a laborer who's ready to put in the first two or three years," she said. All this for a crop that might not produce for ten or twelve years. She'd probably be a grandmother by then. And it was entirely within the realm of possibility that the orchard might not produce at all. Of the hundred or so people in this conference room at the Hilton Eugene, maybe one or two had actually produced a truffle. These lucky ones were like oracles. The rest were waiting. Some had planted a year or two ago, while others, like Margaret, would be planting in the next several months. Just a few owned older orchards, aged five or six years. The growers in this category lived on the cusp. Any year now they might find an odoriferous truffle secreted at the base of a tree tended to like one's own child. Any year now—or not. It was, as they all said, a labor of love.

. . .

I WENT TO THE OREGON TRUFFLE FESTIVAL to eat, of course, but I also went to meet the truffle people, these passionate, determined, sometimes loony people who all had one thing in common: a taste for a wild food that no one has ever been able to fully or properly describe, a taste that has driven some to the edge, or beyond the edge, of madness. I myself had never experienced this sort of loss of control. As much as I loved fungi, I still thought of myself as a relatively sane person. Martha, on the other hand, thought it was all a big scam. She assumed I was going to eat myself silly, and she couldn't believe that I had actually been comped a ticket. All my travels in the overlapping orbits of the mushroom hunters, she said, had just been an excuse to wander around in the woods by day and put away obscene quantities of rich food and wine at night. The truffle festival merely took it all to another level. "What about Doug?" I said. I had never seen Doug eat a single mushroom. She threw up her hands. Every time I went anywhere with Doug, I came home with bags upon bags of mushrooms, which filled up the refrigerator, blocked the front stoop, and successfully transformed our once mushroom-loving children into official mycophobes. "Not mushrooms again!" they would holler at dinner.

"What if we got a truffle dog?" I said to Martha before driving down to Eugene. She perked up and said we'd discuss it when I got home.

The dogs, it was true, brought a friskiness to the event that was hard not to enjoy, and inviting them along to the show had been a stroke of genius on the part of the festival founders, a married couple with a love of truffles and a pedigree of festival management. Charles Lefevre, a boyish-looking scientist built like a wrestler, was a mycologist in addition to being a physicist with experience running a nuclear reactor. Years earlier, his work in forest ecology had led to a side project in truffle propagation and ultimately to a business called New World Truffieres, which was responsible for inoculating the truffle trees used in orchards all over North America. His wife, Leslie Scott, with flowing hair and cat-like eyes, had for the previous seventeen years managed the nationally renowned Oregon Country Fair, one of the great hippie hoedowns, before starting the considerably more upscale truffle festival with her husband. From the beginning it's been a celebration of truffles across the board, not just a booster group for Oregon's native varieties. In fact, Lefevre's cultivar of choice is the Périgord black, since it lends itself most easily to domestication. Inviting the dogs added a touch of frivolity—and it also drove home a point. Lefevre would like to see the end of indiscriminate raking in hopes of finding a truffle. The dogs limit the damage their human handlers can inflict on the forest understory with rakes and garden tools.

Zandra and James, a couple from Oregon City, didn't have a truffle dog yet. They were waiting. Right now they just owned the trees—a six-year-old grove on their twenty-acre plot, about two acres split fifty–fifty between oak and hazelnut, the preferred hosts, and they still couldn't believe they were part of that recently trendy category, the urban farmer. "We don't know shit about the soil," Zandra exclaimed dumbfoundedly, "or what's going on underground, all those spiders and mites and microbes." Her husband, James, a strapping guy with a fireman's chin, said they'd planted because his mother-in-law had read an article in *The Wall Street Journal*. "My stepmother," Zandra corrected. And it wasn't *her* fault. Anyway, this was terra incognita for everyone in America. They had no idea, for instance, what to do about potential pests. Zandra: "You can't exactly Google 'What's that crazy-looking bug at the base of my truffle tree.'" James said that the year before, in a bid to broaden their knowledge, they had gone to the annual truffle festival at San Giovanni d'Asso, in Tuscany, where they stayed at a thirteenth-century villa and ate a meal across the street that is permanently seared in their memories: pecorino heated and then smothered in shaved white Italian truffles and drizzled with honey. They sighed in unison. "We wrote it off on our taxes," Zandra said. They were in the business, after all.

There was that nervous smile again. Margaret listened to the couple's stories of the truffle life with a combination of worry and wonder as we got hustled to the first dinner event by shuttle bus. Earlier that day, the conference had served hot cocoa spiked with black truffles. "I couldn't get enough," she admitted. "I could have crawled into the cup." She needed to get those trees in the ground and get going. The fact that her entire high-flying career prior to this new chapter had been spent in corporate risk management was irrelevant, never mind the irony. She still knew how to read the writing on the wall. As an executive at Washington Mutual, she'd started digging into the books two years before the mortgage meltdown and, after alerting her superiors, quickly jumped ship for Microsoft. Before that, she'd worked at GE and other Fortune 500 companies. Now the truffle was her boss.

"What will you do while you wait?" someone asked her.

"Get a day job!" she nearly cried. "Or go back to consulting." Something, anything, to keep the money flowing—into the ground.

That night at dinner, the epicures joined the growers and dog trainers. This was the third leg of the stool: those helplessly in love with truffles yet sane enough to limit their expenditure to paying a knowledgeable chef for the experience. In North America, however, paying top dollar didn't guarantee transcendence; even otherwise competent chefs didn't necessarily understand how to prepare truffles correctly. Festival culinary director Charles Ruff, another Oregon Country Fair alum, told me, with barely concealed frustration—he was a professional, after all—that he had personally overseen the preparation of one dish, a truffle-infused fillet of sea bass served with a truffle-tomato-butter sauce. He bound the fillets together into cheesecloth sacks before sealing them for twenty-four hours with quantities of Oregon white truffles so the fatty tissue in the fish could absorb the gases emitted by the fungi. Another dish hadn't gone so well. His simple truffle butter meant for the fresh rolls served at table had received at the last minute, unbeknownst to him, a crust of ground-up truffles from one of the guest chefs. Ruff, a tall man on the move with a wispy beard and a thespian's erect carriage, lamented this unsupervised decision. The crust had been executed the day before, ensuring that it would be nearly impotent because of off-gassing by the time it was served. This was just one of the difficulties. Ruff said the festival was a harder feat to pull off than the country fair, because the famously iconoclastic locals didn't embrace it, finding it too pricey to attend and maybe a bit snooty. And the truffle enthusiasts weren't typical either, certainly nothing like the country fairgoers. "Not your docile pot-smoking hippies," he said.

After a round of truffle appetizers, the chef came out of the kitchen to tell his 150 seated guests that ten organic beef tenderloins from Painted Hills Ranch had been infused with the complex gaseous molecules of sixty pounds of Oregon white truffles. The crowd gasped. "I could go to sleep in a vat like that," Margaret sighed. "Better yet, draw me a bath with sixty pounds of truffles and I'll take a tub all night. Light some candles."

This was the sentiment that connected everyone in attendance, a vertiginous swoon in the face of these innocuous-looking tubers. But when it came to describing the flavor of truffles, most demurred.

"What do *you* think they taste like?" asked Gary, a would-be grower from Tennessee, with theatrically arched eyebrows.

I thought about the question for a moment. My tablemates were dressed in blue blazers and evening gowns. They wore nice jewelry and timepieces. "I would have to say that truffles taste like . . ." I started, paused, and finally answered, ". . . a well-used honeymoon suite." There. I'd said it.

"Sometimes you hear *barnyard*," Gary said. "Or *funky*," added another. Funky was a good description. Its derivation is from the word *funk*, a slang expression popularized by African Americans in the Jazz Age. The earliest record, from 1784, is a reference to old, moldy cheese, and the word continued to be used to describe an earthy sort of smelliness until it came to mean, in black argot, the lingering odor of sweaty sex and, from there, the carnally thumping beats of jazz and blues. Funky was just right, and for obvious reasons this hard-to-pin-down yet alluring flavor has been sought after for centuries.

The Greek philosopher Theophrastus (c. 370–286 B.C.), a pupil of Aristotle, is credited with some of the first writings on truffles, in which he described their growth as a cause of both autumn rain and thunder. Plutarch endorsed this theory, adding that soil warmth was also a factor. Lightning was believed to be yet another cause. Truffles fascinated Pliny the Elder (A.D. 23–79); he called them "calluses of the soil." In the sixteenth century, some naturalists thought the semen of rutting deer produced truffles. The oldest truffle recipes, from Imperial Rome, appear in *Apicius*. François Pierre de La Varenne, acknowledged as the godfather of modern French cooking, included more than sixty truffle recipes in *Le cuisinier françois* (1651), including the famous pairing of truffles and foie gras. French novelist George Sand (1804–1876) wrote that truffles are the "black magic apple of love." Black magic seems about right. There isn't much middle ground. Either truffles make little impression or they cast a spell.

Today's chefs are just as enthralled with the lumpy tubers. Paul Bocuse served a truffle soup to French president Valéry Giscard d'Estaing at the Palais de l'Elysée in 1975; it continues to grace the tables of his Lyon restaurant as *soupe aux truffes noires* V.G.E. After California banned foie gras in 2012, Thomas Keller replaced the French Laundry's pricey add-on with Australian winter black truffles. Multi-course, truffle-themed meals of the sort concocted by Daniel Boulud for his Miami restaurant db Bistro Moderne, featuring Alba white truffles ("in celebration of white truffle season" for a cool $325 per person), are now a winter standard across the country. Chefs like Matt Dillon try to spread the truffle love at a less presidential price, using the homegrown variety to jazz up otherwise unembellished pastas, risottos, and potatoes.

In laid-back Eugene, the truffle-festival organizers requisitioned gobs of the things from all over the world, passing around overflowing bowls of both European and American truffles for the assembled to paw over and inhale. Over the course of the weekend, I ate some extraordinary meals. The starter at the Willamette Valley Vineyards luncheon was a slab of Pinot Noir–braised pork belly with white-truffle jam, dried cherries, and frisée with raspberry–black truffle vinaigrette. This was perhaps my favorite dish of all, a perfectly balanced blend of flavors and textures that was expertly knitted together by the truffle jam. Friday night's dinner at the Emerald Valley Resort, hosted by food writer Molly O'Neill, included a soup of parsnip and celery root served with shaved white truffles and pomegranate arils that lingered in the memory. Saturday night's Grand Truffle Dinner plated five courses for three hundred people with the help of a half dozen guest chefs from around the country. An intense aroma of truffles hovered in the ballroom like a heavy fog and drifted out into the hotel lobby, permeating the hallways and alcoves. Its source: three hundred plates lined up elegantly on three long prep tables, each plate decorated with a square of black-truffle panna cotta topped with Dungeness-crab salad and Parisian pears. The cooks, tattooed and pierced like a crew of treasure-seeking pirates, sailed up and down the line, brandishing their mandolines like sabers, shaving paper-thin rounds of black truffle over the plates in quick staccato bursts. A second course of creamy red and white quinoa served risotto-style with a Riesling-poached egg, shaved coppa, wild winter herbs, lemon-thyme emulsion, and shaved white truffles had me reeling. *Uncle,* I wanted to cry, putting my face in the dish to suck in its delights, but it was too late: A meat course of white-truffle-roasted beef short ribs with white-truffle potato puree, salsify, and beet jus was already before me. We joked and moaned at our table, strangers formerly and now intimate in the throes of truffle ecstasy. And dessert? The truffle is one type of fungus that can't be constrained merely to the savory. A chorus of white-truffle raspberry mousse, white-truffle-infused tapioca, and crunchy white-truffle brittle strewn across the top had my dining companions nearly reduced to tears.

All these dishes relied on native Oregon truffles. No less an authority than James Beard declared them a delicacy that demanded equal footing with the more renowned Old World varieties. *Seriously?* I could see Jeremy Faber shooting me one of his withering looks. Though he trafficked in the native varieties, Faber was having none of this. "Have you tried European truffles?" he asked me once with undisguised skepticism. "A really good truffle from Washington or Oregon *maybe* competes with a European truffle on a bad day." Others begged to differ. At lunch, over a soup of chicken and truffle dumplings, I sat with one of the festival speakers, Dr. Shannon Berch from Vancouver, a founding member of the Truffle Association of British Columbia, along with an Australian truffle importer named Winnie who had come all the way to Oregon just to sample the local varieties and decide whether or not to bring them into Sydney.

"How did you like last night's dinner?" Berch asked her.

"I was quite impressed," Winnie admitted. "They were better than I expected."

"They're very bright, aren't they? And powerful. They're too much for some people, but I like them."

"Pleasantly surprised," Winnie agreed. "Now I need to try the Oregon black."

"But you did. This morning's cocoa."

"That's right," said Winnie's partner, David. "Fruity."

"They go well with dessert," Berch agreed.

With a slightly guilty look, Winnie admitted that she was also in the process of cultivating her own truffles, an industry that's taken off in Australia in recent years.

"Really? How many acres is your plantation?"

She turned red in the face. "*Plantation* isn't the right word."

"Oh, well. How many trees?"

Now she was nearly doubled over. "Five, actually."

"In pots," David added.

"A mini-plantation!"

"It's our home in Sydney. Waterfront property doesn't lend itself to a big operation."

"Any hope that a mini-plantation can pay for waterfront property taxes?"

"Don't think so."

"And the truffles?"

"None yet."

Comparing European truffles to American truffles is like comparing Cabernet to Pinot Noir, I heard again and again. One isn't better than the other; they're different. This was the analogy of choice. Truffles and wine grapes frequently grow in the same habitat, so it made sense to hear familiar oenological metaphors. Proponents of homegrown American truffles like to point out that the French idea of *terroir*—the importance of regional influences in soil and climate—is equally important to Oregon black and white truffles. Ground zero was right here in the Willamette Valley.

. . .

THE SOUND MUST HAVE been deafening. A million cracks in the ice coalescing into the fissure that would breach a thousand-year-old glacial plug in great Lake Missoula, an impoundment larger than Lake Erie and Lake Ontario combined. When the 2,500-foot ice dam blew, as it did countless times through the last Ice Age, a torrent of water rushed out of Montana—386 million cubic feet per second, sixty times the flow of the Amazon—and took the scablands of eastern Washington and Idaho's panhandle with it, hijacking billions of pounds of volcanic sediment across the high windblown desert before scouring out the Columbia River Gorge with the abrasive finesse of a Brillo pad. Near the present town of Kalama, a few miles downstream of Portland, a chance logjam of giant old-growth timbers met the fury with a wooden determination that backed up the Willamette River for a hundred miles to the future site of the University of Oregon in Eugene. This scenario repeated itself maybe forty times in the next two thousand years, with Ice Age floods originating from Lake Missoula and depositing huge quantities of silt and sediment—a half-mile-deep crust of soil in some parts—to create the fabled "land of milk and honey" that attracted westward-bound pioneers throughout the mid-1800s.

Like the ancient floods, a half million settlers poured into the Willamette Valley between 1843 and 1870, a force that could not be turned back or slowed. It is said that the first white settlers who saw the valley via what would soon be called the Oregon Trail mistook it for the Pacific Ocean. A sea of blue greeted them in the distance—dense fields of blue camas wildflowers, which grew in the rich alluvial floodplains of the Willamette. The local Indians, who dug up the potato-like camas tubers and pounded them into meal, saw the stark reality of their situation and capitulated in 1855, signing a treaty negotiated by Oregon legislator General Joel Palmer, ceding their land and relocating to a reservation. Palmer, who had founded the Willamette Valley community of Dayton in 1850, built his home near the mouth of the Yamhill River. In a transaction emblematic of the ongoing shaping and reshaping of the West, Palmer's historic residence was purchased in 1997 by a mushroom-crazed Polish American from Pennsylvania and transformed into a fungi-themed destination restaurant.

Jack Czarnecki went west to indulge his twin passions of wine and fungi. Nowhere in the country could satisfy such desires more than the Willamette Valley. These days, the Indians' fields of blue camas are mostly gone and the region is known instead for its vineyards, Pinot Noir in particular, which thrives in the fog-shrouded hills— and increasingly for another tuber-like food: the white and black truffles that grow among the roots of Douglas fir forests covering the untilled slopes of those same hills. The truffles, determined to repro- duce, emit a complex cocktail of olfactory molecules evolved over millennia to entice the order *Rodentia*—and perhaps the species *Homo sapiens*. The newcomer was smitten. He made it his mission to cook the local fungi in imaginative ways and pair his dishes with the best local wines.

Czarnecki comes from a long line of Polish mushroom hunters. His great-grandfather immigrated to America and the family settled in the manufacturing town of Reading, Pennsylvania, where they opened a workingman's restaurant and boardinghouse called Joe's. From the beginning the place was famous for its mushroom dishes, especially the soup, which was made from wild mushrooms gathered in the nearby pine forests. Eventually Czarnecki's father took over the establishment, and Czarnecki himself followed suit by attending Cornell's hotel and restaurant school. But he dropped out in the early 1970s, met Heidi, and moved to California. The couple drifted around a bit and finally settled at UC Davis, then a hotbed for the American wine revolutionaries who would put France's knickers in a twist. At Davis he met Maynard Amerine, a professor of oenology who in 1959 had developed a twenty-point scorecard for evaluating wine. Czar- necki would later adapt this method for evaluating food, especially sauces. He married Heidi and the couple moved back to Pennsylva- nia to work at the restaurant. In 1986 he published *Joe's Book of Mush- room Cookery* and went on the *Regis and Kathie Lee* TV show to promote it. His next book, *A Cook's Book of Mushrooms,* came out in 1995, and this time he went on the QVC channel, selling four thou- sand copies in ten minutes. The book went on to win a James Beard Award. His father died the same year. Two years later, Czarnecki bought the Joel Palmer House and moved his family west.

The first time I went truffling with Jack, he taught me the basics. The second time, he had a surprise for me. We would be hunting Oregon black truffles with a dog. This was a change for Czarnecki, who was generally known as a guy who refused the aid of a canine smeller. He liked to say that he knew all his patches well enough that he didn't need a dog to tell him when the truffles were ripe—and he had ways of ripening them at home if necessary. But this view would be met with mounting skepticism as the New World trufflers learned more about the ancient skill. Europeans had once used pigs, and now they relied on dogs. The problem with the pig is that she likes truffles too (and it usually *is* a *she* because the truffle contains a compound that smells similar to a hormone found in male pigs, or boars). The pig can locate a truffle three feet underground, and after much snuffling and snorfling, the animal will often have to be restrained so she can't eat the truffle. A dog, on the other hand, has no interest in the truffle as food. The dog is after the treat that will follow the successful discovery of a truffle. These days, in most quarters, the idea of hunting truffles without a dog—which has a nose one hundred thousand times stronger than a human's, according to the American Kennel Club—is inconceivable or, worse, criminal. On this subject Czarnecki has become an outlier, even if he's still one of the founding fathers of the native-truffle trade. He's been hunting truffles so long and with such success that he doesn't need any help.

Cooper, the dog, belonged to a woman who had gotten in touch with Czarnecki earlier that year because she wanted to find truffles. They pulled up in an old Volvo. A compact woman layered in rain gear hopped out and immediately went to the hatchback. Her dog leaped from the car and sprinted around Czarnecki's driveway. Cooper was a mutt, though a handsome one. Half black Lab, quarter Bernese mountain dog, and quarter German shepherd, he looked and acted like a black Lab puppy, even though he was four years old. Like Labs everywhere, he seemed possessed of boundless, slobbering energy that would, by day's end, give in to a collapsed torpor.

I rode with Cooper and his master, Anne, to the truffle patch. The day was heavy with rain clouds that covered every inch of sky, making it look like a dark vault. Every now and then a thin ray of sunshine somehow penetrated, as if through a keyhole, to burnish the golden rows of Pinot Noir. A drive through the Willamette, though scenic, is not quite like a drive through France's Burgundy country. From Portland, it's slow going on Highway 99 south through the usual sprawl of fast-food franchises until you reach Newberg. On the outskirts of town, you pass the Someplace Else Tavern and the land begins to reveal itself: the Dundee Hills to the west, the rich agricultural floodplain of the Willamette to the east. Down on the flatlands, little farmhouses sit out in the open like ducks on a pond. Larger homes hide in the hills. Though the town of McMinnville is charming enough, particularly on a December night with its Christmas display, most of the Willamette Valley can't be called quaint in the Old World sense. It's scrappier, rough around the edges, with enough of the original extractive character to still be blue collar.

Our drive took us through major wine-producing parts of the valley and closer to the Coast Range, where the land became increasingly ornery with geologic upheaval. Anne was familiar with the terrain and looked forward to testing her dog's new skills. She said she had trained Cooper by hiding little cotton balls dowsed with truffle oil around the house. Unlike most truffle hounds, Cooper didn't get a treat; he got ball time. "That's the Lab talking," she said.

We followed a dirt road from the agricultural fields up into privately owned hills where the Douglas firs grew, almost all of it second-growth forest that was planted as a timber crop. This was the property of a farmer who worked the fields below and kept the timber plantation as an investment. Rain fell off and on, and the road was slippery. Finally we pulled over, and Cooper led us eagerly into the woods. We carried garden cultivators, those long-handled rakes with four or five curved metal tines for turning over the earth. Czarnecki explained that he had an agreement with the farmer, who had recently thinned the trees on one side of the road. We fanned out on the other side, where there hadn't been any cutting in at least ten years. Most of the trees looked to be about thirty years old and close to typical harvest age. Old rotten stumps between the trees decayed into the moss. Clumps of sword fern painted the ground with splashes of green.

Anne pulled a black film canister from her pocket, inside of which was truffle-scented cotton. She held it out for Cooper. "Get the truffle!" she commanded. "Go find the truffle!" Cooper barked and whined, and then he got down to business. He took off through the woods, his snout to the ground, coursing back and forth until he came to a fir tree and started to circle. You could hear his nose in action as he brought the scent in and circulated it around with a snort. "Get the truffle, Cooper!" The dog paused, then scratched at the ground several feet away from the trunk of the tree. "Good boy!" Anne pulled a red ball from her pocket and tossed it down the slope. Cooper bounded off happily and came back with the ball. Anne threw it again.

Meanwhile, Czarnecki worked the ground where Cooper had scratched. He peeled back the top layer of duff like a carpet, careful not to damage any tree roots. A moment later he had a round, walnut-sized object in his hand. It looked like a small lump of coal. "Oregon black truffle," he said in his gruff voice, as if it were the most ordinary thing in the world. I got the sense he didn't want to surrender full credit to the dog. "Now let's find his brother." Another scratch at the dirt and he had a second truffle of about the same size. "Where there's one black truffle, there's usually a second," he explained.

We all took turns inhaling the aroma. It smelled like overripe pineapple with musty undertones. It was a tantalizing yet peculiar scent that didn't immediately telegraph what might happen when it was added to warm foods and allowed to fully blossom. Truffle lovers from all over flocked to Czarnecki's Willamette Valley restaurant to have this experience. For his part, Czarnecki planned to spend more time in the truffle patch than in the kitchen in the future; he was in the process of handing over the restaurant to his son, not that regulars would notice much of a change. Sometimes a meal at the Joel Palmer House starts with a candy cap martini—a glass of cold vodka infused with the unlikely aroma of a dried candy cap mushroom, a cinnamon-colored *Lactarius* with a strong scent of maple syrup. This might be followed by a hearty New England–style matsutake chowder and then a beef bourguignon with porcini sauce. It's the truffle dishes, however, that encourage many patrons to make the long drive from Portland or points farther away. But Czarnecki had other plans for the truffles we would find today: While a few might find their way onto the restaurant menu, most were destined to be processed into the product that would be the culmination of his life's work, an all-natural Oregon truffle oil.

. . .

MY FIRST TASTES OF TRUFFLE were almost certainly fraudulent. The grammar should have been a giveaway: truffled porcini and chèvre ravioli; tenderloin with truffled mashed potatoes; truffled quail. Note the absence of the noun. My dishes had been *truffled,* which is to say they had been goosed. I was duped by a simulacrum of the pricey fungus—imported truffle oil.

According to chef and restaurateur Daniel Patterson, who wrote a much-talked-about exposé admitting his own former addiction to the stuff, chefs all over the country were (and are) relying on chemical fabrications such as the rather unpalatable-sounding 2,4-dithiapentane to pack a simulated wallop of truffle essence. The truffle oils are big, brassy come-ons, all molecules and no real truffle, a test-tube aroma, likely concocted in a New Jersey flavor factory. When I read this, I immediately went down to my local gourmet grocer and started pulling bottles off the shelf, reading the labels. *Cagey* might be the best description for these artful dodges, or, if we're not pulling punches, *deceitful.* Listed ingredients included *essence* of truffle or truffle *flavor*. Some bottles advertised a few crumbled pieces of desiccated truffle in the bottom for verisimilitude, even though such leavings had long since given up the ghost of their scents. These bottles of imported truffle oil carried the imprimatur of French and Italian flag insignias along with upwardly mobile price tags. Yet there was no getting around the ingredients. The semantic sleight of hand suggested a method rather than an ingredient—a method that relied on pumping up the oil with 2,4-dithiapentane.

The taste of most truffle oils is reminiscent of certain species of truffles, true enough, if a bit too bright and chemical-laden. It's full-bodied and garlicky, round in a general way, even fulsome. It's a bottle blonde with heavy pancake makeup doing her best Marilyn Monroe impression while trying to woo you. In some cases, chefs will stingily use actual truffles along with a drizzle of the faux oil to make the experience go further—in effect, contaminating the good stuff with the imposter, the way a drug dealer cuts his dope with an innocuous household product. Invasion of the Truffle Snatchers.

Czarnecki says his oil is the real deal. This might make him the only producer of truffle oil who doesn't rely on fakery; it's hard to know. His process is a tightly guarded secret, and it turns on the fat-soluble nature of the truffles. When oils, butters, and other fatty products are exposed to ripe truffles, they absorb the aromatic gases. That's the easy part. The hard part is producing an oil that will hold such unstable molecules. Czarnecki figures a small two-ounce bottle of his "100 percent natural" Oregon truffle oil (retailing for about twenty dollars) will last a few months in the refrigerator, gradually losing its punch over time.

While truffle oil has its place in the kitchen, the overall effect is like taking a magnifying glass to a great work of art. Colors brighten, details pop. Yet there is also the risk of oversaturation, a loss of perspective, and ultimately confusion. The oil simply cannot compete with a perfectly ripe truffle used with finesse. The trick is finding ripe truffles.

In North America, where the local truffle market is young and fly-by-night, it's not uncommon to see truffles for sale that are either immature and odorless or over-the-hill and reeking of decomposition. Recently a friend of mine showed me some Oregon black truffles she had picked up at Whole Foods. They were packaged in Styrofoam and plastic—the first bad sign—and you could press a thumb right through the fungus. "Take a whiff," I said. She held one up, inhaled its aroma, and quickly turned away in disgust. My friend was outraged. She had paid an exorbitant price. I suggested she take them back and have the manager do a smell test. The only way to improve the truffle culture here was through education. Most of the mushroom pickers, Doug included, didn't mess with truffles, because the learning curve was so steep. A few specialized in it, but even they didn't bring in the good stuff on a regular basis. Jack Czarnecki was one of the few who had invested a lifetime in the pursuit of quality truffles.

Unlike a *trifolau* of Italy—a professional truffle hunter who is revered, and well compensated, for his centuries-old craft and is likely to be accompanied by a dog with equally honed skills—the average American commercial truffle hunter is not held to the highest of standards, and this mediocrity is shared right up the line. I've sat down to dinner at one of the nicest restaurants on the West Coast and watched the owner go table to table showing off a Périgord truffle the size of a tennis ball. The girth was impressive yet it possessed no magic—it was completely tasteless, probably because it had been dug up too early. *That's a crime,* Jeremy Faber would say. He has little tolerance for the lack of sophistication in the American truffle market. The pickers rake the truffles too soon; the merchants buy the unripe truffles anyway, out of ignorance; and trusting customers allow themselves to be fooled because they've never actually tasted a good truffle and don't know any better. The result is a collective shrug.

Years ago, while visiting San Francisco, I met a friend at her local North Beach trattoria for dinner, where we ate a simple dish of fettuccine Alfredo, among other plates. This was an uncomplicated, Platonic reunion between old friends—even if other restaurant patrons might have thought otherwise. We ordered plenty of Piedmontese red wine to go with our meal, a bottle of Barolo and another of Barbaresco, their vintages long since forgotten in the long, hazy evening of eating, drinking, and catching up that followed. The waiter appeared tableside with a small scale in one hand and a gumball-sized

Alba white truffle in the other. My friend waved him on to continue. After shaving the truffle over our steaming plates of pasta, the waiter weighed the remaining truffle and calculated the not insignificant extra charge. This was my first Italian truffle, and it did not disappoint. The Alba white is a species that growers haven't figured out how to cultivate, which only enhances its mystique. It's wild and subject to chaotic swings in the marketplace. To experience a ripe truffle of this caliber is to be overwhelmed by associations of indulgence, decadence, even naughtiness. Enveloping you like a cloud is the aroma and taste of a night of lovemaking—an earthy musk, a taste of sweetness and of sweat, a complexity that would make a wine snob blush: hints of coffee, chocolate, garlic, peat, overripe fruit.

Perhaps we let slip a few too many secrets that night as we dined, laughed a bit too indelicately in between bites and sips. When you eat your first good truffle, you will say, "Ahhhh." Then you'll say, "Ohhhh," and the four-top next to you will be staring.

CHAPTER 11

Winter Pick

· · ·

IN FEBRUARY 2006, A TRIO OF CZECHS from Washington State and British Columbia was arrested near Santa Barbara, California, on a variety of charges including suspicion of trespass, conspiracy, and grand larceny. Their Eastern European ancestry was reported in every press account, as if this explained it. A fifty-two-year-old Seattle man named Josef Vychodil had thirty pounds of chanterelles in his station wagon, with a "street value" of about three hundred, noted the *Los Angeles Times,* using lingo usually reserved for illicit drugs and other contraband. Later, the police raided a Lompoc motel room, arresting Lucas Vrana, twenty-nine, also of Seattle, and Maxim Mikhailytchev, twenty-four, of Vancouver, Canada, and confiscating "several thousand dollars' worth" of mushrooms. In California, any theft of produce with a value greater than one hundred dollars is a felony. The poachers had been picking chanterelles on local ranchlands—apparently for years, according to the ranchers—and had eluded capture until their boldness got the best of them. The authorities seemed surprised by the "high tech" nature of the crimes, pointing out that the poachers kept detailed journals with notes on the various patches and GPS coordinates. In court, the mushroom pickers plea-bargained for a reduced charge of misdemeanor trespassing and got a sentence of two hundred days in the clink—more than six months' jail time for the nonviolent crime of picking mushrooms on private property. Never mind the crimes of drugs, sex, and violence that happened every day in California; officials in Santa Barbara County sent a message to would-be fungal scofflaws that mushroom picking would not be tolerated.

. . .

MY PHONE RANG THE DAY after New Year's. "This is Howard Womback, District Ten, Western U.S. I'm calling from the Internal Revenue Service. We have a few questions for you, sir—"

"Hey, Doug."

"Had you going there for a second, didn't I?"

"What's up?"

"Winter pick. Where have you been? Trumpets are blowing."

Doug was talking about the black trumpet (*Craterellus cornucopioides*), a mushroom variously known as horn of plenty, black chanterelle, or, to the French, *trompette de la mort*. This last name is misleading. The black trumpet is hardly an object of fear; in fact, this relative of chanterelles is among my favorites of all edible fungi. Blacks, as they're called in the trade, are funnel-shaped, thin-fleshed mushrooms that usually fruit in clusters. Their coloration varies from gray to brown to nearly jet-black. Not as robust as golden chanterelles, they make up for a modest physique with an intense flavor that suggests the distillation of their yellow relatives, a flavor that combines the woodsy essence of their home with a more refined and civilized taste of orchard stone fruit. When I eat black trumpets, I'm reminded of the peeling red bark of madrone trees, dead leaves crackling underfoot, loose-limbed rhododendrons overhead, and downhill scrambles to the pools of remote salmon streams. Like all fungi in the chanterelle family, the black trumpet is an ectomycorrhizal mushroom, and in the Pacific Northwest it's most commonly found in mixed woodlands of tanoak, redwood, and Douglas fir, especially in the coastal forests of northern California. Faber calls the most impressive bunches "California clusters."

Just the mention of them was enough to make me giddy. Like porcini, blacks require skill to find. Do your homework, spend years scouting difficult terrain, learn the quirks of seasonal weather, train your eyes to detect their cryptic form—and then, just maybe, you'll be rewarded with this exalted wild edible. Hit the jackpot and you'll find a hillside bursting with the mushrooms, tightly packed coveys of little black funnels rising above the leaf litter like organ pipes. Mushroom hunters call this a blackout. Back home, in the kitchen, the winning streak continues. Blacks are among the easiest of wild mushrooms to cook, and their presence on the plate enhances virtually anything. A few sautéed blacks crisscrossed on a trio of pan-seared diver scallops, for instance, is all that's needed to give those sweet jewels of the sea a grounded terrestrial counterpoint, a surf-and-turf combo without the need for big slabs of beef and lobster. Not that long ago many diners would find the pairing of shellfish and mushrooms capricious at best. Now the combo has come into vogue, perhaps because chefs have discovered that the result is an unparalleled umami bomb.

These days black trumpets can be found on winter menus around the country—in cafés, bistros, pizzerias, and neighborhood joints of nearly every stripe—where they might figure into a simple crostini, a hearty soup, or a fancier dish of game meat and winter vegetables. Pastas, risottos, spaetzles, and other carb-heavy dishes remain the primary delivery vehicles, where the ink-black mushroom can draw the eye with its sharp color contrast and surprise the palate with its bold taste. Even by themselves, sautéed in a little butter, they're a treat. Sometimes I like to mound them on a small steak—a really good cut of aged tenderloin, because otherwise the mushrooms outshine the meat. They don't require elaborate preparations. I've seen black trumpets deployed on top of a homey mac and cheese, dotting a warm crab salad, and, in my own kitchen, garnishing a cream of chanterelle soup, in which they manage, in just a few bites, to out-chanterelle the chanties. The other thing about blacks is that they dry well, and reconstituted they nearly approach the al dente quality of a freshly picked specimen, meaning that black trumpets can be used throughout the year in the same preparation, unlike, say, dried porcini, which demand an altogether different sort of cuisine from their fresh brethren.

Mushroom hunters can pick black trumpets in scattered localities across much of North America. For commercial quantities, the action is centered on a relatively narrow band of territory that stretches from the coastal mountains of southwestern Oregon down to the Bay Area of California. Practically speaking, the best way to fill my own larder was to drive down to the North Coast. So I set aside a week to join Doug. By this point, the distance didn't seem unnatural. My travels were taking me farther and farther abroad, and California merely represented the lower latitudes of the mushroom trail. When people think of the Golden State, they think of a sun-besotted San Diego or L.A., of orange groves and surfing, or perhaps the Mediterranean climate of the San Francisco Bay. Northern California, on the other hand, is the redoubt of hippies and back-to-the-landers, a place of geodesic domes and communal living or, on the other side of the spectrum, of booby-trapped survivalist compounds. Even Californians don't give much thought to the unpeopled far-northern reaches of their state, a region that shares more in common with the coastal communities of Oregon and Washington. This is the dark haunt of loggers, pot growers, hermits, committed social resisters, and perhaps an elusive ape-like humanoid. It's a place famously cut off from the rest of civilization. A hard place to get to.

My wife and kids stood in the doorway, seeing me off. It was raining. I had my camping gear in an overhead luggage rack and my bucket in the back. Northern Cal would be a nice place to visit this time of year, I had said optimistically before getting in the car, though I would quickly discover the futility of planning far in advance on the mushroom trail.

———

THE LURE OF CALIFORNIA is integral to an American narrative. Where did I go, jobless, with my old rusted Mustang, as soon as I finished school? Cross-country to California, of course. It's a journey that's been repeated with generational regularity since that fateful day of January 24, 1848, when a laborer named James Marshall discovered traces of a shiny metal at Sutter's Mill in the Sierra Nevada foothills. So began a decade-long process of human migration and settlement—the first of many to come—that would transform the landscape and even the nation: the California Gold Rush. In the space of just a few years, San Francisco grew from an outpost to a boomtown, and in 1850 the state of California was officially born as part of the Compromise of 1850, making it a "free state." More strikes would follow, many of them northwest of the Sierra Nevada in an ancient mountain range known as the Klamaths. Straddling Oregon and California, the range is a place of unusual plate tectonics and rich biodiversity.

The forty-niners were a diverse lot, to be sure, with varying motivations, though it's likely that most came from modest means and desired a better life. Like farmland in the Willamette Valley, timber in the coastal old-growth forests, salmon in the rivers, and so many other gifts of nature, the gold fields offered a tangible opportunity for those willing to work hard in abject conditions. Where else could a man be in charge of his own destiny, without a boss to determine his future? And for those lacking in the social niceties—those loners, misfits, and daydreamers who didn't fit in—a rugged life on the frontier offered more than just a chance at material wealth. This was a home. It's also safe to say that most of the forty-niners, regardless of work ethic, didn't strike it rich.

More than a century later, prospectors of a very different sort now visit this same territory comprising northwestern California and southwestern Oregon, where the Klamath Mountains meet the coast. Mushroom hunters, shunted by winter rain and cold farther north, have learned that the region's temperate climate in the lower elevations allows for picking during the darkest months of the year, meaning they can conceivably pursue their avocation year-round. They call it simply "winter pick."

By Thanksgiving the harvest is mostly finished in British Columbia and Washington, except in a few microclimates. Snow dusts the mountains (at higher elevations the ski areas might be open), and killing frosts cruise the lower elevations like battlefield undertakers. Circuit pickers move down to Oregon, to places like Coos Bay and Cave Junction, and then into the Brookings area near the border, and finally into northern California, if they must, quietly picking Del Norte, Humboldt, and Mendocino counties, avoiding local pickers while sneaking among state parks and private timberlands that are mostly closed to mushroom harvest. Porcini beach pickers try to elude ticket-writing park wardens in places such as Salt Point State Park and Point Reyes National Seashore. The risks multiply as the picker moves south; a barrier of state regulations complicates the work and, in a perverse twist, closes much of the woods to recreational mushroom hunting as well, thus stymieing the development of future land stewards and environmentalists with a "museum under glass" approach to the natural world. David Arora has written about this in a paper he subtitled "The Tragedy of No Commons," concluding that "an entire generation has grown up foraging furtively in the shadows, skulkers and creepers playing hide-and-seek with authorities."

Bay Area forager Connie Green, who includes the French Laundry among her clients, calls the California regulatory apparatus "a shotgun kind of approach," and says the rules differ significantly by region. Traditional commercial picking areas such as Mount Shasta and Fort Bragg are governed by extensive regulations, while other areas can be, as she puts it, "wide open." Like so many in the nontimber forest-products business, she questions the motives of those in positions of power. "In California you can get into a lot of trouble with Forest Service officials enforcing imaginary rules," she says. And there are some places, such as Santa Barbara, that she avoids entirely.

Locals there go ballistic if they spot a mushroom basket in a pickup: *These god-awful people are going to steal your babies and kill your chickens.*

The tree composition changes as it moves south, from the spruce-hemlock-fir forests of Washington and northern Oregon to the thin redwood belt that dominates the fog-shrouded North Coast. Pacific madrone, tanoak, chinquapin, rhododendron, and other broadleaf evergreens grow among the second-growth redwoods, making a Mendocino coastal woods an entirely different affair from an Olympic rain forest. The mushrooms are different too. In contrast to the chanterelles of Douglas fir so ubiquitous to the north, a type of oak-loving chanterelle thrives here. Affectionately known as a mud hen or mud puppy, for its habit of growing up among the oak-leaf litter and humus that is common in its range, this chanterelle (*Cantharellus californicus*) is the largest in the world and lands on the menus of San Francisco restaurants well into March. Hedgehogs continue to fruit through much of the winter, as do yellowfoot chanterelles. The species most identified with winter pick, however, is the black trumpet. Restaurants from coast to coast prominently feature black trumpets in their specials, a wild foraged food at a time when most local plants and fungi lie dormant. On the East Coast, the black trumpet is a summer and fall mushroom, with unpredictable swings in abundance; on the West Coast it's a predictably common mushroom in winter among the dense tanoak forests of the coastal mountains.

Most of the commercial winter pick is focused on the Siskiyou National Forest just east of Brookings, Oregon. Up the Chetco River is a labyrinth of logging roads that leads into the headwaters of the Kalmiopsis Wilderness. Pickers spread across the national forest with widely dispersed camps. The Chetco marks the far northern boundary of the Redwood Empire, with winter mushrooms that thrive in the mixed second-growth forest. Each night, after coming out of the woods, the picker must drive into the ticky-tacky seaside resort town of Brookings to sell his day's labor. Restaurants and cafés with names like the Hungry Clam and the Salty Dog line the harbor. Flag lines

snap in the wind against faded white poles. One time, on my way
south to meet Doug for one of our winter-pick outings, I found five
buyers in town and one working out of the increasingly popular shipping container in the Riverside Market's parking lot, a couple of miles
upriver. Four of the town buyers operated out of the same motel, the
Blue Coast Inn & Suites, setting up their grading tables and scales
right outside their rooms—a convenient way to make sure no one
was paying too much, or much at all, for mushrooms. After a long
day of combing the hills, pickers pulled into the motel parking lot and
received a meager one dollar per pound for yellowfeet, two for hedgehogs, three for black trumpets, and four for the dregs of the golden
chanterelle crop (at the Riverside Market, closer to the patch, the
prices were even lower). At such prices, it hardly seemed worthwhile
to pick at all, but as one man who was unloading several baskets of
yellowfeet at the Riverside Market for seventy-five cents a pound told
me, "When you ain't got a job, that's a lot of money."

Joyce, a small elderly woman in a pink cardigan, was the manager
at the Blue Coast. She was new, though it was her understanding that
the Laotian and Cambodian buyers had been setting up shop here for
years. "They are just the most wonderful people," she said. "I haven't
had a whit of trouble out of any of them." Besides, the Blue Coast was
the only establishment in town with weekly rates, she explained, carefully writing down the prices on a business card for me. "If someone
wants a weekly rate, the other hotels will send them our way. That's
how it is around here." A room was $250 for the week.

Doug, however, doesn't pick Brookings. "Too many Asians," he
says without animus. He prefers to take his chances down in California, where most of the out-of-state immigrants won't venture. In
many ways, the influx of Southeast Asians into the mushroom trade
mirrors the original Gold Rush, when waves of Chinese immigrants,
mostly from Guangdong Province, flocked to the California and Oregon gold fields. The white Europeans, recent immigrants themselves, viewed the "coolies" as an invading horde. This fear dated
back to the first wave of Asian immigration, when the immigrants

accepted lower wages to work in mines, railroads, and textiles. They endured arson, lynching, and routine purges that culminated in the Chinese Exclusion Act, first passed in 1882. "I almost bit into that," Doug once admitted to me, "and then I started wising up to it when I saw the ugliness and how they were being treated." The history of western American expansion can be written as one long series of tribal squabbles within the human family. Doug came to this realization while picking morels in Montana. "I'm sitting around the camp-fire in Libby, and I swear there was two thousand Asians parked there. We were talking about our options and where we could go. Someone said, 'There's so many fucking Asians. They just keep coming and coming, and there's no stopping 'em. You can't fight 'em. They've won.' And I said, 'I guess you know how them Indians felt about two hundred years ago.'" Doug got visibly angry as he told me this. "Manifest destiny," he growled, clearing his throat and spitting in the dirt. "You can shove that right up your ass."

The Asians stick to the Brookings area because just a few miles to the south, across the border in California, the mushroom picker finds a very different legal landscape. The national-forest boundary dives inland—too far inland and too high in elevation for a long winter of mushrooms. Unlike Washington and Oregon, California offers very little public access along the coast that is open to mushroom pickers, and the small parcels that are public are mostly state parks in the red-woods that restrict such activities, not that old-growth redwood is on any picker's wish list. Doug calls the ancient redwoods "bad medi-cine," a phrase he picked up from a Klamath Indian. Little in the way of commercial mushrooms grows under the big trees. The profitable lands are up in the cutover hills—mostly private timberlands and ranches—and California law encourages the landowners to keep the public out. Logging tracts are posted and carefully monitored, in part because of liability. If a picker should trespass and, say, break his leg, by California law he could sue. Large private landowners have re-sponded by limiting public access. To pick winter mushrooms com-mercially in California is almost certainly to flout the law.

. . .

THE KLAMATH-NORTH COAST BIOREGION is a lonely, unpopu-
lated place that has long puzzled scientists trying to fit it into a larger
scheme. The writer and naturalist David Rains Wallace calls its confusing jumble of rivers, forested slopes, and secluded meadows the
"Klamath knot," named after the region's dominant geographical
feature, the Klamath Mountains. Unlike the relatively young Cascades to the east, the Klamaths are a very old range, more like the
Appalachians. To roam here is to step way back in time. In some parts
you are literally seeing the ocean floor, now thrust up on top of the
continental plate by an uncommon process called obduction; looking
at the red-tinted ultramafic rocks is like looking at the bones of the
Pacific. Over the years, these foreboding peaks and ridges have ex-
acted a human toll of travelers, especially in winter. One waylaid RV
driver got caught in a storm and tried, unsuccessfully, to last out the
winter on his meager supplies, far up an unplowed logging road. In
another, highly publicized case, a family from Silicon Valley took a
wrong turn in an attempt to cross the mountains from I-5 to the coast
and ended up in a snowbank, burning all four tires to stay warm, before the father set out on foot for help. He ultimately succumbed to
the elements several miles away in the rugged country of a Rogue
River tributary, just as rescuers were zeroing in on his missing family.
Like the fabled Lost World of Sir Arthur Conan Doyle, this is a land
of hidden jungles and relict species. The region boasts some of the
highest diversity of coniferous trees in the world. Species found nowhere else continue to hang on in the Pleistocene-carved valleys, even
as they disappear everywhere else throughout their former range;
these species are typified by the once-widespread redwoods as well as
by other very localized species such as weeping spruce and Siskiyou
cypress. Another relict species thought by some to inhabit the area is
Bigfoot.

Amid the maze of geology and conifer diversity, there are bounti-
ful mushroom patches. Late matsutake harvests occur in the moun-

tains around Cave Junction, Happy Camp, and Weitchpec; closer to the coast, the mushroom hunters mine the rich deposits of decaying redwood that descend down the western slopes to the Pacific like seams of gold, always moving toward the sea. These redwoods are the same trees that built the gold miners' camps and flumes, though now they exist only as stumps in woods recolonized by tanoak, madrone, and Douglas fir. More than 95 percent of the original redwood forest was cut down in the previous century and a half, leaving behind decomposing evidence of a great forest that stretched 450 miles, from Oregon's Chetco River to Monterey County, and survived multiple ice ages only to fall in swift order at the hands of man. When you walk among the last standing old-growth redwoods, through groves of trees with names like Hyperion, Apex, and Stratosphere Giant, you pass wooden benches and plaques with the names of individuals and couples who had the foresight and generosity to buy these parcels before they could be cut. In an ironic twist of fate most appreciated by a mushroom hunter, it is the logged-over land, with its redwood decay, that now fuels the winter pick. Come winter, the lower slopes of these mostly private mountain forests all the way to the coast are decorated with fungi.

Doug's rationale for picking these closed patches involves a complicated algorithm that would never hold up in a court of law. At its core is a strong belief that the timber companies have looted the public coffers for generations, beginning with the first lumber barons. Men like George Weyerhaeuser were known to have obtained thousands of acres illegally in the nineteenth century by using to their advantage the federal government's largesse, including such laws as the Homestead Act, and then making Gilded Age end runs when new laws didn't suit them. Back in the day, when the settling of the West was a haphazard and sometimes ruthless affair, the timber barons rounded up local town drunks to petition for homestead lands and then acquired the land out from under them. Even worse, the timber barons were now locking their gates. To Doug, this is an unconscionable breach of public goodwill that demands action. "We all break the law at one point or another," he says. "Even the most self-righteous bastard in the world. So it's all a matter of what's acceptable to you personally. You can't let someone who takes a bulldozer to these woods dictate to you what's healthy for them." Doug knew this sounded sanctimonious, and he didn't care. "What would Freud call it? Righteous and right, or something like that? A friend of mine was taking psychology in college and she said, 'This is you, Mr. Self-Righteous.' We can't help who we are."

MY FIRST TRIP TO CALIFORNIA with Doug ran headlong into the double-dealings of nature. While the Pacific Northwest was hit with a series of Pineapple Express weather systems out of the South Pacific—unseasonably warm temperatures and moisture that dumped buckets of rain even at the mountain ski areas—California endured a January of drought and warm winds, with temperatures into the seventies as far north as Eureka. The one-two punch of heat and wind stopped the mushroom season in its tracks. Yellowfoot chanterelles withered where they stood, hedgehogs turned brittle, and the star of the show, the black trumpet, burned to a charcoal crisp as it emerged from the leaf litter. The mushroom's curled funnel-like cap turned coal black, in contrast to the healthy grayish-black of the stem, with cracked and tattered edges that gave it the look of dirty old confetti strewn across the ground.

"Blacks are gakked," Jeremy Faber said with typical fatalism. Winter pick was done for him; he would start concentrating on the first wild greens of the season. Doug decided he would go anyway. He'd already made a couple of extended trips to California this winter, and he figured this would be his last before morel season started up in the spring. If he couldn't pick viable quantities of blacks, he would load up on stinging nettles. A hundred pounds of nettles would still be worth the trip. Plus, he planned to scout new areas in Humboldt and Mendocino. Scouting was a necessary chore. There was always the hope of finding new microclimates that produced mushrooms even in the most adverse conditions. Circuit pickers have early patches and late patches; they have hot patches and cold patches; high elevation and low elevation. A good picker was continually adding new patches to his portfolio. Besides, whatever we found would be sold, no problem. Matt Dillon, for one, would be getting an order. When I asked Dillon in an email what he might do with a box of blacks, he ticked off a few possibilities: crispy-fried and paired with cider-poached oysters and cultured cream; scrambled with eggs, dried ham, and tarragon; braised with Jersey cabbage in buttermilk. And that was just a start. Black trumpets, so appealing on the plate and with such big flavor packed into a small package, could be used in all kinds of ways. It was an ingredient that showed off a chef's imagination.

I picked Doug up at the Greyhound bus depot in Olympia. He had a camo-colored external-frame backpack, a threadbare felt-lined sleeping bag with the stuffing bursting out, and several hooded sweatshirts. We stopped at a Grocery Outlet, where he could use what he referred to as his "new card"; he had finally persevered through various bureaucratic hurdles to receive some disability for his Parkinson's. The state now gave him a few hundred dollars a month for food and other essentials. Doug pushed a cart through aisles of towering overstock at the Outlet, loading it with Twinkies, cans of sardines and mandarin oranges, instant coffee, and other favorite camp foods. At the checkout, he insisted on paying with his new card. He didn't have any cash, telling me instead to take gas money out of the nettle pick that I would be delivering to Faber at the end of the week. I offered to split it. "This is my treat," he boomed, breaking into a wide, tight-lipped grin.

We had eight more hours together in the car to talk about mushroom picking before arriving at our first camp. Though I was always eager to hear his stories from the rural fringes, the more I got to know Doug, the more I found myself in the uncomfortable position of remaining silent—or, when pressed, disagreeing—on certain basic matters of conduct. This didn't bother Doug at all. I was an outsider.

Spend any time on the Olympic Peninsula and I would change my opinions. He was sure of that. He told me about a friend of his who had a dispute with the state over some shellfish leases. "State screwed him out of a couple grand in clams," Doug explained to me, as if the outcome was obvious. Under the cover of darkness, his friend got his due, as he saw it, on state-owned clam beds.

"That's poaching," I said. I was a clam digger. I depended on those public shellfish beaches.

"It ain't poaching when it's owed to you."

"I'd need to know the particulars. Still sounds fishy."

"Nothing fishy. No particulars. He got screwed and wasn't standing idle. Simple as that."

There was one particular game warden whom Doug liked to taunt. "Everybody knows him," he told me. "My kids know him." Doug was proud of the outdoor skills his sons possessed. It wasn't an easy childhood for them, he admitted. If the boys got hungry, they poached a deer. The freezer always had plenty of salmon. He assured me that the poaching of fish, animals, and timber were minor transgressions in the big picture. Despite the Great Recession, there were legit jobs for a man who wanted to work. Lately, between mushroom picking, Doug had been working as a part-time scrapper, cutting steel. The work of a scrapper was a form of recycling. China was buying any metal it could get. Doug said he'd never seen such high prices for steel, aluminum, and even tin. As we drove south, he noted the small gold mines of rusted metal: a long-abandoned bulldozer, a decommissioned oil tank, copper wire from an upside-down house. "Cut steel with me if you ever need some quick dough," he advised. He was always offering me employment. I could commercially dig razor clams, or catch crab, or go out on an iceboat. An iceboat fishes for only a week, ten days max, he explained, so I could be reunited with my family after making a small bundle of cash. Freezer boats, on the other hand, were out at sea for a month or more. Though I begged off these enticements, there was one job I told Doug I wanted, if only for a little while: In the spring I would join him for morel camp, picking alongside the other mushroom hunters rather than observing, competing for poundage and pay.

DRIVING THROUGH GRANTS PASS, Oregon—"Grants Ass" to Doug—we passed a few tough-looking bikers and hoodlums standing on street corners in their black leather vests, flashing their colors. Doug looked at them scornfully. "I'm seriously considering packing a piece again," he said. The world was a dangerous place, and though it was a crying shame, he figured a gun was a practicality, like clothes on your back. While I didn't agree with Faber's assessment that Doug was a hairbreadth from running amok, the possibility of violence hovered over him nevertheless. The day before, he said, he'd had an altercation with a pet abuser as he was getting into the man's truck. The dog had come to the window. "It was happy to see somebody," Doug said, outrage in his voice. This acquaintance of his then "doubled up his fist" and punched his dog right in the nose. "I said, 'Hey, motherfucker, don't hit that dog with your fist.' And he says, 'You don't tell me how to raise my dog.' I don't like people picking on dogs. I grabbed him by the back of the shirt and spun him, like this. I put my boot in the back of his calves. He went down like a ton of bricks. Didn't hit him at all. He's one of those Vietnam vets who can't talk to you without mentioning 'Nam. The Lord didn't want me riding in the car with that guy."

Doug freely admitted he'd been a tough kid. "I was boxing at the time, so I could handle myself." Once, he said, he'd punched out five rednecks at a dance before they could jump him. "They were gonna give me a beating, so I hauled off and started hitting them first." These stories often stretched credulity, yet there was usually a detail or two that made me wonder. About the rednecks, Doug remembered that two of them were identical twins. He said he gave each one the same black eye, so they were still identical. Doug reckoned he'd had two dozen concussions, at least. Now he wondered if all his past brawling was in part to blame for his Parkinson's. "I'm not hanging around too long," he liked to say. "No *wah-wah* story. I've had a good run. Put me on the iceberg and *hasta la vista*."

When I asked Doug if he believed in an afterlife, he frowned. Some things in life were meant to remain a mystery, beyond the scope of either science or religion. "What about those experiments when people lose an ounce and a half at death? What is that weight that disappears? I've seen ghosts myself. I watched one coming down the hallway. It come to the doorway, and fear started kicking in. When it come into the room, I was flat-out scared. I was too scared to yell out. It moved right up beside me. White, grayish, the form of a person but no features. I bailed. I grabbed the covers and pulled them over my head and started saying, 'Our father, who art in heaven,' over and over and over." But heaven? Heaven was on earth, and people ought to start treating the planet as such. He cussed and then caught himself. Doug said he knew he had anger issues, that he was forever trying to contain the feelings of wrath and injustice that bubbled up from some deep crack in his soul. Overall, he figured he'd done a pretty good job keeping a lid on it. "I need a piece strictly for self-defense."

As we made our way south and then west, I wondered whether there was a road anywhere in the American West that Doug hadn't mapped out in his head, complete with shortcuts, mushroom patches, and potential hazards. We followed the Applegate Valley through Cave Junction ("Major cop trap," he said. "You better have your shit together when you drive through here"), past the agricultural checkpoint that marks the California border ("Not even a twig of firewood is allowed"), and along the Middle Fork of the Smith River Canyon ("That Jedediah Smith sure got around—just like a mushroom picker!"). Not far from the coast we caught a glimpse of why Highway 199 is called the Redwood Highway. All at once the trees jumped up, these California trees famous the world over, one of nature's seven wonders, now reduced to a handful of small, scattered groves. Jed Smith would have been among the first Americans to encounter this narrow "green prison" that connects the Klamaths to the North Coast. It took his party a month to cross forty miles of redwood forest from Gans Prairie, where they could glimpse the Pacific, before actually reaching the ocean. Downed trees presented obstacles few white men had ever seen. Even smaller, surmountable deadfall still required long detours for the stock.

That night we camped on Redwood Creek just outside the sleepy town of Orick. This was one of Doug's usual camps. Tweakers had found it since his last visit. Radiator hoses, beer cans, and other assorted junk lay scattered around a fire pit suitable for only the biggest of bonfires. There was an old mattress in a grotto of alders. I didn't want to think about that piece of tweaker furniture. We built our own fire elsewhere, closer to the creek, and kept it low so it wouldn't be seen by any passing cars on the road a quarter mile away. Doug slept in my car while I slept in a tent.

The next day we drove winding roads up into the coastal hills to visit the first of several black-trumpet patches. Twelve miles in from the highway, we passed a pickup coming the other way. "That's a bad sign," said Doug, craning his neck. "What does he have in the back?" I'd seen something too, in my rearview. Maybe it was a burlap bag; maybe it was a poached animal. "Don't like the way he was looking at us. Bad vibes. Hope he's not a mushroom picker. Looked like he was packing something else." All of a sudden I wondered whether it had been a bright idea to bring my laptop computer along. Even though it was stowed away in the cargo carrier atop the roof, I now felt vulnerable. Doug wasn't too optimistic about the locked cargo carrier either. "I know a patch where we can park nearby, so we'll hear any cars. Tweakers will try to get into anything. It's just sorry the way it is. They're quick too. What the tweakers want to do is strike and leave; they don't want to hang around a crime scene." It seemed that wherever the mushroom patches were, meth users weren't far away. Their cooking sites littered the woods with highly noxious chemicals, and the users themselves were totally unpredictable and dangerous. They gathered in lonely farmhouses to stay high for days on end, losing all sense of control after a while and committing crimes in broad day-light to get money for more meth, sometimes perpetrating senseless violence merely because of a misunderstanding or a sudden onset of paranoia. You had to avoid them at all costs.

I pulled off the road at the edge of a clear-cut. Doug hesitated before getting out. "I know you're not into guns at all, but I'm really thinking about packing a piece. All you need is a .38. You don't need much. End of soapbox." With that, he got out, pulled on his pack, and made the short trudge through stumps to the edge of the woods. This was one of the few patches on private timberland that wasn't posted. Down the road toward the Trinity River, Doug had another patch, on ranchland owned by a vet. "Yeah, the guy's got a nasty temper and can handle an automatic," he said. "Best not be caught poaching that patch unless you have an arrangement with him. We'll smoke weed together. A real nice guy but a little crazy in the head, if you know what I mean. 'Nam did that to a lot of these guys. He knows me. We'll be okay."

Mushrooms appeared right away. Yellowfeet clustered around fallen, decaying trees. Slender and demure, these winter relatives of chanterelles were a dirty yellow, sometimes nearly brown on the cap, with hollow egg-yellow lower stems. They had the characteristic chanterelle wrinkles, rather than gills, beneath the cap. It was easy to be dismissive about yellowfeet, especially in a part of the world known for cranking out the flashier golden chanterelle. Yellowfeet seemed pale and limp in comparison. Chefs, on the other hand, love them. Since yellowfeet are thin-fleshed and lightweight, it's possible to dress up a plate with plenty of them without eating away at profit margins. Like other members of the chanterelle family, the yellowfoot boasts a surprising fruitiness that runs counter to typical fungi. They grow in colonies in similar habitat to that of hedgehogs: damp conifer forest with ample deadfall and decaying wood. In a good spot, yellowfeet can be gathered by the handful.

We worked our way down a slope of mixed second-growth forest dominated by redwood, tanoak, Pacific madrone, and Douglas fir, grabbing yellowfeet as we went and the odd hedgehog that wasn't too far gone, before locating groupings of another species—the mushroom we had driven more than seven hundred miles to pick. We found it among thick drifts of fallen madrone and oak leaves, nestled inconspicuously in leaf litter and yet reaching up as if begging for discovery: black trumpets. In a good year these horn-shaped mushrooms can fruit in plentiful abundance, often in troops that make them a little more visible. The heat wave had been hard on the blacks, with most of them not up to restaurant quality. Doug let me keep all his discarded mushrooms for my dryer. "Prospects ain't good," he groaned, passing over yet another cluster of heatstroke mushrooms. I stuck them in my bucket anyway.

THE NEXT NIGHT WE made camp in a remote corner of the Lost Coast, the wildest remaining stretch of California coastline, a place too rugged for Caltrans to impose its multi-lane will. Only a couple of rough roads grant access to the Pacific here. Otherwise you have to walk. The King Range, running parallel to the coastline, vaults from the ocean like a jack-in-the-box to reach a startling height of 4,088 feet atop King Peak, a mere three miles from the ocean as the raven flies. The lack of blacktop didn't deter loggers, who still made off with most of the valuable old-growth redwood and Douglas fir. All the same, the Lost Coast, with its King Range National Conservation Area and Sinkyone Wilderness State Park—eighty miles of remote shoreline between the two—remains a rare and unpopulated stretch of California coast. It's just the sort of place for a mushroom picker to hunker down.

Right after dinner, the weather turned. First spit, then brimstone. I slid down into my sleeping bag and listened to the drops of rain gather strength until it was an all-out assault. Twice I crawled outside to re-stake the fly, as gale-force winds thrashed my tent and a heavy downpour turned the ground to liquid. Doug slept in my car again. He'd forgotten his tarp. In the morning two bull elk, one of them a seven-point, munched grass in the campground. It was still raining hard. We evacuated quickly, before the way out became impassable. A small redwood had fallen across the road in the night. Luckily, it was broken in several places and we were able to lever it to the shoulder and get by. We picked more patches down the coast. This was difficult, unpeopled terrain. Recently, a fugitive accused of two murders in the Fort Bragg area had managed to elude hundreds of law-enforcement officers for weeks by hiding in these hills and ransacking cabins for weapons and supplies. When the SWAT team finally caught up with him, they shot him on sight.

You can't think about fugitives and bears and bogeymen if you want to pick mushrooms. The woods are dark and deep, but mostly the darkness is in our heads. I told myself this as I traversed a steep slope through dense garrisons of tanoak, brushing the branches out of my face and wending my way ever downward toward a mossy swamp at the bottom of a dark alleyway. It seemed so easy for something to go wrong: a misplaced foot, a sharp branch, a gun-toting hobgoblin lying in wait. There was no one to hear your cries. Even when picking with a partner, as I was doing now, a yell for help barely penetrated the heavy cover. On a day like today, the risk hardly felt worth it. Everywhere, the blacks were, in Faber's words, gakked. All we picked was destined for my dehydrator and not subject to the fussy inspection of restaurant chefs. At last, a couple of hours down the road from Fort Bragg and the Jackson State Forest, we pulled into the coastal hamlet of Gualala, near the Sonoma County border. After three days and two nights of nonstop rain and arduous picking, I was ready for the shelter of David Arora's home.

Arora has been championing people like Doug for three decades, and for this reason factions within the community of fungi enthusiasts regard him warily, even if many of them would agree that his book *Mushrooms Demystified* is largely responsible for introducing recent generations to the charms of mushroom hunting. Recreational hunters, it appeared to me, had the mostly mistaken idea that they were in competition with the commercial pickers. In my own travels with Doug, Faber, and the rest, rarely had I seen pros and recreationals picking the same patches, barring the occasional burn site for morels. (Then again, I live in Washington; commercial picking to the south in Oregon is much more intensive.) A study by the U.S. Forest Service revealed that recreational chanterelle pickers in the Pacific Northwest in the late 1980s blamed the commercial harvest for lower recreational yields, when in fact most of the data suggests that a few years of drought were to blame. Such perceptions combined with lurid media accounts of territorial pickers have conspired to give commercial harvesters an increasingly bad rap. Arora takes a contrarian position. In the early 1990s he visited the matsutake camps in Crescent Lake, Oregon, and morel-picking camps in subsequent years. He's traveled abroad to visit with commercial pickers all over the world, especially in the Chinese province of Yunnan. He admires the carnival aspect of the trade, the rough-and-tumble do-it-yourselfness that makes mushroom picking such a welcome reprieve from our increasingly buttoned-down society. This hasn't endeared him to some of the mycological society members who view commercial pickers with distrust.

Arora is also known for needling the establishment. He likes to point out that the otherwise politically and environmentally progressive San Francisco Bay Area is at the center of increasingly punitive regulations designed to curtail the gathering of edible fungi on public lands, whether commercially *or* recreationally, regulations that are now being enacted from California to Maine. In places like Fort Ross and Salt Point State Park on the Sonoma coast, Italian immigrants have enjoyed a long history of picking porcini mushrooms for the table, some of which can grow to a few pounds or more, earning the nickname *gambone* ("big leg"). Despite such traditions, California regulatory bodies have steadily moved against mushroom harvesting. Arora traces the rise of these regulations to environmental groups such as the Sierra Club as well as to recreational mushroom pickers themselves, who organized in the 1980s via mycological societies "to oppose commercial harvest of mushrooms only to see regulations passed that severely restricted their own activities." The California Department of State Parks went so far as to outlaw any picking of mushrooms whatsoever. After pressure from Club Italia of Marin, the department relented and reopened the most famous hunting ground, Salt Point, to limited picking, with a daily bag limit of five pounds, the equivalent of just a few nice gambones. As Arora explains it, the decision to limit picking on public lands had the unintended consequences of, first, funneling all the mushroom hunters into one open area, Salt Point, increasing impact there; and second, making off-limits areas more desirable to those willing to pick illegally. His forecast for future generations is dire: "Children's direct experience and knowledge of nature, already seriously compromised by larger social and historical processes, is now being further stymied and eroded by a preservationist, anti-foraging model of public land use that aggressively discourages knowledge acquisition and hands-on experience of nature even when the particular activity is exciting, of low impact, and fosters enduring ties with the natural world."

As at so many rural compounds, the head of Arora's driveway was marked with a warning sign, albeit one that made sport of such signs:

Notis! Trespassers will B persecuted to the full extent of 2 mongrel dogs which was never over sociable to strangers & 1 dubble brl shot gun which ain't loaded with sofa pillers DAM if I aint gitten tired of this mushroom pickin' on my place.

HE CAME TO THE door rubbing his eyes, his thick eyeglasses in hand, and ushered us in from the rain. The house was cold and dark. We'd caught him during a lull in the season, when the usual circus of mushroom hunters and other assorted hangers-on had dispersed. Arora started building a fire in the kitchen stove. "I've been busy," he said, "though I'm not sure with what." He gave a little chuckle at this. He said he was supposed to be working on the revision of *Mushrooms Demystified,* though it was such a massive project he had grown weary of it. Maybe he would go back to China instead.

While Arora prepared tea, Doug and I wandered around. Casa Madera, as the house is called, isn't especially notable as you pull into the driveway, just the way the rabbit hole didn't look like much to Alice. Once inside, though, you quickly discover Arora's true avocation. He is a collector. A collector of artifacts, people, stories. The single-level house, a rambling rustic log cabin gone AWOL, begins in the kitchen and spirals out into a labyrinth of rooms, each one thematically different from the last and housing various collections of what Arora has brought back from his mushroom missions around the world. There is a wall devoted to his collection of Kenyan scissors, another decorated with handmade brooms. One room contains only edible mushrooms in their various global guises: dried, canned, and commercially packaged in colorful labels. Another is filled with antique children's marbles. Cobwebs wreathe the corners, and dangling from the rafters are birds' nests, beehives, and giant African seedpods.

Meeting up with Arora had been my idea. Somehow I knew that he and Doug would have plenty to talk about, though I hadn't anticipated the myriad connections they would share from three decades on the mushroom trail. People, places, events: They talked a common language, and Arora's sharp memory helped elucidate long-forgotten details in the foggier corners of Doug's head. We sipped cups of hot tea, and Doug told Arora about his biggest payday, the matsutake pick of the early 1990s, when prices went batty.

"Ninety-three," Arora said. "I was there too." He'd gotten a call from someone who said he'd better get up to Crescent Lake, Oregon, that strange things were brewing. Doug recounted his high price of $520 per pound and how the price had even hit $600 earlier in the day, how he'd been picking the matsutake in a little-known patch in California and driving it up to Chemult, Oregon, to sell. What Doug didn't realize—and what Arora explained now—was that this high price was something of a bamboozle. It was a good year for matsutake, and the buyers were desperate to get their hands on as much as they could ship to Japan, but the pickers weren't getting the mushrooms out of the woods. To attract pickers to their buy stations, the buyers started offering outrageous prices for number-one buttons, prices they rarely had to pay, because most of the crop had already popped and was rotting in the woods. The ploy worked, and the buyers managed to get a lot of traffic in lesser grades of matsutake that were nevertheless in demand. Doug and his friends, however, were picking to the south, where different conditions meant they could still find number ones.

"The buyers must have lost a lot of money on you," Arora said, smiling.

"You're damn straight."

. . .

THE NEXT DAY I had to drive down to Santa Cruz, where I was to give a talk at the Fungus Federation on mushroom cookery. I left Doug at the bus station in Gualala so he could make it back to camp and start to pick stinging nettles. At the federation, I showed slides of my favorite mushroom preparations: gnocchi with porcini and oxtail ragu; morels with scallops and maple-blossom pesto; Sichuan pickled cauliflower mushrooms. The crowd murmured restlessly. "Unfair," someone in the audience called out. "Food torture." One of my latest was an Indian chana masala with fresh porcini, which I served alongside a stinging nettle paneer. I neglected to mention that a commercial picker was at that moment holed up in my tent a couple of hundred miles to the north. Even in a place as liberal-minded as Santa Cruz, the topic of commercial harvesters raised hackles. Three days later, after nearly constant rain and high winds, I rolled back into the Lost Coast. It was already dark. In my headlights, our camp looked abandoned. I put down my window.

"Doug?" During the entire drive north from Santa Cruz, I had envisioned various worst-case scenarios: not finding Doug and driving all over kingdom come in search of him, or arriving to find him deathly ill in my tent after enduring nonstop cold and rain.

"Doug?"

"Howdy," came a voice from within a stand of redwoods on the other side of the road. He was completely out of sight—and out of the elements—beneath the sweeping hem of trees.

I felt immediate relief. "Hey!" I yelled into the bushes, happy to hear his voice. "How're you doing?"

"Just as snug as a bug in a rug. Some guys came rolling through earlier, just tearing up the place, but they didn't see me." So we weren't alone. That was okay. It was late and time to sleep. I pulled my car into a meadow across from Doug's secluded camp and stretched out my sleeping bag in the back. We would get up before dawn, load Doug's nettles and my camping gear into the car, and split.

I heard the music first, just before falling asleep. Loud, angry rap. The bass rumbled through my car. Floodlights lit up the trees around me with an eerie glow. It was a Jeep of some sort. It pulled over onto a spur a hundred yards away. Next came the gunshots, and then the vehicle was off, doing donuts nearby before racing down the dirt road to another likely target. My heart was thumping. It would be a while before I would settle down to sleep again. I looked at the clock. Eleven-thirty. At midnight the Jeep was back. I could hear the muffled voices of two men, then the sharp ringing of at least thirty rounds of automatic gunfire unloaded into the woods mere yards from my car. The sounds punctured the night and echoed through the darkness. The men had to be jacked up on something, probably meth, and didn't know I was there. A row of trees stood between us. As far as I knew, I was the only other car in the area. If they came around the corner and saw the silver gleaming Subaru exposed in this meadow, they might conceivably take a pot shot at it, not realizing—or maybe beyond caring—that I was trying to sleep inside. A few more gunshots and they were back in the Jeep. I watched the lights fade into the woods. The time was now. I pulled on my sneakers and jumped out of the car. I ran quietly toward Doug's hidden camp. The overhanging branches parted like a curtain and he stood before me, ashen-faced, his eyes wide in an expression like none I'd ever seen before. His voice quaked. "We're thinking the same thing," he said.

Seeing Doug like this told me my instincts were dead-on. "We need to get out of here. I'm like a sitting duck in that car." We left Doug's camp where it was, secreted beneath the redwoods—tent, cooler, backpack, garbage bags full of nettles.

"Those fuckers! Hurry up."

"Should we drive through the creek or go around?"

"Just decide. No time."

I could barely make out the small stream and its embankment in my headlights. The quickest route to the main road was to follow a dirt track and drive right across the creek. But the embankment looked like a hazard. If we got high-centered, it was over. I threw the car into reverse, spun around in the mud, and gunned the engine. We skidded onto a forest spur, turned a corner—please, no headlights facing us—and joined the main dirt road leading out of the basin. Up ahead was a rickety one-lane wooden bridge over the creek and a stone memorial to a local girl killed in a car accident on this same stretch of bad road. I accelerated across the bridge and up the opposite ridge.

"Any headlights back there?"

"Not yet."

"Let's hope there are no more trees across the road."

Several miles of tight hairpins led us back to the highway. We pulled over on the shoulder of Route 1 and tried to sleep for a few uncomfortable hours in the front seats, with my sleeping bag stretched across us for warmth, before returning the next morning. This time the Jeep was nowhere in sight. In the light we could see that my campsite was gouged and gored by knobby four-wheeling tires.

"They passed out somewhere," Doug said hopefully.

We broke down his camp as quickly as possible, loaded the car, and fled California with a cargo richer in weeds than mushrooms.

CHAPTER 12

Into the Fire

...

JEREMY FABER CALLED ME out of the blue on a Thursday afternoon. It was late June. He didn't sound pleased. "Probably best not to mention this to Doug," he started. I hadn't seen Doug in months, not since our aborted California winter pick. The morel season was in full swing. In the past seventy-two hours, Faber had bought morels in La Grande, Oregon ("Garbage"), checked a burn site near Wenatchee, Washington ("Got a couple buckets, nothing special"), visited multiple burns around the Idaho panhandle ("Too much snow in the high country"), and was now stopping in McCall for dinner before driving home to Seattle. Originally he had planned to scout western Montana as well, but he was too depressed by what he'd seen already to continue eastward. He had a simple question for me: Did I want to go to the Yukon tomorrow?

"Yukon Territory?"

"I'm going broke. Should have been up north two weeks ago." Faber had gotten a tip from another mushroom broker, a guy who went by the nickname King Morel, who told him about this burn up near the Yukon–B.C. border that had good road access and few pickers. It was a chance for a big takedown, and Faber needed a score.

The New York operation was limping along, and even his Seattle business seemed stuck, despite increasing demand for his products. A haul of morels would go a long way toward digging Foraged and Found Edibles out of a deepening financial hole.

"What about Doug?" I asked. Doug knew I was keen to join morel camp. He'd been keeping me apprised of his movements all spring, leaving weekly messages about the latest rumors and assuring me he'd relay any hints of Faber's travels as well. I was really hoping the three of us would camp together. Both Faber and Doug had told me stories about their campouts of years past, how they had made hidden base camps in the mountain woods, just a couple of pup tents pitched off-trail and a small fire ring, how they kept a low profile by hiking the mushrooms out to the road at night, how they had made money hand over fist.

"Doug is broken down," Faber said. "His body is finished. I can't afford to carry him." Doug was in his fifties, it was true, but he seemed in pretty good shape to me.

"I think he's waiting for a call," I said.

"He can wait. How will Doug get up to the Yukon, anyway? Drive his shitty car? Hitchhike? He's got no money for a plane ticket—am I supposed to buy his ticket and his food and everything else? It's morels. I need to make money."

Late in the spring and into summer, the wild-food trade is dominated by what are known as "burn morels"—morel mushrooms that appear in staggering numbers the year after a forest fire. The burn morels are the last of the many different morel varieties to show themselves. When conditions are right, they make up for this coyness with a wanton abandon that is truly heart-stopping in its promiscuity. Serious mushroom hunters from all over the country, lured by the promise of such crops, learn to become expert fire watchers, studying local newspaper reports for clues, scrutinizing maps, and even using newly available tools such as Google Earth to survey conditions on the ground via satellite. Most of these fire watchers would undoubtedly agree that the previous year, from a morel point of view, was an especially poor one for wildfire in the American West, which is to say a year without enough fire, and the lack of burned forest was further compounded by an unusually heavy spring snowpack in the mountains. Conditions certainly didn't look favorable in the Lower 48. Up north, however, in British Columbia and the Yukon, several large fires had the most dedicated morel pickers salivating.

"If I have to pick illegally, might as well be the good stuff," Faber added.

By "illegally" he meant, well, illegally. In many of Idaho's forests, where much of the action would soon be focused, you could get a permit to pick recreationally for personal use only, and some were closed altogether. Opening a forest to commercial harvest was at the discretion of the district ranger. This was a technicality. In coming weeks, commercial pickers would swarm over the lower flanks of Idaho's heavily forested mountains wherever the whispered promise of morels might lead them, whether these places were officially open or not, avoiding authorities while picking the first flush and hoping the snow would hurry up and melt off before it became a moot point. Not only did Faber not want to push his luck on the permit issue in Idaho, he wasn't buying this line of wishful thinking. He'd just scouted the burns and seen for himself that they were mainly in stands of beetle-killed lodgepole pine. Such woods rarely produced well. It wasn't worth hassling over the legalities or competing with the Cambodians, who would likely be selling to one of their own anyway. He'd also put off going to burn sites in southern British Columbia because of the regulations that constrained non-Canadian citizens. But the Yukon was different. For one thing, it was big. For another, it was empty. Hardly anyone was up there, certainly not a bunch of mushroom pickers, American or otherwise. He figured he could skirt the nationality issue and buy enough morels to give his company a shot in the arm just when it was needed most. His New York operation could kill the competition with a steady supply of fresh morels in an off year such as this. With wild greens mostly spent and berry season still a month away, the month of June was all about morels and spring porcini mushrooms. This year the snowpack was sure to put a damper on the porcini pick. He said it again: "I need morels." He needed them badly. In many ways June was the most important month of the year. It was a month to sell huge volumes of the most marketable mushrooms on the planet. Unlike matsutake, morels always commanded a high price, and with low supply this year the prices were sure to be even higher than usual. For a buyer like Faber, who increased his margins by doing his own picking, the morel season was money in the bank.

It would be a chance for me to pick commercially too. Not just for an afternoon but for a week or more. I had said from day one that I wanted to learn the pickers' secrets. I wanted to know how they exited a tract of woods with a hundred pounds of edible fungi, an amount that seemed either superhuman or as likely as unicorns. Morels gave me my best shot. Unlike other species, with a surfeit of variables in their gathering, morels limit the picker's options. In commercial quantities they require burned forest, plain and simple. A picker need only keep track of the fires each year. A basic understanding of tree composition narrows the field. The burned trees are almost always certain types of conifers, sometimes poplars and willows. Once on the burn, though, many little decisions start to add up to separate the guy who harvests fifty pounds a day from the one who does twice that, efficiencies of the sort that sequester grades of carpenter or mechanic or other skilled laborer.

I told Faber I'd need a few minutes to wrap my head around this possibility. All along I'd talked about how much I wanted the wilderness picking experience, the military-style campaign of pulling mushrooms out of the bush and rushing them to market against the clock. Here was my chance. I just hadn't expected it to be so far away: a drive across the border to Vancouver International Airport, a plane ride on Air North (a carrier I'd never heard of) to Whitehorse, capital of the Yukon Territory, and a five-hour drive in a rented van to Watson Lake, a community that, at less than two thousand souls, was the province's third largest. This wasn't some token "wilderness" in the

Lower 48, surrounded by towns and roads. This wasn't a nice little forest preserve. Weren't there grizzlies up there? What if I got lost? These were the questions on my mind. Equally worrisome: Would I measure up? This last question was the worst of all. Lately I had entertained the queasy feeling that I was going soft. I'd reached a certain age at which it was tougher to rebound from injury, tougher to get competitive on the pitch, tougher to get up before dawn and go. This getting older and softer rankled.

I called him back. I was in.

. . .

THE WEEK BEFORE FABER'S CALL, I took my kids morel hunting in eastern Washington. This was something I'd been doing each spring for several years. When they were babies, I carried them on my back. Now they were old enough to hunt for themselves. It was a rite of passage, the spring morel hunt, and I looked forward to it every year. We returned to the mountains as the snow melted. Yellow balsamroot blooming in the sagebrush hills told us it was time to go. White trilliums and pink calypso orchids colored the forest floor. Elk gathered in meadow clearings to calve and feed on newly emerging grasses. Gaudy western tanagers, back from the tropics, chased each other through long-needled pines, flashes of red and yellow against an evergreen canopy. Townsend's warblers in the treetops repeated their flimsy, insect-like trills. At higher elevations we heard the melodious notes of the continent's preeminent vocalist, the hermit thrush. Seasonal streams ran fast with runoff. Everything was greening up, pouring forth, and singing of renewal.

We found the morels in their hiding places—hundreds of them popping up around tree stumps, along the edges of meadows, and beside rushing creeks. I couldn't imagine being anywhere else. The vernal mountain wilderness was invigorating. My children raced each other to the crest of a hill, pinballing from one clutch of morels to another. Despite the beauty and serenity that surrounded us, it didn't take long before a fight broke out. Riley, the older one, was by this point an experienced mushroom hunter, but his younger sister, Ruby, that much shorter and closer to the ground, had developed the eye. She snatched up handfuls of morels that quickly became too numerous for her little fingers to juggle. I gave her my bucket. Meanwhile, I could see a sour expression creep across Riley's face. "Ruby's taking them all," he complained, stomping his foot in the dirt. I gave him my pocketknife to keep the peace, and this seemed to work for a while, until he saw the disparity between their hauls and decided he was done for the day. Ruby, almost always the one reduced to tears in other contests of will, beamed in triumph.

Faber thought this was a cute story. He liked my kids, liked most kids. But the Yukon wasn't child's play. He wanted me to understand what it was like to hump a hundred pounds of mushrooms out of the bush. This wasn't going to be a recreational pick. It dawned on me that all my questions, all my hanging around, had made him realize that there really was something unusual about his occupation. Initially he had been standoffish. *It was a job like any other. Hard work paid off.* That sort of stuff. The more I pestered him about specifics, the more he began to see what his work looked like to an outsider. I started to hear from him more often. He'd send me texts with a little bit of local color or give me a call from some backwater. He liked to keep me informed on Doug's movements too. "Doug shows up, zero cash," went one text sent from California. "Picking so so. Ranger stopped us, let us go." In another text, he said Doug had found some buried copper cable and was harvesting that instead of mushrooms. "He's digging up 200 pounds of copper," the text went. "WTF?!?"

Earlier that spring, before the Yukon beckoned, Faber had tipped me off that he'd be down in Oregon—along with a few hundred other pickers and buyers—trying to fulfill an impossible demand for morels and spring porcini. "Don't move," I'd said. "I'll see you in six hours." I got in my car and drove south to the Deschutes National Forest near Sisters, Oregon.

Twenty miles northwest of Bend in the center of the state, with a

Main Street of faux-Western storefronts straight out of *High Noon,* Sisters is the epitome of the New West. A former ranching town, it was first settled by sheep graziers in the 1870s. Industrial loggers made their way into the region's open, park-like forests of large Douglas fir and ponderosa pine following the 1911 completion of the Oregon Trunk Line at Bend. Years of boom-and-bust resource extraction continued apace for most of the twentieth century, until the mines and mills closed and a recreation-based economy took over. Today, Sisters is a bustling tourist destination of boutiques, restaurants, and galleries. Visitors hike in the summer and cross-country ski in winter. In town you can buy an ornately decorated saddle or a watercolor painting of Mount Bachelor or a vegetarian Cobb salad. The Three Sisters peaks to the south, rising precipitously above the flat ranchlands, dominate the view, and to the north is the stark Mount Jefferson Wilderness.

Since the 1980s, mushroom hunters have gathered in droves in the woods surrounding Sisters to pick morels and spring porcini. A series of droughts, beetle kills, and forest fires combined to make this a productive area for morels for many years, notably the early 1990s after a die-off of white fir. The original hunters were mostly seasonal pickers who saw this as both vacation and a way to earn some extra money. The national forest offered quality camping sites along scenic creeks. As the pressure increased, the Forest Service decided that the commercial pickers needed to be rounded up and corralled into a single camp, where their footprint wouldn't be so wide and they could be monitored. This decision was met with disapproval by the pickers. The encampment now occupies about a quarter-mile stretch of lonesome Forest Service road off the main backwoods arterials and, like some of the other mushroom camps scattered around the Northwest, has semipermanent structures—the standard post-and-stringer variety—that get covered with tarps in spring to shelter tents, outdoor kitchens, and drying operations. Most pickers arrive in mid-April and stay well into June.

Faber had purchased a ten-day permit for one hundred dollars from the Forest Service to run a buying station in the camp. His stand, number nine and one of the last to be sold, was far from most of the action up the road where the majority of the pickers congregated. Faber liked it this way. Unlike the other buyers, who put up wall tents and camped behind their stands, all he had was his van and a foldout table, with a simple Costco canopy in case the weather turned. Most nights he didn't sleep there, since he was busy driving his mushrooms to one of two airports, where he would wait in the lot until morning and catch a few Zs. Faber liked his relative anonymity because he planned to raise the price and outbid the other buyers. He didn't see spending more than a week in Sisters. It was a poor spring for mushrooms, and his goal was to buy as much as he could in a short burst and then move on to Ukiah in the Blue Mountains or elsewhere. "I don't want to step on anyone's toes is all," he said to me with a straight face.

Even though the harvest was only mediocre in Sisters this year, Faber suggested I spend the afternoon picking for profit. He needed to stick around camp. With a brainless blue sky overhead, I drove a few miles over to the Metolius River and started hiking the river trail. Though few pickers will ever use a trail open to the public, I'd never hunted mushrooms in this area, and I thought it might allow me to scout the conditions a little.

Spring on the eastern slope of the Cascades brings a welcome shot of sun and heat; it can also seem bright and oppressive after a long winter of twilit skies and little warmth. Harsh yellow light filtered through the pines and lit up the ground with polka dots of washed-out sun. Pollen drifted languidly through the shafts of light, like dust motes. The spring air was so sharp and sap-filled it nearly hurt my throat. After walking a couple of miles along dry pine flats above the river, I turned uphill and off-trail and started bushwhacking. *Trails are for tourists,* I could hear Faber say. Almost immediately, near a hulking, fire-scarred Douglas fir, I found a stout blond morel growing along a game trail. It was seven inches tall and in perfect condition, a real beauty. I put it in my bag and continued following the game trail. Sometimes morels will grow right out of a track left by a deer or elk. Even if it's tempting to think the morels are being eaten by wildlife and then reseeded wherever the animals leave their droppings, mostly it seems that the morels like the disturbance of the game trail itself, and a slight depression in the ground left by a hoof might be all the mushroom needs to have the proper shade or humidity to gain a foothold. Sure enough, up ahead there was another blond, and beyond that a third. What I didn't realize was that these three gorgeous morels were leading me down—or up, to be accurate—the primrose path. I scrambled another hour along a series of intersecting game trails and didn't find another mushroom. A costly boondoggle.

Back down by the river, in a sunspot among the pines, I found a large spring king—a *flag* in picker's parlance, since the cap was fully open and the pores underneath were turning yellow. Though a flag is a signal to look around for other nearby, fresher specimens, even these older mushrooms were still fetching a few dollars as dryers, so after scanning the area to no avail, I put it in my bag. Worse than the flags were the *blows,* big bubble-headed boletes that had become soft and worm-infested. These got the boot.

The king, like the morels earlier, was a red herring. I was so excited by it that I drove the logging roads looking for spring porcini habitat, specifically groves of older grand fir in moist conifer forests with nearby water sources. I didn't consider the fact that my spring porcini patches that I picked back home had been acquired over years of careful hunting. I was determined to find some right now on this alien ground where I had never set foot. Needless to say, it was a nice, two-hour walk with nothing to show for it. Faber's admonition that you must know individual trees to commercially hunt spring porcini rang in my head. It was time to get serious.

I jumped back in my car and started looking for logging roads that would take me higher into the mountains. Porcini were off the list, and though blond morels were beautiful, they were crapshoots. I needed to search for the steady black morel. At a higher elevation amid forest that reminded me of home, I parked the car and dashed into the woods. Black morels hid under the greenery wherever I turned—old, dark, waterlogged morels. I needed to go higher. Another thousand feet in elevation and I found a very enticing woodland of mostly true fir, and among these trees I found morels. Not a lot, and not nearly as large and stately as the blonds, but fresh and enough of them to line the bottom of my bag. Sometime after five I drove back to camp.

It was more of a scouting trip, I said to Faber. He laughed as he tallied me up. He was paying eleven dollars for blonds; my 0.305 pounds yielded $3.36—less than four dollars for being led on a wild goose chase that ate up much of my afternoon. The single number-three king, just shy of a pound, earned me $3.96, and my scant half pound of black morels, at nine dollars per, took a purse of $4.23. A whopping $11.55 for an afternoon's work. Faber handed me a receipt and twelve dollars.

Battered trucks started pulling in to check out the new buyer in camp. Faber was paying two dollars more across the board. Soon a line of mostly Cambodian, Lao, and Latino pickers waited with baskets in hand to sell to him. A newer white Toyota pickup cruised by slowly, then cruised by again a few minutes later. "That's a buyer," Faber said, unconcerned. After he had paid out the first rush of pickers, the truck reappeared and idled in the roadway. The window went down. Faber walked over. They chatted for a while, then the truck drove off and Faber returned to his position behind the grading table.

"So?"

"Some white guy. I've seen him before. He told me I was pissing off the Cambodian buyers. Why? Because I raised the price and they had to match me? So what? It's all bullshit. That's just his way of telling me to leave." Faber had no intention of leaving.

Later, the truck was back. The buyer, an independent in a Yankees ball cap who worked for himself, offered to sell Faber four hundred pounds of morels. In this way they came to an agreement. Faber accepted the offer and kept his prices firm.

"I don't want to step on anyone's toes," he said again.

. . .

MERIWETHER LEWIS, CO-CAPTAIN OF Thomas Jefferson's Corps of Discovery, wrote in his journal on June 19, 1806: "Cruzatte brought me several large morells which I roasted and eat without salt pepper or grease in this way I had for the first time the true taist of the morell which is truly an insippid taistless food." Despite his great accomplishments, Lewis's palate was as suspect as his spelling.

The royal kitchens of Europe welcomed morel season for centuries. Preparations using this taste of spring date back to the very first cookbooks. Today in the United States it's nearly impossible to visit an acclaimed restaurant in May and not see morels on the menu. Simply sautéed in butter, they offer a supremely woodsy, nearly smoky flavor that is mushroomy and yet so much more. As with good wine, the taste spectrum of morels is largely subjective. Over the years, food writers have used adjectives like *loamy, nutty, musky,* and the obligatory *earthy*. Renowned gourmand "Johnny" R. W. Apple, Jr., who spent most of his years writing foreign dispatches for *The New York Times* but loved nothing more than a literary detour into food, used a few of these same modifiers plus a surprise or two when he wrote about a morel hunt with Jack Czarnecki: "The taste is haunting—musky, loamy, faintly sweet, hinting of caraway and bell peppers."

It takes a dedicated and well-traveled palate to pull out those final qualifiers, but I know what he means. There is both a down-home and an exotic side to morels. For myself, they conjure the spring awakening. Their taste of the woods tells us it's time to throw off the last vestiges of winter and return to the renewing pleasures of fragrant forests, sun-warmed meadows, and cool mountain streams. To eat a freshly cooked morel is to imagine places apart from the hubbub of the city. Recreational hunters will often carry their cookware into

the woods, making a day out of the morel hunt and its fleeting pleasures. A picnic of morels fried up over a camp stove with just a tiny
bit of oil and garlic along with a crusty baguette and a good bottle of
rosé wine is a perfect lunch. Really, morels don't even taste like
mushrooms—they taste like something else that hasn't been named,
something closer to meat yet with a less chewy texture. The flavor is
delicate, so too much fanciness in the kitchen can obliterate an ethe-
real delight. I've eaten fresh morels at home over a fillet of grilled
Copper River sockeye; stir-fried with geoduck clam in a Sichuan "fish
fragrance" sauce; with lamb ragu and handmade pappardelle; in risotto with fiddleheads and asparagus tips; decorating a Hangtown
fry; on a cheeseburger, over pizza, and simply out of the pan. In the
woods I've had them with fettuccine tossed in a creamy red-wine
sauce; over aged sirloin cooked on the campfire; with spring porcini
in a sausage stew; in an omelet, over coals, and on a stick. In restaurants I've had them so many ways—creative and otherwise—that I
can't begin to count. When reconstituted, dried morels make a rich
stock that's lighter than porcini and well suited to a touch of white
wine and cream. In the depths of winter I'll make morel sauces to go
over a New York strip or simply tossed with egg noodles.

Morels are more valuable than chanterelles and more abundant
than matsutake. Year in and year out they are the backbone of the
commercial mushroom harvester's dossier. Those not sold fresh can
be dried and sold later for equally tidy sums, meaning that in a year
of abundance and lower prices a forager with foresight (and money in
the bank) can put aside some of his work for later, when prices have
rebounded. This is not the case with either chanterelles or matsutake.
Morels inhabit much of the temperate world, and their association
with fire has been noted in many a far-flung locale. In western North
America, this association borders on something out of science fiction.
An early botanist spoke of *stupendous* fruitings, and by stupendous he
meant that you could stand in the middle of a burned forest and see
ten pounds of morels on the ground immediately before your eyes,
hundreds of the buggers tucked under snags, hiding inside hollow

stumps, lazing in the shade of a blackened trunk, as if the mushroom were mustering its armies and preparing for a global takeover. It's an impossible embarrassment of riches for the fungiphile, a freakish event that has a first-timer pinching himself. Every wildfire in the high country of the West is monitored by thousands of morel pickers, some of them recreational pickers, many of them commercial. As the snows begin to melt, the morel hunters hop in their jalopies and drive, sometimes for hours or even days, to scout the burns. Well-heeled buyers might go by helicopter, scanning the view from above. Google Earth has simplified this process, but there's no substitute for scouting on foot.

Most of the morels coming out of Sisters were what is known as "naturals." These are non-burn morels. Though often larger and more handsome than burn morels, they're also more prone to worms and don't fruit with anywhere near the same abundance. The term *natural* is somewhat misleading, because in the West the morels are almost always the product of some sort of disturbance. Morels thrive in the multi-use forests favored by resource extractors as well as off-road vehicle enthusiasts, equestrians, and hikers. Some years produce a good crop of naturals in such busy woods—and this wasn't one of them. Neither the quality nor the quantity in Sisters was up to Faber's standards. He needed to find a burn that wasn't "covered with Cambodians," as he put it, which meant gassing up the Astro van and hitting the road.

Most of Faber's clients had little time or inclination to track his peripatetic movements on the mushroom trail, even if they counted on a dependable supply of his products. Each week, usually on Sunday or Monday (depending on whether he had been able to sneak off to ski), Faber sent them an email with the product outlook for the next week as well as a longer-range forecast, so the chefs and purchasers could plan ahead, along with a heads-up on short supply or special offers. Smart chefs used the brief periods of abundance to put up quantities of Faber's products so they could have wild foods year-round. They made chutneys and pestos, pastes and preserves. As with the trend in house-made salumi, kitchen staffs all over the country were learning the fine art of pickling. Navarre in Portland lined its walls with mason jars of canned goods; Vie, near Chicago, was famous for its extensive pickling; and in Seattle, Matt Dillon's restaurants were always putting up something—pickled ramps one day, herring another.

Before leaving for the Yukon, I stopped in for lunch at Nettletown, which could boast of perhaps my favorite pickled food of all. I ordered a bowl of udon noodles topped with a five-spice pork rib, a soft-boiled egg, crispy shallots, and a medley of wild greens and mushrooms, including sautéed morels and the most exquisite fiddleheads I'd ever tasted. Pickled in rice vinegar and Asian spices, they retained a hefty crunch and didn't exhibit any of the bitterness that often plagues West Coast lady fern fiddleheads. This was one of Christina Choi's signature dishes; a small bowl of them often accompanied a meal, on the house.

In the early years of Foraged and Found Edibles, Choi had accompanied Faber on many a harvest. Now she was wrapped up in the restaurant and rarely got out. Faber enjoyed telling the story of the day Choi had schooled him on a morel pick. They were somewhere in the eastern Cascades, and all day, each time they met up back at the van to dump another load, Choi would have twice as many morels as he did. Finally Faber gave in to his pride and asked her where she was picking. For Choi, there was no such thing as a secret patch. Wild foods were meant to be shared. Follow me, she said, and she brought him to a narrow little chasm beside a stream where the morels were having a convention. "That was one of the best picks ever," Faber said wistfully.

"Where are you and Jeremy off to next?" she asked me now, placing a steaming bowl of udon before me.

"Nowhere special," I said. "Just the Yukon."

"Really," Choi said absently, without her usual enthusiasm. I could tell the restaurant business was wearing on her. "Be careful up there. Is Doug going?" I shook my head. "Poor Doug," she said. "I hope he's okay."

I explained that this was a last-minute decision on Faber's part. I had hoped the three of us would camp somewhere in the Cascades together. But Nettletown, like so many other restaurants across the country, needed morels. "If all goes according to plan, we'll have all you can eat before long."

Her face briefly lit up at the prospect of a box of fresh morels, then she wandered back to the kitchen to take more orders.

. . .

JUST BEFORE THE BORDER CROSSING, we got our stories straight: He was buying mushrooms; I was covering the event. In the presence of the customs guard, though, Faber buckled and said we were camping in the bush. This wasn't exactly a lie, and the guard waved us through without even a cursory look in the back, where two hundred baskets—hardly the stuff of your average camping trip—awaited shipment to Whitehorse. These baskets would cost nearly four hundred dollars to ship empty at the Air North cargo office, where Faber caused a brief ruckus by paying in U.S. dollars. He pulled out a wad of more than five thousand in cash from his wallet before realizing he'd forgotten to exchange currencies at the bank. The cargo office shrugged it off. They could work with dollars. At the airport Park'N Fly, he explained to the parking attendant how his van started without need of a key (it was broken off in the ignition) and we boarded a shuttle. An hour later we were coasting north over British Columbia in a small jet, overlooking a mountaineer's wet dream of misted peaks in desolate ranges that rarely saw a piton or rope. Faber gazed down longingly at untracked glaciers, picking his routes on first descents among innumerable glades and snowfields that beckoned to the back-country skier. I thought about Doug driving around looking for some crummy burn close to home while we jetted to the mother lode. I hadn't told him I was going, didn't have the heart. Later he would laugh it off, in the way that all people with hurt feelings and pride laugh it off. He would say I'd given him the *hokey-doke*.

No one on that plane could have guessed that Jeremy Faber was a mushroom merchant poised to spend the next week (or month, as it would turn out) camped in the Yukon bush. Carrying a calfskin satchel under his arm, he cut a natty figure, dressed in designer black jeans, leather shoes, and—the centerpiece of his ensemble—a straw beret. His hair was starting to get long again, falling in brown curls below the back of his cap and across his eyes. He actually looked the part of a downtown hustler. "No mushroom talk," he begged me. We talked about girls instead. For all his swagger, Faber wanted to play the role of attentive boyfriend. There were so many girls—and so few who warranted an audience with his mother. "She's a good girl," he'd say about one who passed the test. Seattle was filled with too many not-so-good girls, like the barista he sometimes chatted up downtown. "She's hot, but not marriage material." His old-fashionedness was almost heartbreaking in its sincerity.

NAMED FOR A FLOWING mane of rapids on the Yukon River, now submerged by a dam, Whitehorse (population 26,000) is the largest city in Yukon Territory and sits on roughly the same latitude as Anchorage, Alaska. It's the land of the midnight sun. At nine o'clock, after finding a room for the night in town, we walked down Fourth Avenue, looking for a place to eat dinner; outside, the light suggested something more along the lines of a late lunch. The next morning I bought a map at the local bookstore, Mac's Fireweed, while Faber picked up the rental car. "This trip is getting more expensive every day," he grumbled, stepping out of a GMC Acadia, the biggest rental in town, a midsize SUV that clearly was not big enough for the volume he intended to buy. They were charging him for mileage too. He did some quick math: "I'll buy a car if I have to."

After a morning of preparations that included a trip to the vener-

able Canadian Tire to buy a cooler, stove gas, and other camping supplies, we started out of Whitehorse, briefly paralleling the headwaters
of the Yukon River along Robert Service Way (the poet known for
gold-rush ballads such as "The Cremation of Sam McGee") before
turning east. At Carcross Cutoff, the road forked, with the Klondike
Highway heading south to trace the original route of the 1898 Klondike gold rush between the gold fields of Dawson City to the north
and the entry point of Skagway, Alaska, to the south. We continued
east on the Alaska Highway, the storied thousand-mile-plus artery
built during World War II that connects Alaska to the contiguous
United States through Canada. Spurred in part by war, the highway
was completed by U.S. Army construction crews in less than a year
following the Japanese bombing of Pearl Harbor.

The country spread before us. Neither benevolent nor malicious,
the wide mountain valleys seemed distant and unknowable, places
apart, which would remain apart and inviolable. I found myself in-
ventorying provisions in my head once again and, distressingly, remembered something I had forgotten to purchase in Whitehorse.
Faber suggested I toughen up. "I don't need any modern conve-
niences," he said. The cooler I had requested was outrage enough. "I
don't need cold beer or hot food. I'll sleep on the ground. And I definitely don't need bug juice." In the next five hours we passed only a
handful of cars. Yukon Territory unfolded in the vaguely geometrical
patterns of receding glaciation that reminded me of ever-expanding
origami. It was a panorama of broad valleys surrounded by austere
mountains drained by a vast, incomprehensible network of rivers and
lakes. Almost none of it was protected in any official status as designated wilderness or provincial park, yet most of it looked utterly wild
and untrammeled. It was hard to imagine a human being out here in
this big country—it felt like land meant only for ravens and bears.

Some anthropologists believe the oldest evidence of human habitation in the New World comes from the Yukon: the remains of animal bones carbon-dated to twenty-five to forty thousand years ago,
found at the Bluefish Caves archeological site near Old Crow. Main-

stream archeologists find such dates—much older than previously thought—hard to believe. The *how* and *when* of human habitation in the Americas remains a tantalizingly open question. The word *Yukon* is Athabaskan and means "great river." This language group includes tribes such as the coastal Tlingit and the northern-dwelling Gwich'in, as well as, intriguingly, tribes in the American Southwest such as the Navajo and Apache. One theory holds that a major volcanic eruption encouraged southward migration. These eruptions also dumped layers of volcanic ash that promote substantial mushroom fruitings today. European contact began with fur traders in the 1800s, such as those from the Hudson's Bay Company. Missionaries and botanists came next. After a series of minor gold strikes, Skookum Jim Mason's party discovered gold in 1896 on Bonanza Creek, a Klondike River tributary, and the region's transformative historical moment commenced. Forty thousand prospectors stampeded into the territory over the next few years, weathering the dangerous trail over Chilkoot Pass and later a safer detour over White Pass, to pan for a few short months before winter swallowed the camps once again. With the turn of the century, the population declined as the gold dwindled. Today it's around thirty thousand—about the same as it was in 1900.

The burn was five hours by car to the east of Whitehorse, across the northern border of British Columbia and south of the small community of Watson Lake, famous for its "Sign Post Forest." The jam-packed collection of road signs from around the world was started in 1942 by a homesick U.S. Army G.I. working on the Alaska Highway. Black spruce, lodgepole pine, and poplar dominate the actual forest here, growing out of a sponge-like carpet of sphagnum moss. The presence of black spruce (*Picea mariana*) in particular was important to Faber. This is one of the key species of the great boreal forest that encircles the northern portion of the globe, covering parts of Alaska, Canada, Sweden, Finland, Norway, Russia, Kazakhstan, Mongolia, and even slivers of both the continental United States (Minnesota and Maine) and Japan (Hokkaido Island). In Russia, the boreal forest is known as the "taiga." It's the largest ecosystem, or biome, in the

world, accounting for almost 30 percent of the world's forest cover—
and it's a mushroom producer par excellence. It has been observed
that morels fruit best in areas with distinct seasons, notably cold
snowy winters and hot summers. The boreal forest has this in spades,
since its low temperatures can exceed that of the tundra while its
highs are significantly higher and, due to long days in summer, sus-
taining.

Novice question: "Where can I find morels?"

Old-timer answer: "Morels are where you find them." Or, as
David Arora likes to say, mostly outdoors. They've been spotted
growing out of sidewalks, Sheetrock walls, flowerpots, even an old
shoe.

If mushrooms are a mystery, morels are an enigma wrapped
within that mystery. Their taxonomy is a mess. Little is known about
when, where, and why they will fruit. And even their purpose is not
well understood. Are morels saprophytic or mycorrhizal? Or both, at
different stages in their life cycle? Technically speaking, morels are
not even mushrooms. As members of the *Ascomycota* phylum, they're
actually cup fungi, differentiating them from true mushrooms, which
are members of the *Basidiomycota* phylum. But that's mostly a matter
for mycologists. To the rest of us, they might as well be called
mushrooms—enticing, delicious, elusive, maddening mushrooms.

A technical paper on morels in Alaska reports that there is "little
well-established information on morel reproduction, spore dispersal,
colony establishment and growth under forest conditions." In terms
of classification, the genus *Morchella* is up for grabs as well. We don't
know what to call individual species or even how many there are.
Many of the North American species went by European names until
only recently, when a 2012 paper proposed a number of new classifi-
cations based on the most up-to-date DNA analysis. Former
conundrums, like a species commonly known as the western "mountain blond"—*Morchella frustrata* in this new regime, because it used
to frustrate morel taxonomists with its amalgamation of morel
characteristics—now had scientific names for the first time. At the

moment it seems clear that the North American varieties are distinct from those on other continents—and, in fact, it has been suggested that North America has more distinct species than anywhere else in the world and may represent the point of origin for the group's evolution.

Meanwhile, North American morel hunters, both commercial and recreational, use all kinds of pet names to describe their darlings, mostly based on outward appearance and coloration. They refer to yellows, blacks, blonds, grays, reds, whites, pinks, and greenies, among others. There are morels called bananas and morels known as pickles. In the South they're sometimes called peckerheads. The morels I picked in Michigan are denizens of eastern hardwood forests; the morels of the West are very different. They prefer conifers, though not always. What's known for sure is that, given the right habitat, morels in the West will respond to disturbance. The disturbance could be logging or trail maintenance or road building. Most often it's fire.

West of the hundredth meridian, the continent is governed by fire ecology. Wildfires are a part of life. Trees such as lodgepole pines have adapted to fire; their seeds germinate in conditions of high heat. Morels, it would seem, have also adapted to this regime, though for reasons that are unclear. Is the mushroom making a last-ditch attempt to spread its spores after the death of its host tree? Is it suddenly capable of carpeting the ground because competing plant or fungal life has been eliminated? Is a change in soil pH responsible? No one knows. What is known is that a forest fire in the right coniferous habitat (usually dry, montane forests of fir, spruce, and sometimes pine) can produce a bonanza of morels that will draw morel hunters from miles around, just as the gold strikes did more than a century ago.

Faber got visibly excited at the first sight of burn. Though winter snowstorms had extinguished the last embers months earlier and the smoke had long since cleared, the air here felt heavier and thicker than usual, probably due to floating ash particulates. Up ahead, the fire line stood out like a stop sign. Healthy green forest turned to red—the dead needles of spruce and pine where the fire had crept along. Farther along, the red turned to black, the total devastation of what morel pickers refer to as the "hot burn," a place of gray ash and blackened spars. The topography looked relatively flat compared to Faber's regular haunts in the Cascades, with an elevation of twenty-five hundred feet, give or take a few hundred, and a smattering of minor rounded peaks that rose to five thousand feet. The Cassiar Highway bisected the burn from north to south, and the Blue River, a nice-looking trout stream, bisected it again from east to west. This was too good to be true: a huge burn with good road access and prominent geographical features. Black-spruce country is considered one of the world's great morel factories, and it's equally infamous for the logistical nightmares that accompany the harvesting of its morels. Entrepreneurial (or just plain crazy) harvesters have been known to helicopter into remote Yukon burns or try to float out their haul by whitewater raft. This burn was large (official estimates put it at nearly seventy-five thousand acres), on relatively flat ground, accessible by a highway as well as forest roads, and less than twenty miles from an outpost of civilization, Watson Lake.

Faber shifted anxiously in his seat, scanning as he drove. "*No one is here,*" he said finally. We'd driven five miles through burned-over forestland without seeing a single car on the side of the road. "If this was Oregon, we'd have cars lining the highway. You'd have four thousand Cambodians picking a two-thousand-acre burn." We passed a collection of wall tents off to the right that Faber initially mistook for a very serious mushroom buyer, until we saw a sign identifying it as a fire camp. Finally, at the junction of the Blue River, we saw a couple of cars and a single buyer. Another mile and we turned left, passing a few picker camps on either side of the gravel logging road. We pulled in to an empty turnout on the right. Neither one of us could wait any longer. We quickly strapped on our heavy boots, grabbed buckets, and made for the woods. I found my first morel just a few feet from the car, then another. I stayed close to the road and hunted the general vicinity, filling half a bucket. Faber reappeared half an hour later with a full bucket. He had made a beeline through the woods to a ridge, climbed the steep slope (because many inexperienced mushroom pickers will avoid climbs), and found a hillside exploding with morels. Together we went back up the ridge and picked until ten P.M., filling several baskets.

Back at camp, Faber started to organize the buying part of the operation. He had baskets arranged all around the SUV, and it didn't take long for pickers to see them as they drove by. A new buyer was in town. They approached cautiously at first, not wanting to commit, with one main question: *How much?* Faber had a few questions of his own. *How many buyers are there?* Three or four. *What are they paying?* Four dollars a pound. "Don't bullshit me," he said. "I'll find out for sure tomorrow." They said it again: four dollars. He thought this over, looking around at the landscape, pausing for dramatic effect, mulling it over. The pickers lifted their chins. "I'm paying five," he said, and everyone relaxed into a good humor as the weighing began. Word spread fast. Even at eleven P.M., a number of pickers were just returning from a day in the woods, with full baskets in hand.

OVER AN INDIAN-STYLE CAMP dinner of chicken, peppers, and onions with naan and yogurt, Faber told me that tomorrow would likely be my best shot at a hundred-pound day. I'd never picked more than thirty pounds in a day, an amount that most recreational pickers would consider extraordinary. To achieve the magic three digits, I'd be using a packboard that could carry six baskets. We would get up early, five A.M. or so, and pick for most of the day, until it was time to open the buy station. We wouldn't even drive anywhere—we'd pick right out of camp.

The next morning, the sun was already above the trees when we finished our coffee and walked out of camp at six A.M. It would be a warm day for the Yukon. I was dressed in light pants, heavy socks, and boots. In my pants pockets I kept two granola bars, a mimeographed map of the burn, and my wallet, with identification (just in case). I wore a long-sleeved Capilene T-shirt and a compass around my neck. My mushroom knife was sheathed on my belt and a water bottle tied to my pack. I had a rain slicker stashed in one of the baskets. We passed by the spot-burned woods adjacent to camp, strode through blackened hot burn to the ridge, switchbacked up, and then began to follow the drainage. Before leaving me, Faber suggested I keep to the edge of the hot burn. The picking would be better on the edge, and, perhaps more important, by keeping to the edge I wouldn't get lost.

Unlike the evening before, I was now looking for the highest densities of mushrooms before dropping my pack. I walked by onesies and twosies, scouting for the large clusters that would make the picking go faster and increase my chances at a hundred-pound day. Each time I dropped my pack, I would make circles around it, carrying my bucket to points beyond and then leaving that on the periphery to make even wider concentric circles, using my shirt as a receptacle. These orbits around orbits ensured that I would cover the most ground possible without the burden of carrying my pack. With the hem of my shirt clenched firmly between my teeth, I sliced off morels as fast as I could and dropped them into the makeshift pocket of the shirt. Pretty soon I got in the habit of walking with my knife unsheathed, to save time. I could hear my seventh-grade teacher telling us a story about how her son had stabbed out one of his eyes in a swing-set mishap involving an open pocketknife. All my life this story had made me cautious around open blades—but not today. Honor trumped eyesight.

The shirt bulked up quickly. I could smell its contents as the mushrooms piled up to my chin. Unlike chanterelles or porcini, fresh morels don't have a particularly appetizing scent, certainly nothing that suggests the wonderful and complex aroma of cooked morels. The smell is dank, almost milk-like, and hardly hints at what lays ahead in the pan. Nearby, the white bucket stood out against the earth tones of the burn like a beacon, calling me in after each sally through this one small wrinkle of scorched forest. I'd circle back to the bucket with a full shirt, then make another foray before picking up the bucket and going elsewhere, until I'd covered an area around the pack the size of a football field, at which point I'd hoist the pack again and look for a promising new area.

The day heated up, and the burn offered little respite from the sun. For the Yukon it was hot, about seventy-five degrees. Downed timber lay higgledy-piggledy across the earth, like a Goliath's game of pick-up sticks. Under the burned logs and in the depressions left by uprooted stumps grew morels. They poked their impish heads through the ash, phallic in the extreme. A pornographer would see penises everywhere—rudely shaped penises popping out of every nook and cranny, mocking our taste in psychosexual foods. I followed the ridgeline and picked as fast as I could. My teeth began to hurt, as if I had spent the night anxiously grinding them together. After four shirtfuls, my five-gallon bucket was nearly full and I emptied it into a basket. Each basket took a bucket and a half of morels to fill. When the basket was full, I covered it with a lid, nested it among the empty baskets, and lashed them all to the packboard with bungee cords before moving on. My cords were color-coded. I had two long red bungee cords to cinch the baskets to the pack and two short blue bungee cords to keep the baskets nested together with their lids tight. These were not the sort of bungee cords with weak, bendable hooks and short-lived elastic that you might find at a typical hardware store; they were bungee cords that Navy SEALs could endorse. Faber wouldn't even tell me where he'd found them. The packboard was the kind preferred by big-game hunters, and the extendable top braces were crucial for stacking a maximum number of full baskets, not that I required this carrying capacity—yet. Soon, though, I had two full baskets tied together, and then three.

The idea of lurking grizzly bears had long since vanished from my mind. There was no time to worry about such beasts. I was driven to pick as many morels as I could. Strategy now occupied my head. When I wasn't in the middle of slicing morels off at the ankles and filling my bucket, I was scanning the burn, trying to deduce its secrets. Looking at a burned-over forest is like seeing the landscape naked. It can't hide. The drainage reveals itself in all its crimps and creases. I studied the topography for clues—slope aspect, moisture pockets, percentage of standing timber, whether any of that timber was alive. The deeper I progressed into the burn, the more I learned from experience. The forest—this badly wounded northern boreal forest—was eerily beautiful in its most desperate moment. Blackened trunks rose in silhouette against a gray sky. The dense mat of sphagnum moss ran like a green maze where it hadn't burned into ash. Clumps of perfect morels sprouted from divots in the singed moss and on tufts of reddened spruce needles. This disfigured patch of earth was determined to live again.

Despite Faber's warning to stick to spot burn on the edge, I was finding it easiest to cover ground by walking right through the hot burn. Here the trees had mostly burned up and it wasn't necessary to negotiate downed timber. The ground underfoot felt spongy and tentative, as if it might just give way once and for all and send me hurtling to untold depths. Little wisps of smoke followed my footfalls, as if I were stepping on ripe puffball mushrooms. There were morels in the hot burn, though not as many as in the spot burn, and many of them were dried out from direct sunlight and wind. The hot burn was apocalyptic—the popular-imagination version of forest fire, with virtually nothing left alive and only a few skeletal trees to tell you this was once a forest at all. Just the same, next summer it would be pulsing with new plant growth. Fireweed would be the first to erupt, in colorful bursts of green and pink, providing shade for new saplings to sprout. Beetles and worms would recolonize the earth. In time the ash would melt into soil, shrubbery would take hold, and moss would reclaim the ground. In this way a new forest would rise from the ashes of the old.

The other reason I preferred walking through the hot burn was the need to keep moving. A cloud of flying insects harried me constantly, buzzing in my ear. Now I realized what a miscalculation I'd made in allowing Faber to shame me into not buying any bug spray.

At the time, I had decided he was right—dealing with insects in the bush required changing one's state of mind. Bugs only bothered you, I told myself, if you let them. How mistaken I'd been. The phrase *eaten alive* came to mind. A hoary phrase—and yet so correct. I couldn't shake them. *Insecta* had it out for me: mosquitoes large and small, blackflies, sand flies, no-see-ums, deerflies, horseflies. Morel-picker flies. The list went on. They pursued me like the Furies, darting in when my hands were full of mushrooms, penetrating my ears and nostrils, going down my throat, clawing at the corners of my eyes, finding sweaty folds of skin and clothing under which to burrow and hide. They gave no quarter. Just before one P.M. I reached my limit, turned around, and headed back toward camp, where we had agreed to meet for lunch. I was a mile or more away. I had four full baskets and a half-full bucket—about fifty pounds, half my goal.

I passed Faber a quarter mile from camp. He'd already eaten lunch and was on his way back into the bush. All along, with nobody to talk to except the voice in my head, I had been wondering what Faber would say about my first full day of picking professionally. I replayed little scenarios over and over, imagined bits of conversation. Would he be critical? Dismissive? I was on his turf, trying to prove something. Now he looked at my load and said, "Well, you've out-picked everyone else around here. Go get some lunch and take a break." It's understood that the level of picking doesn't impress him. Still, he's not one to offer empty praise. I was feeling good.

The way home was treacherous, however. I carried my heavy load over countless deadfalls and beneath leaning snags. The top of my pack, with its extended frame that rose a foot above my head, was now a liability. Like a buck that must lower his antlers in thick cover, I was forced to duck and weave among the downed timber, several times getting hung up while trying to scoot under suspended logs. Potential widow-makers littered the ground. It was easy to see how a picker might come to a grisly end in the burn, impaled on a sharp branch or crushed by a tree. By the time I reached camp, I was exhausted. The bugs had had their way with me. At times there were so many crawling over my skin that I felt as if I were walking through spiderwebs. My body was covered with raised red welts—more than a dozen on my right wrist alone where the skin was exposed. Behind each ear collected a dry, crumbly crust of blood, matted hair, and squashed flies, and beneath that was the Braille-like pattern of bumps where they had pierced tender recesses of epidermis before I could swat them away. The bumps followed my hairline all the way around the nape of my neck, while the larger welts of horseflies and deerflies adorned my shoulders, back, and arms. I had a collection of bloody lumps in the pit of my chest, where they had gotten under my shirt, and more on my abdomen. Mosquito bites were indiscriminate. They were everywhere, wherever the bloodsuckers could get purchase. I had flecks of bright red blood all over me. My hands were black with soot, not to mention my own dried blood from swatting so many mosquitoes. My pants had turned from a light khaki color to lead gray. My feet ached.

But, hey, more than fifty pounds before lunch. I was still feeling good.

The boots and socks came off first. My feet were red and swollen. I changed my shirt. A morning like this demanded a serious lunch. I cooked a chicken thigh on the camp stove and made a sandwich with the leftover naan, rice, peppers, and yogurt, with a half lemon squeezed on top for extra measure. This was a ridiculous lunch in the bush, but I couldn't help myself. I was exhausted and hungry. A picker needing to make his car payment, on the other hand, would probably pause for a nanosecond to wolf down an uncooked hot dog or a Twinkie. At a certain point I had to acknowledge the absurdity of my lunch prep, which was crawling along. I popped open a beer. What the heck. The day was hot and windless and somehow not of this world, as if unchained from time, the bugs relentless. After lunch I sought refuge in my tent, though without significant shade it was like a boiler room or a sweat lodge. *Tick-tick-tick-tick.* Blackflies hurled themselves at the tent to get at me, in such numbers that it sounded like rain.

Finally, after another drink of water and a pear, I pulled on a clean pair of socks (a ridiculous luxury that wouldn't be scalable through the week) and laced up my heavy boots for round two. It was after three P.M. Even though I was dragging, there was no choice. My honor was at stake. I headed for the cooler spot-burned woods on the other side of the road. The picking here was slow going, for reasons that weren't immediately clear to me, though I would learn soon enough that it had to do with other pickers. No one picks a hundred pounds next to a road. I managed a basket and a half for about seventy pounds on the day, before thunderheads piled up overhead like a slow-moving train wreck and detonated over the burn. The sky turned black, lightning danced across the horizon, and thunderclaps evicted the quiet of the bush. I hightailed it back to camp—one, to avoid the lightning, and two (more important?), to protect my mushrooms from rain, which was now falling in a steady drumbeat of fat drops that made muffled explosions in the ash fields with little puffs of smoke in their wake. The mythical hundred-pound day was not to be. As rain pummeled our campsite, I collapsed in my tent and immediately fell asleep.

When I awoke, I crawled out of the tent and found Faber standing in the rain, getting soaked. It was time to buy morels and he couldn't afford to hide. The tailgate of his SUV provided little cover. He had neglected to buy a canopy because of the cost, and now he had to live with that decision. Pickers pulled into our camp and waited in their vehicles until it was their turn to sell. In addition to the typical burn morels, known as "conicas" to the pickers (for an out-of-date Latin name), many of them had a few of the season's first gray morels mixed into their baskets. Faber was paying six dollars for those. He pulled out the big grays and tossed them into their own dedicated basket. "These are going to Matt," he said.

Little is known about what western pickers call "grays." This species of morel that seems to be associated exclusively with burns in the Pacific Northwest hardly appears in the literature, though it was granted full species status in a 2008 paper by Michael Kuo. Currently it carries the binomial *Morchella tomentosa* and goes by common names such as fuzzy-foot morel or black-foot morel. It's definitely not the same mushroom that is known as a "gray" in the Midwest or on the East Coast; that morel is likely an immature version of a yellow morel, *Morchella esculentoides*.

The grays of the burn are large, some of them bigger than an outstretched hand, and densely pitted. Younger specimens exhibit small hairs on the cap and especially at the base of the stem, hence the name fuzzy foot. Pickers and buyers talk about their "double walls"—that is, when you slice them in half, you can clearly see two layers of flesh, especially in the stem, making grays heavier than most other varieties. Chefs in the know covet this meatiness. Grays are usually one of the last species of burn morel to fruit. Conicas, the bread-and-butter species of the burn, more closely resemble natural black morels, though they have thinner flesh. Chefs like conicas because they're lightweight, relatively small, and don't cost as much as other morel varieties. A few halved conicas can spruce up a plate and bring a chef plaudits without breaking the bank. Then there are chefs like Matt Dillon, so enamored of *Morchella* that they forget to make any money off the fungi at all, using the conicas whole to dress up a dish with an impossible smothering of morels, or gladly spending seventeen dollars a pound to be one of the few restaurants offering grays on the menu, a delicacy among delicacies that most restaurant patrons would be hard-pressed to recognize anyway.

By eight P.M., Faber had bought enough mushrooms to make a run to the Whitehorse airport, five hours away. I did the driving. The AC rattled away on high to keep the mushrooms from overheating. Packed into baskets, they generate their own heat and can quickly turn rotten if not properly cared for.

Faber tried to dry out. Everything he owned was thoroughly drenched, since he was forced to use his tent fly to shield the mushrooms from rain. His tent, sleeping bag, and extra clothes were all wet. He could have moved some of these items into the car, but in his zeal to buy, he forgot.

We stopped in Teslin, the only gas after Watson Lake, narrowly pulling in before its eleven P.M. closing time. We warmed ourselves in the café and drank a cup of coffee, then I washed up in the men's room. It was my first look in a mirror, and I was shocked. My face was covered in soot. Worse, I had multiple red bites in the corners of my eye sockets, and my neck was visibly swollen. I looked like a junkie, an escapee from a leper colony.

We drove on and arrived at Whitehorse well after midnight. It was twilight out, the sky a dark blue with traces of orange—the longest sunset I'd ever seen, if it can even be called a sunset. The rains let up, the clouds broke, and bright silver and gold linings appeared etched in thunderheads low on the horizon. We drove around for a while, marveling at the forlorn quietude of the Yukon's most peopled settlement and looking for an all-night diner. There was none to be had. We settled for the blandness of a Tim Hortons donut shop, where the cops glanced at us uneasily even as we tried to make polite conversation in line. *Really, I'm not a junkie.*

It was three A.M. when we pulled into a vacant lot next to the Air North cargo office and cadged a few hours of cramped sleep with the front seats reclined to their limit, a few degrees past vertical. At six the gate opened and we backed into the lone bay to unload 630 pounds of morels onto two pallets. The morels were packed into fifty-one zip-tied baskets. After unloading, Faber was dismayed to see a few dozen small white worms struggling on the bed of the SUV. Not a good sign. Burn morels usually have the advantage of not being wormy, unlike morels picked in more natural conditions. This is an obvious commercial advantage, and now Faber was worried that this particular burn, for reasons not readily apparent, might have some flaws.

Next we waited in a Starbucks parking lot until seven to poach Wi-Fi, then it was back to Canadian Tire for bug spray and a tarp. A return trip to the car rental was fruitless; they had nothing larger. By eight A.M., the first orders of the day started flooding in on Faber's BlackBerry. It was Monday, and everyone wanted morels. Unfortunately, Faber's right-hand man, Jonathan, was on vacation, an extended long weekend with his wife to celebrate her birthday. Faber was incredulous that one of his two full-time employees in Seattle would take a day off in June. "When he first asked me a few weeks ago, I couldn't believe it. All I said was, 'Dude, June is the busiest month of the year.' I thought I was clear." This left the young and relatively inexperienced Shane as the only one available to take orders and make deliveries.

To further complicate matters, Chase Bank had frozen Faber's account, and AmEx was reporting a negative balance. The Chase situation was especially nettlesome. For whatever reason, they were putting holds on incoming checks, including holds on payments from some of Seattle's biggest restaurateurs. Faber was forced to tap a third account and open a fourth in Canada at Toronto Dominion. He was seriously contemplating buying a van. Little cash, a too-small car. The anxieties were mounting. Back in Seattle, a courier picked up a five-thousand-dollar loan from a friend and delivered it to Toronto Dominion in the form of a cashier's check. "It's like cash, right?" Faber queried the teller over the phone. Unbelievably, TD slapped a thirty-day hold on the cashier's check. "Welcome to Canada!" Faber yelled into the phone after hanging up.

Sunday's rain had been hard on the crop, the burned, defenseless woods a wet, muddy mire of decomposition. After spending all of Monday morning with money woes, a glut of orders, and mounting logistical issues, we returned to the bush in the early evening to find that the quality of the morels had plummeted following the rainstorm. Needing product quickly to fulfill so many orders, Faber decided he should make another return to Whitehorse that night. He set up his buy station on the main road, hoping to get as much as he could as quickly as possible. The conicas looked terrible. He turned away pickers with obviously compromised mushrooms—waterlogged morels with brown stems; old, pink-hued specimens; softball-sized sponges with gaping holes at the stipe. A carload of pickers piled out of an old Pontiac and opened the trunk. Even before the first basket came out, Faber could see their stuff was awful.

"I'm only buying fresh market," he tried to forestall before they could start stacking baskets on his table. He told them about a buyer down the road who was buying everything, even brown stem, for drying. The pickers already knew this buyer was paying a dollar less.

"What's the problem?" one of them wanted to know, getting in Faber's face.

Faber explained what he was looking for: firm morels with white stems. Another picker got out of the car. "This guy's an asshole. Let's get out of here."

"Shut up for a second. I want to know why he won't buy from us."

"Come on, man."

"Well?"

"Like I said, I'm doing fresh market. I can't sell these fresh."

Three of the four pickers got back in their car. The belligerent one pointed his finger at Faber. "We'll be back."

Faber couldn't get enough mushrooms to warrant a return to Whitehorse. We drove up to the junction of the Alaska Highway and Cassiar Highway to use a pay phone at the gas station. "It's amateur hour," he grumbled, pumping loonies into the slot. Plenty of mushrooms, no good picking crews. Now that a heavy rain had done in part of the crop, the picking would be more difficult, and Faber expected to sift through pounds of garbage. "Amateurs," he said again, fishing around in his pocket for more change. He spent four Canadian dollars to get Shane's voice mail and left the pay-phone number on the message. We sat in the car and waited.

When his employee called back, Faber could tell immediately that something wasn't right. Shane had been detained at the border. After driving two hours north to pick up the first Air North shipment, Shane got grilled on his way back into the States. A young border patrolman thought he had a pigeon. "I'm not stupid," he told Shane. "I know those mushrooms cost more than four dollars a pound."

Faber had fudged the price slightly, knowing that the going rate for the last month was four dollars, not the five he was paying. Since it was his first run to Vancouver, Shane wasn't exactly sure what to say.

"Did you tell him to look up the price on the Internet?" Faber asked impatiently.

Shane said he did. He was clearly unhinged by the experience and having trouble explaining himself. He said he waited around for a couple of hours while the young hotshot guard accused him of forgery—a felony—and then, during a lunch break, when another guard came on duty, he pleaded his case again; the guard took one look over the paperwork and sent him along, just like that. The vagaries of the border crossing. But, in his haste, Shane blew by the next checkpoint in the van, not realizing he wasn't finished, and an armed border agent came running after him, shouting, with his hand on his holster, before Shane realized he was being ordered to stop. Now he was a wreck.

Faber hung up, shaking his head and smiling uncontrollably. Poor Shane. But it *was* kind of funny.

Still, the Yukon wasn't working out the way Faber had hoped. This was supposed to be a big cash takedown, a chance to refuel. Faber had been bleeding money since opening the East Coast branch of his business. Even though he was a born New Yorker, the intricacies of operating in Manhattan had come back to haunt him. At the moment he was fighting a fourteen-thousand-dollar fine from the state for neglecting workers' compensation for his lone employee, who had meanwhile racked up nearly a thousand dollars in parking tickets because his delivery van lacked the proper identification on the side. Faber thought he had remedied that situation with stick-on decals; instead he'd earned another couple of hundred in tickets because the lettering, by law, must be stenciled. Stenciled! Faber had used up nearly all his retirement fund to launch the New York gambit, and now he was looking for investors. Twenty thousand dollars, he said. That's all he needed. But the fines stung. "If New York tries to collect any of that fourteen thousand dollars, I'll shut down and move to New Jersey. Fuck them. I'll file Chapter Eleven before I give them a dime. I'm employing a resident in their state. They should work with small businesses, not fight them." He shouted a few choice words, then sagged back into his seat. "I don't need this shit." It was time to drive back to camp.

Though Faber could work at a breakneck pace with little sleep for days on end, the management of day-to-day small-business minutiae was clearly not his interest. He wanted to be in the woods. And then there were those deep glooms. The mood swings came on sudden and savage. His intensity during the up moments was mirrored by the things he did to relax: skiing backcountry avalanche chutes in the Kootenays, spearfishing in the Bahamas. Dusk was his favorite time of day and winter his favorite season. "Summer sucks," he said to me in his binary way. "I'd much rather be in the mountains in spring or fall. Winter is the best." Now he went into a dark silent place, and I didn't try to follow. I spent my time watching the Yukon's rawboned scenery scroll past the window as we drove back into the burn.

. . .

MY ORIGINAL PLAN WAS to pick for profit. So far, with all the logistics and trips back and forth to Whitehorse, I'd gotten in only a single full day of picking, which was a partial rainout in the afternoon in any case. On Tuesday I walked back into the bush, this time putting more miles on my boots in an effort to find virgin ground. I walked through my previous picking area behind camp and followed the drainage until it crested out onto a broad plateau of hot burn. Across the hot burn, a half mile or more, a fringe of lush green forest shimmered like a tropical mirage: a prime picking ground away from the road. To get there I would need to traverse the hot burn and what looked like a vicious blowdown of monstrous proportions, its story written in the devastation visible all around. The plateau, I could see, was the highest ground for miles. The fire might have kicked up a windstorm that swept across it like a tidal wave, or perhaps the winds came later after the trees had burned, toppling anything with the audacity to still be standing. Whatever the cause, there was no protection on top of the plateau. The compromised forest got flattened, and now it was a huge logjam between me and where I wanted to go. *Shit.* I stood in the ash and looked out across a morass of charcoaled logs for a long while before common sense turned me away. It was an impenetrable fortress. No, I would continue to follow the edge of the burn all the way around instead of trying to take a direct route across the blowdown. Anything else would be foolish.

Though it took me the better part of two hours to reach the far side of the plateau, with poor picking along the way, eventually I got into the spot burn, a few miles at least from the road, and immediately started to see prodigious fruitings of conica. Or, rather, prodigious fruitings of *gak*. I could hear Faber's swift judgment in my ear. The rain had done its dirty work, helping to spread the morel spores. The mushrooms were in various stages of decay, almost all of them way past their prime. Acres and acres of gak, with some of the clusters sprouting dozens, even scores of mushrooms from a single focus in the charred earth, the morels radiating in tight formation like petals on a dandelion. It was a depressing sight. Two days ago in this spot I might have gotten my hundred pounds. Now it was mulch. The walking here wasn't easy either. The effects of the windstorm had rippled even through unburned forest, toppling trees everywhere.

Finally I accepted defeat and moved into the hot burn, where many of the trees had been incinerated, leaving openings to pass through. I wasn't exactly sure where I was, though looking at the sun as it slipped through the western sky, I had a general sense of which direction I needed to walk to return to camp. I had two full baskets and a half-full bucket—less than half my carrying capacity. The day was shaping up as a loser. Somewhere to my left was the blowdown, which I wanted to avoid. I continued north. And that's when I started to see them: giant gray morels in the hot burn. They grew in little families, and some were huge, bigger than a russet potato. They had two colors, gray and yellow. I had read that direct sunlight might account for the color differences in gray morels, but these varicolored specimens were growing together in the same conditions, with the same light. The difference had to be age or genetics. Regardless, they both carried the same price, which was a dollar more than conicas, and they weighed substantially more. A single family of a dozen mushrooms might weigh in at a few pounds or more. Here was my chance to make up for an otherwise poorly executed day of picking. I plucked the large grays, trimmed their ends, and then started roaming the hot burn for more. There was no rhyme or reason to their appearance, not that I could figure out. The only link I could see was a preference for fruiting beneath the long, twisted branches of some type of deciduous shrub that reminded me of vine maple.

When I'd filled my four baskets and the bucket—about fifty pounds in all—it was time to return home. I figured I was about two miles southeast of camp. Looking out across the fire zone, it appeared I might be able to make a beeline directly across the hot burn and arrive at the forest road for an easy walk home. I started across. This was easy. I hummed a song and swung my bucket. My pack felt good and secure, four full baskets. Six baskets would have been better, though four was acceptable.

When I came to the first of the downed trees, I didn't think much of it. It was normal to scale a few deadfalls in the hot burn. Little trees turned into bigger trees, and soon I was looking at a wall of stacked dead timber that might have been two stories high. A realization dawned: I had walked right into the blowdown. I had allowed myself to be cornered by lifeless trees. How could I be so stupid? And now I'd gone too far to turn back. I pressed on, trying my best to squeeze between logs or pull myself over deadfall, balancing, jumping, highstepping from one tree to the next until I might be perched ten feet above the ground. I saw myself plunging through a latticework of burned timber and impaling myself on a sharpened snag. Skewered in the patch.

After an hour of struggle, sweat pouring off me and stinging my eyes, the green edge of unburned forest came into view. Here the blowdown was at its most formidable. This was the last hurdle: a towering maze of wood. I stood on a log and surveyed my options, looking up at the jumbled mass of timber the way a mountaineer studies the peak he's about to attempt, finally settling on a route. I started to climb. Again and again, I was forced to take off my pack-board, haul it over blackened tree trunks, and carefully lower it to the ground before pulling myself through a narrow gap in the wall. It was grueling work. When I finally escaped into the cool shade of healthy forest, I dropped my pack, took a swig of water, and fell on my back into the sphagnum to rest. Fifteen minutes later I got to my feet and looked over what I had just struggled through. My eyes alighted on two prominent tracks in the ash at the edge of the forest: my hiking boots. I had arrived back at the exact point where I had judiciously decided, earlier that day, to avoid the blowdown.

Faber weighed my work back at camp. Not so bad, he said. I'd still outpicked the others. My only competition was a tall, bikini-clad woman from Vancouver. Margo was in her forties and wore a home-made mosquito-net cover-up over the bikini and black leather motor-cycle boots. "Yeah, she's a badass," Faber said with admiration. He gave her an extra fifty cents per pound.

The next morning, while Faber was in Whitehorse getting the runaround from TD Bank, I came out of the woods to find new neighbors. A loud diesel pickup truck was in the process of backing a trailer into an opening next to our camp. Once the trailer was posi-tioned and level, the truck drove off, leaving two men and a woman behind. Their trailer—long, white, and windowless—looked more like a storage unit with a meat-locker door. The occupants worked on their camp all day as I made trips into the woods. With chain saws and power tools, they built a private latrine, a covered porch off the trailer, and a big fire pit complete with spit. That night the new neigh-bors invited me over for a beer. Tommy was Takla Indian, his friend Slim was white, and the woman was Tommy's sister (and maybe Slim's girlfriend). They kept a sawed-off grizzly rifle by the trailer door and wore bear bells. "That's for moose," Tommy said, seeing me stare at the gun. "See any around?" I said we'd seen plenty on the roadside. He nodded without interest.

"Those packs are handy for the mushrooms, eh," Slim remarked. All they had were buckets.

"They're not pickers," Faber said the next morning over coffee. No one was stirring next door. "Must be on the lam." I hadn't even considered this possibility. To me, they looked like some serious campers who planned to spend the summer hunting game and picking a few mushrooms for profit.

"Come on," he said. "No vehicle? Left in the bush? They're running from something."

Each night after dinner and a few smokes by the fire, they disappeared into the trailer to watch DVDs. They seemed friendly enough. Slim wore the same black TAPOUT T-shirt each day. He was happy about his alliance with a First Nations member and wore it like a badge of honor. I asked him about moose-hunting season. "Closed for me," he said. "But I'm with him. We'll be netting salmon on the Telegraph next month."

"Probably robbed a bank," Faber said later. Banks were on his mind. He was still suffering money woes and didn't have nearly as much cash in hand as he expected to by now. Word had spread and pickers pulled into our encampment in droves, taking a place in line to sell their goods. Faber paid out all his cash, borrowed some from me, and then started writing IOUs to some of the pickers he'd gotten to know in the last week. He didn't like writing IOUs. Anything could go wrong. If he didn't have the cash tomorrow, then trouble would brew. The pickers, however, were insistent. They wanted that extra dollar or two per pound. It was getting late when one more pickup pulled in, a Tlingit man, a new face. He was with a buddy. Faber explained that he was out of cash and suggested the man visit another buyer down the road. In fact, he knew from picker chitchat that the other buyers were all closed tonight; one had shuttered indefinitely and the other two were done for the evening.

"You fucking buyers," the man growled. An air of menace burned off him. "Always trying to rip someone off."

"I'm not trying to rip anyone off," Faber said. "I'm out of money."

"Yeah, yeah. We heard that."

"Seriously."

The man jumped onto his tailgate, walked over to his baskets. He bent over to inspect his mushrooms, then suddenly wheeled around. His face was contorted into two hundred years of fury. "Get out of here! Get out of our country!" The words hung there: *our country*. There was no mistaking the meaning. He wasn't talking about Canada.

Faber sprang forward with his outstretched hand. "I'm Jeremy. I'm paying two dollars more than the other buyers. I want everyone to be happy."

The Tlingit man studied Faber for a moment, then took his hand. He hopped off the tailgate into the dirt, still cursing under his breath, stepped back into his cab, and roared off with a load of mushrooms that he wouldn't be selling tonight.

. . .

BY THE END OF THE WEEK, Faber had shipped nearly eighteen hundred pounds of morels back to his warehouse—far less than the wish number of three thousand pounds, and a couple of hundred pounds short of his two-thousand-pound goal. On the other hand, he had eighteen hundred pounds more than his competitors. No one in the Lower 48 had fresh morels in any quantity at this point in the season. Wholesalers were calling him up, trying to get a piece of the action, though most of the shipments were already spoken for.

On our last night, we stood around the fire with a family from Whitehorse, a husband and wife and their teenage daughter. They wore colorful homemade fisherman sweaters and roasted wienies on sticks. When they'd eaten all the hot dogs, they tossed the plastic package on the fire without thinking twice. This is what you did in grizzly country. The parents were hippies once, no doubt, now hard-ened. Even so, they still exuded an air of idealism in this harsh land-scape. Though they had already sold Faber their day's work, the warm fire and conversation kept them around. They told us about their wild-food business in Whitehorse. Most of the morels they planned to dry for resale later in the year; as long as Faber was here to offer a better price, they would sell some of their work now. Their main income was derived from fireweed honey and arctic char, which returned to their lake every year to spawn. The daughter was starting college in the fall. Her name was Sierra or something like that. She was beautiful and fit, with black smudges of soot smeared across an otherwise unblemished face. The dirt didn't bother her at all. She fingered a small hole developing in one of her boots and wondered aloud whether her footwear would last until it was time to go to school. Her father said a few more baskets would pay for a new pair. Faber glanced at me. Her expression was utterly guileless. Later, with admiration, he would call her gnarly.

Margo showed up too—in pants this time—accompanied by a woman wearing a red bandanna over her hair. Three children, the youngest still a baby, waited in the backseat of their truck. They all had soot smeared across their faces and impossibly dirty hands, and they smiled as if this was the best vacation ever. Faber was glad to see them. "Your kids will remember this forever," he said, playing peeka-boo with the baby. Margo and her friend had something special for us: pickles. Also called greenies by the pickers, these were a rare type of morel, exclusive to burns in the Northwest and not yet recognized by science. Like the gray morel, a pickle was substantial, and even heavier for its size owing to its triple-walled flesh. Dark, with a forest-green hue, they took forever to dry. As with grays, Faber paid extra for them.

Even after the last basket was weighed, taped, and loaded, every-one continued to linger by our fire. The pickers were sorry to see us go. They liked the extra dollar or two that Faber was paying, sure, and they also liked the feeling in our slapdash camp. This wasn't a typical buy stand. They talked about the mountains and the wildlife and the relative merits of caribou meat versus moose steaks. Faber packed up his stove and carried some supplies over to the neighbors, things he couldn't take on the plane, such as fuel. Everyone said their goodbyes and exchanged numbers. Finally it was time to leave. We pulled slowly out of camp, our car filled with morels and camping gear, the pickers still standing around the fire, watching us go.

On the way back to Whitehorse, Faber sat in the passenger seat while I drove. The car felt cold and damp to the bone with the air-conditioning on high—and here was Faber in wet clothes again. It wasn't a matter of not learning. There was no time to care, no time to fuss with even a halfhearted attempt at comfort. He'd hardly slept all week. We passed a family of bears and two moose on the road out of the burn. Shadowy figures appeared by the roadside. It was that curious twilight again, when the sky turns cobalt blue for a couple of hours before the sun rises again. Faber jerked around in his seat, thinking we might have passed a grizzly on the highway. Just another big black bear. The bears were drawn to the side of the highway, where tender young weeds grew in tall green clumps. Only one griz this trip. He was disappointed. I hadn't seen any.

Faber faded in and out of a restless sleep as I drove. He talked to me and talked to himself, and after a while I didn't bother listening. He was in that fugue state again, miserable about the holy grail of burns not quite panning out and yet plotting his next moves, cursing the banks, bitching out his employees, dressing down all the stupid people who didn't know the first thing about these extraordinary products he was bringing to market. And in New York! How could they be so fucking dense in his own hometown, the culinary capital of the New World? Outside Whitehorse, we stopped at a lake he had found on one of his solo trips to town earlier in the week. Everything outside looked a different shade of dark blue—the sky, the lake, even the distant line of trees beyond the far shore that receded into blue mountains beyond. Just like that, with the moon out and a cool chill on the air, Faber emerged from his funk. We stripped by the car and

ran naked down a black-sand beach. The water, though not quite alpine cold, was still cold enough, and the approach was long, nearly
fifty yards of hurdling to reach water deep enough for a shallow dive.
We rubbed our legs and arms with handfuls of gravel, trying hope-
lessly to scrub ourselves of all the dirt and sweat and blood, then ran
back to the car just as fast. This pure mountain water had the intended effect. We broke into fits of hilarity now as we tried to dry off
without towels or fresh clothes or anything even remotely clean and
dry, hopping up and down on one foot and then the other, trying to
climb back into clothes soiled beyond comprehension, laughing at the
absurdity of a week in the Yukon bush scrounging mushrooms
capped off by a midnight swim in a testicle-shriveling lake.

BY THE TIME WE boarded our morning flight out of Whitehorse,
Faber had already made up his mind. He bought a return ticket while
we waited for our luggage in Vancouver. He had to be home for the
July Fourth long weekend—his parents and sister were visiting from
out of state—and then he would fly back the following Tuesday and
stay the rest of the month. This time he'd do it right. He'd buy a van
if necessary, and a dealer of his from Idaho would pull stakes and
come up to the Yukon to set up a drying operation. The two of them
would combine forces to take over the market.

Throughout July, other buyers played a game of musical chairs,
with one buyer selling out to another, and a third trying to partner
with Faber to avoid "looking bad" in front of his pickers because he
couldn't match Faber's prices. It was not the epic burn that Faber had
hoped for, but it wasn't bad. His friend from Idaho showed up eventually, though that didn't blossom into the partnership that Faber had
imagined either. "He was so green," Faber told me. "I had to help him
so much." One night, after a full day of rain, Faber offered to buy all
of his friend's morels, since he knew the wet mushrooms would lose
20 percent of their weight as they dried out during shipment. Unlike
Faber, who was selling directly to restaurants for seventeen dollars a

pound, his friend was selling to a wholesaler in Oregon for much less. His friend declined the offer. "The Canadian dollar hit an all-time high that week. It was ninety-one cents to the dollar. When you factor in the gas and air cargo, the mushrooms were probably costing ten seventy-five by the time they landed in Seattle. He lost his shirt." But that wasn't all. "He started smoking weed and drinking too much with the neighbors. I'd come back to camp at three and he'd be sitting there. I'd run into the woods and pick twenty pounds. You have to. That's how you make money. There wasn't a single day that we picked together that he came close to beating me. You start putting the pipe in your mouth and forget it."

It was his friend, though, who figured out what was going on with the neighbors, probably because he was spending so much time next door getting high. The white guy, Slim, they called Mel Gibson. Except for the ponytail, he was a dead ringer for the actor. "Mel Gibson had the connections," Faber explained. "They were selling in town. I was sitting in the van one night, and no one is out because it's been raining for two days. I knew they had a refrigerator in there with cold beer. I knock on the door and they say, 'Come on in.' They didn't care. They had everything out. I said, 'Ohhh, I haven't seen this stuff in a long time.'" The neighbors were cooking crack cocaine in their windowless trailer.

A Death in the Family

...

T HE NEXT TIME I SAW DOUG, it was fall and he had a new
friend, a mutt named Buddy Ramp that he had found as a stray
in Michigan while digging ramps during the off-season. Buddy was
some kind of Chihuahua–Jack Russell mix, with a thin brown and
black coat and bulging eyes. Doug carried him through the patch and
let the little dog curl up in his lap during the long drives in between.
He said he was still planning to get a piece too, even though he didn't
have the money to buy one. He assured me that carrying a firearm
wouldn't change his behavior in the face of danger, and he wanted
me to understand there was no alternative. "It's just like during winter
pick," Doug said. "I won't stand and fight if I don't have to. The
law says you must take reasonable routes of escape before discharging
your weapon in self-defense. We made the right call. But I'm still packing."

By mid-November on the Olympic Peninsula, the days are so
short and wet that, even on a sunny morning such as this, stepping
foot in the woods is like walking through a car wash. Doug was a
little perturbed with me because I wanted to pick winter species like
yellowfeet and hedgehogs. He was getting seven dollars for the hogs,

which was double the price for chanterelles, but it wasn't a hedgehog year, and he doubted we'd find enough of either the spreaders or the belly buttons to pay for gas. The possibility of yellowfeet got him a little more excited. "We'll call it a scouting day," he said, expecting a poor pick overall.

We drove into an area he called, without a trace of irony, the Promised Land, following a head-spinning network of rough logging roads through heavily cutover timberland, most of it owned now by ITT Rayonier. This vast tree farm on the edge of the Pacific had been continuously leveled by industrial logging for nearly a century, and the cut rotations were getting shorter and shorter, making for a cramped, ugly forest with little use for wildlife other than weedy species like crows. But, *whoa!*—Doug slammed on the brakes—there was a mink crossing the road. It stopped to look at us and then slunk back into the undergrowth. "Well, isn't that cool," Doug said. "The day is looking up. We'll go easy on ourselves and walk the grades today." These were former railroad lines from the days of steam donkey and railroad logging. Since they were unmarked, you had to know where they were in the matrix of uneven-aged timber stands. Doug had found them over the years while hunting elk, and though most of the grades had been lost to road-building or reclaimed by the forest, a few still penetrated the woods—flat, wide, raised beds that made for easy walking in an otherwise unforgiving tangle of re-growth and swampland. Moss had long since colonized the old gravel, making for well-drained arteries through the woods that grew mushrooms like a crop.

Buddy Ramp barked sadly as we left the Blue Pig, our buckets swinging in anticipation. "Buddy has separation issues," Doug said. As we walked the grades, he got excited. Maybe my idea to pick winter species wasn't so bad after all, because in coming to an area known for hedgehogs and yellowfeet that grew in the decaying cedar bogs, we had inadvertently stumbled on a late matsutake flush on the edges of the grade itself. "You're not as dumb as you look," Doug said to me happily. Each time he spotted a hint of white cap peeking from the moss at the sides of the trail, he pretended to ring a bell and then reached down beneath knots of salal and huckleberry to retrieve his prize. He excavated carefully around the button until he could pull it out without breaking the stipe. The excavation often revealed two or three more mushrooms hiding nearby. Though I tried my best to spot them, Doug was too quick for me. Finally he let me walk ahead of him. Even then he found most of the matsutake, ringing that bell over and over. His mood elevated with each new discovery. Because it was late in the season, the prices for matsutake had gone up in recent days. "We're making money today!" he sang through the woods. "It's a day to pick mushrooms. Full buckets for everyone!" In short order Doug had more than a basket of mostly number-one and number-two matsutake buttons, some of them larger than my fist and maybe a half pound. "That's a ten-dollar mushroom," I said, feeling the excitement well up.

Doug turned it over gingerly in his grip. "You might be right . . . you might be right."

The rain started up again after lunch. We called it a day and took the long way out of the Promised Land, exiting the woods just south of Moclips near the Aloha Tavern. Doug hadn't set foot in this watering hole, he figured, in eight or ten years, not since his logging days. I got a beer and bought Doug a Pepsi. It was peanut night. We grabbed handfuls from red plastic baskets on the bar and admired the paintings on the wall, which dated to 1982, those fat years just before the end, just before the spotted owl swooped into view and put a stop to everything. One, called *The Clam Digger's Sweetheart,* showed a woman, shovel in hand, bent over a razor-clam hole, her ample bosom spilling out of a too-small top and a randy grin on her face. "We used to have T-shirts with that," Doug said. Another painting had the words SHAKE RAT written across the top. A mischievous rat in red suspenders, with a pallet of shingles on his back, was running a chain saw at dawn as a peeping cartoon sun came up over the horizon with surprised-looking eyes. "Know why the rat's got that hose off his chain saw in a bucket of water?" Doug asked the bartender. The bartender didn't know, and neither did anyone else at the bar, which Doug found hard to believe. "It's a muffler," he explained. "He's been cutting all night on someone else's claim." The bartender thought about this for a moment, studying the picture up on the wall behind his bar, then turned around to face us.

"He's a thief!"

Doug finished his cola with a wink at me. We paid and left. "That'll give them something to talk about for a while," he said. His good mood didn't last, though. Doug now had a cell phone, his first, and on the way back to Hoquiam he got a call from Faber, who said most of the matsutake coming out of the coast was infected with cap worm. "I understand," Doug said into the phone. "I figured on fifty percent anyway." There was a pause. "Thirty percent? Well, look, I don't care. You grade it however you want. I'll give it away, I don't give a shit." Doug passed me the phone before I could object. He was done with this conversation. "It'll be garbage," Faber said to me. "In Aberdeen they're paying ten. I'm paying twenty for worm-free."

It was late afternoon and nearly dark. The rain had stopped. We passed a friend of Doug's on the Moclips road. Doug wheeled the Buick around and we pulled in next to a Ford pickup with a dented tailgate. A large oxygen tank was chained to the bed. "That's for cutting steel," Doug explained. The men knew each other from scrapping together. Before Doug could open his door, a dark-haired guy built like a fireplug was striding over to us, shooting the bird and grimacing. "Where are my rocks?"

"Be nice," Doug replied, staying in the car.

The man knocked at Doug's closed window.

"Behave yourself!"

I was starting to think he might bust the glass, when both men broke into peals of laughter and Doug got out to shake hands.

"I've got your rocks at home."

"Got a buyer lined up." The man spoke in a deep guttural voice, as if he'd recently had throat or stomach surgery.

"Already?"

"Cash in hand."

"Well, why didn't you call me, man?"

"You never answer that thing."

"What, this piece of shit?" Doug tossed his cell phone onto the car floor. "I'm not much for this new technology, you know that. How you been?"

"Good. Wanna go poaching?"

Doug looked over at me, back at his friend.

"I'm kidding, man. The silvers are stacked thick under the bridge. We caught sixteen yesterday."

"No shit."

"Yeah."

With that, we turned around again and we all drove back to the coast to go salmon fishing, where we found the Moclips River too high and muddy already from the day's light rain to fish. Doug waved goodbye to his friend and told me how the man was driving illegally without a license. The state had taken it away after he failed a physical. The physical was required because he had been paralyzed briefly after a hunting accident and still couldn't properly turn his head. In a bizarre series of events that echoed Jeff's near-death experience at sea, the guy had shot a bear and then, while winching it out of a ravine, was knocked clear off his feet after a cable snapped. The impact broke his neck.

It was dark when Doug pulled into Grand Avenue in Hoquiam, where I had left my car. Buddy Ramp was asleep in his lap. I tried to slide a twenty for gas under a wiper blade, but he turned them on before I could finish. *Swish-swish-swish* went the wipers until I pocketed the money. He put his window down. "I usually pick alone. I like my solitude, but it's good to have company in the woods too." With that, the Blue Pig rattled off to the south.

. . .

LATER IN THE SEASON, I met Doug in California. The sun had been
out, so I went exploring on a trail along the coast. I was late getting
back to camp and our agreed-upon meeting place. I used my flashlight to find my way down the last half mile of trail. Doug's fire had
burned down to coals and he was sitting in his car, with the engine
running. I knocked on the window, putting Buddy Ramp into an up-
roar. The little dog bared his fangs and lunged at me. Doug made
hand gestures, telling me to come around to the other side, while he
leaned across the seat and rolled down his passenger window. "Driver
window don't roll down no more, door don't open," he explained.
The Blue Pig was on its last legs. "She's been good to me." He patted
the dashboard with his hand. "I might need you to follow me out."

The next day we decided to pick a favorite patch of Doug's on the
Lost Coast. After we'd crested one ridge after another, sweating and
brushing broken twigs out of our hair, Doug would survey the territory for a moment and shake his head. "It's right around here somewhere," he'd say, or "It's just one more ridge over." The amount of
time it was taking to find this one patch was cutting into his profits.
Surely there were plenty of easy road patches we could still hit to sal-
vage the day. But Doug was determined to find this one patch. He
called it the "god-awfulest patch o' blacks you ever saw." I was starting to realize, though, that it was something else entirely. It was like
the passage of seasons or a birthday. Returning to this patch that had
been good to him over the years was a way to mark the calendar and
also a way to place one's life within time's continuum. This was a remote patch in a sparsely picked drainage. For all he knew, Doug was
the only human being to have ever picked it. To pick it again was to
demonstrate mastery. In a way, Faber was right. Doug wasn't working anymore. He was participating in an age-old drama.

And so was I. Each time we stopped to assess the situation and
decide which way to go, I found myself making suggestions based on

what I had learned since first peering behind the curtain of the mushroom culture. The landscape looked different to me now. I noticed crinkles in the topography, seeps of underground water, transitions in tree composition, the presence of a certain species of woodpecker that might mean a change of habitat. These small nuances of nature—nearly imperceptible details that add up to create the miracle of life in a cold universe—had become just ever so manifest to me. *Let's follow the north-facing slope,* I might suggest, *because it will be wetter, with more redwood decay.*

"Now that's a thought," Doug would say. "You're thinking like a mushroom picker."

That night, after walking down to a lonely cove and watching commercial smelt fishermen haul in their beach-casting nets and fling them back out into the breakers—a style of fishing that had barely changed in hundreds of years—we drove out of the Lost Coast in advance of a terrible storm that was bearing down from the north. Flooding was predicted along with record snowfall in the high country. The clayish mountain roads would turn to mud, and we might not get out at all if we didn't leave now. We camped on Redwood Creek in a steady downpour. The next day I said goodbye to Doug. He needed to get his load of mushrooms and watercress back to Seattle, and I planned to walk among the redwoods in the rain, which I did in the middle of the storm, a terrific wind howling through the tops of these great Jurassic trees, throwing balls of lichen to the ground and hurling widow-maker limbs like javelins all around me. Even though I knew I should turn back and evacuate, the redwood forest in the storm was exhilarating, and I kept walking, passing an uprooted stump that could shelter several families and windfall branches as big as telephone poles. Every rivulet, seasonal creek bed, and crack in the earth overflowed with water. After crossing paths with a park ranger a few miles in, I finally turned around at her urging and hurried back. The ground gurgled and spat and made a million other noises of wetness. A deep puddle had gathered around my car in the parking lot, and the way out was now a shallow river. I made it to the Redwood Highway and turned east. Water poured off the mountains and sheeted across the road. People gathered on the bridges above the Smith River to watch it rage through its canyon, carrying the detritus of both wilderness and civilization out to sea like a riptide from the hills: trees, couches, whatever got in the way, it didn't matter.

Somewhere just south of Cave Junction, on the far side of the California border and back in cellular range, the messages appeared on my phone all at once: five calls from Doug and three from a number that I recognized as Doug's brother. Doug had never made it home. He was broken down on the side of the road, on one of those radiator-killing hills just north of Grants Pass, an undulating ribbon of highway where you'll see strategically placed gallon jugs of water left on the shoulder by wary long-haul truckers, who know they'll be in need at some point on this stretch. Water. There always seemed to be too little or too much.

By the time I found him, at Bulldog Automotive on the outskirts of town, Doug's twenty-four-hour ordeal was nearly over. He'd spent the previous night sleeping in the Blue Pig, in a "check brakes" area. Someone—his brother?—must have wired money to have him towed and repaired. Doug seemed to be worried more about his cargo of mushrooms and greens than his own safety. I could hear Faber's admonition: *I told you not to go to California. You have no money and a crappy car.* To someone like Doug, who didn't like being bossed around, this was incentive enough to make the trip.

"You see many mushroom pickers around these parts?" I asked the mechanic.

"Nope, sure don't." He and Doug shared a knowing look.

"They grow some good bud, though," Doug said. He opened his passenger door and slid across ripped vinyl into the driver's seat. "I can't be late," he said. "This week is my most important appointment of the year." He was getting a new set of teeth.

I followed him out of town a ways, until I was confident the Blue

Pig would make it over the hill, then honked twice as I passed him and drove north on I-5 toward home.

. . .

A COUPLE OF WEEKS LATER I got a call from Faber. Had I heard from Doug lately? As a matter of fact, I had. Just the day before, Doug had given me a call from somewhere out in the boondocks. He sounded upbeat. "Yeah, new choppers. And I changed medications. We're trying something new. So far, so good. Hey, this is something really cool," he said, changing the subject. "You'd like this a lot. We're using my new video camera to . . . what's the word? We're *documenting* these old historical things out here. Indian salmon weirs and derelict railroad trestles. The old railway grades." The camera had been a Christmas gift from one of his brothers. I told him I thought that was a worthwhile project. He knew better than anyone where most of these artifacts of a nearly vanished era resided.

Faber thought about this for a moment, then told me that he planned to drive down to California for a couple of days, spend a day picking black trumpets and then another day whacking down stinging nettles. It would be a quick trip. "You wouldn't believe the prices," he said. Blacks were down to two dollars a pound. "I figured I'd do Doug a favor, throw him a bone. He's not returning my calls."

"Maybe he doesn't care about the money," I said.

Faber was dealing mostly with Southeast Asians now. He needed more product to keep the New York operation afloat, and the Asians were reliable. While I watched him grade mushrooms one evening at Sang's house, Bill, the free spirit, one of the last of the white pickers who still sold to Faber, showed up with a few baskets of kings. He said he was a wanted man. The IRS had come after him for tax evasion. "No pictures," he told me, seeing my camera on the kitchen counter. He expressed relief that Doug hadn't shown up. "He wants to kick my ass."

"Come on. Doug?"

"We used to pick together all the time."

The man's girlfriend chimed in, "Bill picked sea beans for Jeremy, and Doug had a fit over it."

"He showed everybody my patches."

I asked Bill if he'd run into Doug since their falling out.

"At the gas station," said the girlfriend, a tall woman with raven hair.

"And how did that go?"

"It didn't go well. He barked at me, called me nasty things."

"Don't think that Bill's clean," jumped in Faber. "Don't think he's totally clean. I'm not taking sides, you know that."

Bill told the story of how they met while picking neighboring patches. "Doug's a pretty good-sized guy," he started. "I had to choose between friend and foe. I chose friend, and from that day forward it was always chaos trying to get anything done in my patch. You pick more mushrooms than him and he's pissed off and bent out of shape. He's a very good picker, one of the best I've ever known. When I'm in Montana or Idaho, up in the Sawtooth Wilderness or somewhere, I feel pretty safe over there. I don't have to worry about running into this big guy. He's told me that when I do run into him I better be packing, only one of the two of us is coming out. Doug's a guy that chases down elk. I know the herds around here, and you've got to outrun them. He's on foot and he chases them through the brush until they stop and he's on them again. He'll keep running until he catches up. I don't want to be one of those elk—"

"I'm just here to buy mushrooms," Faber interrupted. "I'm not saying Bill's perfect; I'm not saying Doug's perfect. They're both at fault, but Bill's not threatening. He might be dumb, but he's not threatening."

"If you hang around this guy long enough," the wanted man said, looking over at Faber, "you'll learn that everyone is a fucking retard."

. . .

THE LAST TIME I saw Doug and Faber together was at a funeral in Seattle. Faber's former girlfriend and his original founding partner in Foraged and Found Edibles, Christina Choi, had died unexpectedly after complications following surgery on a brain aneurysm. She was only thirty-four years old. Both Faber and Doug were broken up. We all were. Nettletown had closed a few months earlier, after its brief yet beloved run, with Choi citing an exhaustion that mystified her friends and family. After months of feeling run down and not herself, she submitted to tests. The surgery was scheduled immediately. Though everyone knew it was risky, no one was ready for this.

Doug arrived at the memorial in his usual hooded sweatshirt, jeans, and work boots. The church was packed with restaurant workers from all over town. Faber, helping out as an usher, greeted people at the door. Matt Dillon, who had acted as a gatekeeper at the hospital, trying to control the flow of well-wishers, arrived in a three-piece suit. While we sat in the pews listening to a choir sing uplifting songs, Doug confessed that his belief in a benevolent higher power was badly shaken.

Later, at the reception, a slide show cast images from happier times onto the wall. Faber was in many of the pictures with Choi—camping, hiking, picking mushrooms. Choi's bright eyes lit up the room. Faber's father, who had flown out from New York for the service, looked at his son. "I always thought you two . . ." he started, unable to finish the sentence. Everyone nodded solemnly and Faber went off to embrace one of Choi's sisters.

Near the end of an open microphone for remarks and remembrances, Doug shambled up to the podium. "I'm a forager," he began. "That's how I knew Christina, and this is the type of person she was. Jeremy and me were coming back from California from picking mushrooms one time, and it was Jeremy's birthday. Christina called to wish him a happy birthday and told us about this place where you could get a rib eye for cheap." Uh-oh. I could see where this was going. I tried to catch Faber's eye, but he was in the back of the room. Doug forged ahead. "It was a really good, juicy steak for only about five bucks. The other thing was that, while we were eating these really good steaks, there were these gals dancing on our table. Now, how cool is that?" The crowd laughed without reservation, and Doug finished by telling a story about how Choi had once asked him to stop acting so territorial about his mushroom patches. "And you know what? She was right. I asked myself the same question. Why was I so territorial about my patches? I've got millions of patches. What difference does it make? Why not share the beautiful things in life? That's the kind of person she was." I could see the tears in his eyes when he came back to the table. He leaned over and whispered to me, almost apologetically, "I didn't prepare anything. I didn't even know I was gonna say anything until I was standing up there."

"You did great," I told him.

After the reception, the gathering moved on to Dillon's restaurant, Sitka & Spruce. Doug, though he didn't have a dollar to his name, had brought elk tenderloins and a bushel of Dungeness crabs from the coast, and now the kitchen staff was busy preparing these and many other dishes for the crowd, while Dillon greeted everyone with bear hugs and plenty of booze. Some of these people had been up for days. Guests grabbed handfuls of Choi's personal stash of pickled fiddleheads, knowing they would never taste such miraculous food again. It was a night to celebrate the life of a friend and colleague. In a few months Dillon would travel to a gala event in New York, where he would mingle with some of the culinary world's biggest names and be feted with a James Beard Award for Best Chef Northwest. But tonight he was just a guy trying to marshal his years of kitchen experience to feed people. Friends of Choi's, their mascara smeared and shirts untucked, lined up at the kitchen counter because, at some point, if nothing else, you had to eat. They laughed suddenly, uncontrollably, at a joke or a story, then turned away as their eyes filled again. Faber and Doug looked exhausted. They stood in a back corner, the mushroom buyer and picker, talking like old friends about the coming weeks. That's what you did in these circumstances: remember the good times and then look ahead. The mushroom trail never ended. It was January. Time once again for winter pick.

Acknowledgments

MUSHROOM HUNTING IS A FAMOUSLY secretive activity, and I am indebted to mushroom hunters far and wide, both commercial and recreational, who bucked tradition to allow me a glimpse into their seldom-seen world. First and foremost, I couldn't have asked for two more knowledgeable or companionable guides on "the trail" than Jeremy Faber and Doug Carnell; their generosity cannot be overstated. Matt Dillon took time from his busy kitchen to give me the chef's-eye view, and Christina Choi's joie de vivre, remembered fondly by so many, infuses these pages throughout. David Arora, Jack Czarnecki, Mary Ellen Geist, Eirik Johnson, Jonathan Julia, Jeff Lacey, Somphone Nhamnhouane, Aaron Schaal, Leslie Scott, Joy Thavisick, Sang and Srey Tran, and Tony Williams all welcomed me into their fungal orbits. To the many other pickers and buyers who shared patches, camps, and talk: thank you.

My agent, Lisa Grubka, was an early, devoted supporter of this book—and a taskmaster of the best sort. Ryan Doherty (aka Ninja Editor) pushed me in his subtle yet persistent way to whip the manuscript into shape. Big thanks to both for their adroit shepherding from beginning to end—may your cupboards overflow with fungi. Thank you to the Random House team: Evan Camfield, Mark Maguire, Kathy Lord, Barbara Bachman, Quinne Rogers, and Greg Kubie. Also, thank you to Kate Rogers for pointing the way.

Many others contributed wise counsel. My dear friend Svenja Soldovieri provided a cozy Santa Fe casita, close reading, and happy-hour margaritas. Mary Smiley and Jonathan Frank graciously lent me their mycological eyes. Steve Duda gave me the Eastern European perspective. Through the years I've been fortunate to work with accomplished mentors; my deepest gratitude for guidance and example to Jay Parini, John Elder, David Bain, Sally St. Lawrence, Laura Kalpakian, and Katherine Koberg. I am sincerely grateful to Artist Trust and 4Culture for funding and support during critical phases of field research and travel.

Finally, to my wife, Martha Silano, and our children, Riley and Ruby: I would be lost in the wilderness without you.

Selected Bibliography

THE FOLLOWING BOOKS, JOURNALS, AND ARTICLES were helpful to me as source material:

Amaranthus, Michael P. *The Importance and Conservation of Ectomycorrhizal Fungal Diversity in Forest Ecosystems: Lessons from Europe and the Pacific Northwest.* U.S. Department of Agriculture, 1998.

Arora, David. *Mushrooms Demystified.* Ten Speed Press, 1986.

————. *All the Rain Promises and More.* Ten Speed Press, 1991.

Arora, David, and Glenn H. Shepard, Jr., eds. *Economic Botany* 62, no. 3 (2008).

Bone, Eugenia. *Mycophilia.* Rodale, 2011.

Hosford, David, et al. *Ecology and Management of the Commercially Harvested American Matsutake Mushroom.* U.S. Department of Agriculture, 1997.

Kuo, Michael, et al. "Revision of Morchella Taxonomy." *Mycologia* 11-375 (2012).

McLain, Rebecca J., et al. *Commercial Morel Harvesters and Buyers in Western Montana: An Exploratory Study of the 2001 Harvesting Season.* U.S. Department of Agriculture, 2005.

Molina, Randy, et al. *Biology, Ecology, and Social Aspects of Wild Edible Mushrooms in the Forests of the Pacific Northwest: A Preface to Managing Commercial Harvest.* U.S. Department of Agriculture, 1993.

Molina, Randy, and Pilz, David. "Commercial Harvests of Edible Mushrooms from the Forests of the Pacific Northwest United States: Issues, Management, and Monitoring for Sustainability." *Forest Ecology and Management* 5593 (2001).

Money, Nicholas P. *Mushroom.* Oxford University Press, 2011.

Parks, Catherine G., and Craig L. Schmitt. *Wild Edible Mushrooms in the Blue Mountains: Resource and Issues.* U.S. Department of Agriculture, 1997.

Pilz, David, et al. *Ecology and Management of Commercially Harvested Chanterelle Mushrooms.* U.S. Department of Agriculture, 2003.

Pilz, David, et al. *Ecology and Management of Morels Harvested from the Forests of Western North America.* U.S. Department of Agriculture, 2007.

Schaechter, Elio. *In the Company of Mushrooms: A Biologist's Tale.* Harvard University Press, 1998.

Schlosser, W. E., and K. A. Blatner. "The Wild Edible Mushroom Industry of Washington, Oregon and Idaho: A 1992 Survey." *Journal of Forestry* 93, no. 3 (1995).

Stamets, Paul. *Mycelium Running.* Ten Speed Press, 2005.

Tsing, Anna. "Beyond Economic and Ecological Standardisation." *Australian Journal of Anthropology* 20 (2009).

Witta, Amy L., and Tricia L. Wurtz. *The Morel Mushroom Industry in Alaska: Current Status and Potential.* Institute of Social and Economic Research, University of Alaska Anchorage, 2004.

ABOUT THE AUTHOR

LANGDON COOK is the author of *Fat of the Land: Adventures of a 21st Century Forager*. His writing has appeared in numerous magazines and newspapers. He lives in Seattle with his wife and two children.

www.langdoncook.com